ADVANCE PRAISE FOR *THE DIGITAL SONGSTREAM*

"Brad Hill is the most musical technologist and the most tech-savvy musician. Where others write with notes or strum with guitar picks, he crafts words and ideas in ways that will leave your ears intrigued and your head begging for more."

—Jim Griffin, CEO, Cherry Lane Digital

"If you're wondering whether or not to plunk down hard-earned cash to buy this book, do it. Pay attention to what Brad Hill has to say—he writes not only as a digital music journalist, but as a fan. His no-nonsense, step-by-step approach to understanding how to quickly and expertly join the digital music revolution will have you up and running in no time, with all jargon explained and all hype removed. I have Brad on my show as an expert guest because he knows what he's talking about and he writes in plain English."

—David Lawrence, Host/Executive Producer,
Online Tonight and *The Net Music Countdown*

"Brad Hill takes a refreshing, consumer-focused perspective on a subject that often finds music fans excluded from the discussion. This book cuts through the rhetoric and gets to the heart of the digital music revolution."
—Steve Grady, General Manager, EMusic.com

"Like it or not, digital delivery is the future of music. I know of no one who comprehends the Byzantine complexities of the digital delivery of music better than Brad Hill, nor anyone who conveys that comprehension better to the reading public. He has the remarkable ability to digest complex and granular material and turn it into clear concepts. You want a blueprint for the future of music? This is your book."
—Eric Olsen, Blogcritics.org, Editor/Author,
The Encyclopedia of Record Producers

D1311358

The Digital Songstream

Mastering the World of Digital Music

Brad Hill

Routledge • New York & London

Published in 2003 by
Routledge
29 West 35th Street
New York, NY 10001
www.routledge-ny.com

Published in Great Britain by
Routledge
11 New Fetter Lane
London EC4P 4EE
www.routledge.co.uk

Printed in the United States of America on acid-free paper.

10 9 8 7 6 5 4 3 2 1

Library of Congress Cataloging-in-Publication Data

Hill, Brad, 1953–
    The digital songstream : mastering the world of digital music
      / Brad Hill.
         p. cm.
      Includes index.
         ISBN 0–415–94203–9 (pbk. : alk. paper)
         1. Music—Computer network resources. 2. Music—Computer programs. 3. Internet—
      Computer programs. I. Title.
         ML74.7 .H45 2003
         025. 06'78166—dc21
                                                   2002015996

Contents

Acknowledgments

Many thanks to Richard Carlin, who acquired and edited this book. His steadfast collaboration, and willingness to test new waters, are rare and prized qualities.

This book would be very different if not influenced by the Pho community, whose daily explorations of new frontiers stimulate new thinking, new seeing, and new listening. My thanks to every participant.

Introduction

About twenty years ago the digital compact disc was introduced to the music-buying public. Embraced by record companies that urged us to replace our beloved but scratchy vinyl collections with shiny, durable five-inch discs, the CD transformed gradually from a novelty item to a staple in the musical home. A simple format change altered the expectations and buying habits of the music marketplace. Specifically, four major improvements were introduced and quickly adopted as the music industry moved into a new phase:

- **Indestructibility.** CDs are not literally unbreakable, nor do they last forever. But they are much more impervious to time and rough handling than vinyl records are.
- **Quietness.** The absence of background noise was the first sonic revelation of digital CD reproduction. And, of course, CDs don't develop noisy scratches.
- **Random access.** Home programmability took a giant step forward with CD players that could leap among an album's tracks in any order.
- **Portability.** Compact discs really are compact compared to vinyl LPs. It suddenly became possible to slip one into a purse, or keep a disc library in the car. Later, the mobility trend got a push from portable CD players with headphones.

None of this changed how music entered our homes: it still streamed in on radio waves and was purchased at music stores selling both vinyl and CD albums. Not until 1988 did CD sales exceed LP sales, marking the end of a six-year wrestling match between the two formats. Once in the home, however, the CD changed how purchased music was turned into life's soundtrack. Despite the audiophilic complaint that CDs lacked the aural warmth of vinyl, most people embraced the pristine sound, lasting format, flexible track-juggling, and convenient size of the compact disc, upgrading their music collection and playback equipment accordingly. The new format was a boon to the industry and welcomed by consumers.

The music marketplace is on the verge of its next transformation, and it's a whopper. Arguably more consequential than the shift from LPs to CDs, the shift from CDs to nonphysical music files is likewise based on a new format. In this case the innovation remains decisively unembraced by the record companies, but it has nonetheless arrived—legally, noisily, and with the power to once again reinvent the music marketplace.

As with CDs, the format shift by itself means nothing. It needs corresponding playback support to gain traction in our daily lives. So, the invention of MP3 and other file-compression formats is given life by software players, desktop organizers of computer music collections, portable MP3 players, a generation of portable CD players that understand MP3 and other new formats, and a host of services that encourage online music collecting and home programming.

As music consumers are poised at the beginning of a new era, new expectations that will govern consumer demand are still being formed and learned. Audio quality is not an issue as it was when CDs were introduced in 1982. The new marketplace expectations all pertain to convenience:

- **Extreme portability.** A 12–song CD was fine in its day, but now a blank CD stands ready to clutch 150 or more songs in its glittery grasp. An hour of MP3 music can fit into a portable headphone device smaller than a credit card.
- **Extreme replicability.** Perfect copies of any music in any format are a reality, thanks to the digitization tools of a typical home computer. Furthermore, the time required to make a copy is usually a fraction of the duration of the music being copied.
- **Extreme random access.** By unbinding songs from discs, home programmability reaches an unprecedented level of versatility. Music is no

longer tied to playback devices capable of shuffling tracks of just one, or a few, prerecorded discs. It can now be centrally stored in massive volume, tagged by many identifying criteria, and sorted by mood, genre, artist, year, album, or any number of other divisions.

- **Extreme accessibility.** The newest and most controversial expectation in the new marketplace, accessibility refers to the suddenly near universal selection of informally shared music. Taken to its ultimate extent (whether by record companies or without their cooperation), extreme accessibility would mean the almost instant availability of every sound recording ever created.

How might a musical household be changed by these small, simple new formats that are so roiling the industry? The changes will be more profound than the conveniences brought about twenty years ago with the shift from one type of disc to another; shifting away from discs entirely has the potential to bring an entirely new order of consumer behavior and advantages. Music need no longer be contained in plastic discs with terrible packaging sold in physical stores; it has attained pragmatic evanescence. Music is bits and bytes residing on the global datanet, organized into virtual delivery packets that slide into the home music system with fluid economy. Music has become a digital songstream.

This book is not primarily about file-sharing, though authorized downloading of music from various sources is a big piece of the puzzle. This book is about new standards of portability, replicability, programmability, and accessibility. In other words, how to carry around your music, copy it for your own use, manage your collection, and legally acquire music in the cheapest and most fluid manner.

The Little Format That Could

One might not think that shrunken music files would impact consumers and the recording industry with such revolutionary effect. But the relatively small size of an MP3 song file matches up with mainstream residential downloading to enable the sharing of music products like never before. After the invention of MP3, eager fans could, for example, copy a song from a CD to a computer hard drive, squash it down in size, and e-mail it to five friends simultaneously. Or, leveraging the distribution power of the Internet even further, a person could place an MP3 song on a personal Web site and invite all visitors to take copies as they pass through. From there it was a small step to creating a central directory of such Web-posted song files, driving a greater flow of Internet traffic to download sites. All of this quickly came to pass, and it was just a beginning—merely the overture to the operatic drama of digital music on the Internet.

The MP3 compression scheme was based on the work of the Motion Picture Experts Group, an engineering alliance of which MP3's full name (MPEG Audio Layer-3) contains an acronym, and completed by the Fraunhofer Institut in Germany. The first patent was granted in 1989, but neither the Internet nor any necessary supporting software was mature enough to bring MP3 into consumer consciousness.

It wasn't until 1997 that a developer named Tomislav Uzelac created AMP, the first reasonably user-friendly MP3 playback program. (It doesn't do much good to own an MP3 file if you can't listen to it.) At that point the earliest, most geekishly astute adopters of digital music began experiencing the benefits of compressed, sharable music files. (MP2 had attracted some attention too.) When Justin Frankel added a Windows interface to AMP's core playback engine, and dished it up without charge to the global online community in 1998, the MP3 revolution shifted hard and fast into high gear. Winamp, as it was called (and still is, several freeware versions later), closed the circle. Music fans could e-mail and download at will, with no barrier (of either technology or cost) preventing the recipient from enjoying the music immediately, right through any computer equipped with Winamp, a sound card, and speakers.

MP3 gained its toehold just as high-speed home Internet connections, delivered through cable-TV wires and DSL lines, were starting to worm into homes. A typical MP3 song file is about 4 megabytes in size: roughly 1 megabyte for every minute of music. (Sizes and durations vary according to the method of MP3 creation, as described in chapter 2.) Four megs is a handily small size compared to the corresponding 40–meg uncompressed file, but still is a hard swallow for pokey telephone modems. What took between twenty-five and forty seconds to acquire through the cable modems gaining popularity in 1998 could take from ten to thirty *minutes* through a dial-up modem. Suddenly, as use of the keyword *mp3* began to overtake *sex* at online search sites, the allure of downloading music files became an urgent reason to step up, if possible, to a high-speed connection at home. College students (and office workers to some degree) made avaricious use of the institution-grade Internet lines freely at their disposal.

The fact that much of the enthusiastic sharing was illegal seemed, to many giddy MP3 enthusiasts, nothing more than a negligible technicality. Such unchecked blitheness was eventually called to the bench as the record companies, which own recording copyrights, belatedly awakened to the infringement of their distribution control. Of course music bootlegging long preceded MP3, the Internet, and personal computers. But copyright infringement online seems uniquely threatening in its global scope, viral speed, and almost ridiculous ease.

Whether the recording industry is actually harmed or helped by unauthorized grassroots distribution of its product is a debate that rages intractably and with daunting complexity. The point here is that the increasing attention given to the illegality of a popular activity has contributed to a sense that MP3 itself, having become a controversial buzzword, crosses over to the dark side of legality. Nothing could be less true. Like any other format (such as DOC for certain word-processing files or JPG for certain picture files), MP3 is a totally neutral container, in this case holding both infringing and noninfringing music content. The Fraunhofer Institut continues to own the patent and—after a period of allowing unregulated use—now charges a royalty to software developers who incorporate MP3 functionality in their programs. MP3 is legit.

It should likewise be emphasized that many activities and services falling under the umbrella of "digital music" are perfectly benign and legal as well. Many independent artists, unsigned to an exclusive recording contract, intentionally give away MP3s of their songs: in these cases the fear of going unheard is greater than the fear of losing money. (Chapter 6 describes how to plumb the online "indie" scene.) Several third-party companies license, from record labels, the right to encode commercial product in the MP3 format and sell it to downloading customers, with pricing set on a per-download and/or flat-fee basis. (Chapters 3 and 4 cover this area.) Even the "majors"—the five large, international music conglomerates that control most of the CDs found in stores and heard on radio—are hesitantly wading into the waters with plans to sell directly to the online citizenry. (Again, see chapters 3 and 4.) And, of course, all of a person's at-home MP3 creations, made from CDs for personal use and not for trading, are lawful. MP3 carries conveniences that extend beyond file-sharing over the Internet, because compressed music is portable music. (Chapter 2 explains making MP3 copies of CDs.) Listening to MP3 streams over the Internet is also sanctioned, though not without the political difficulties described in chapter 7.

A New Approach to Music Ownership

The freedom and scope delivered into the home by digital music are maximized by an important mind shift. Most of us over the age of twenty-five are at least partially accustomed to traditional ways of relating to music products, ways that involve discs, stores, and shelftop players connected to stereo components. These vestiges of the vinyl and CD eras are still viable, of course, widely used, valuable, and pleasurable. I don't mean to slam them or prematurely claim their demise. But the crucial components of the new era operate in parallel to inherited musicware, without necessarily touching it.

It's worth remembering that music has been delivered digitally to consumers since the first audio CDs were released in 1982. (That's when Europe and Japan got them; the United States enjoyed its first CD products the following year.) The term *digital music* as used in this book and in most press coverage refers to the products, services, and consumer behavior derived from a compression of the CD format we have known for the last twenty years. When you buy a commercial music CD, you have in your hand what is essentially a computer disc holding a collection of files. Those files are not fundamentally different than word-processing, digicam, or text files. Average computers have been equipped with CD drives for only a handful of years, but CDs have always been computerized, in a sense, because their sole mission is transporting data. CD players are basically specialized computers designed to understand music as software.

So retail music has been bits and bytes for two decades. The online realm has been a social force for about half that time. It was the technology of file compression that first rubbed the two combustibly together. MP3 compression reduces native CD music files to roughly one-tenth their original size, after which they can be saved to a hard drive or blank disc with the famous ".mp3" file identifier. When opened in MP3–playing software programs they deliver music just as a CD player does when "opening" a song from an audio CD. In most situations and to most ears, MP3s sound pretty much like the originals from which they derive.

There is, actually, some integration of the MP3–centric universe and the CD realm. Ripping and burning are CD-oriented activities. But even they don't make much sense, and cannot be carried through to their ultimate usefulness, without a new understanding of what music has boiled down to: the file. I've found that many people are slowed in their exploration of digital music not by equipment, or the speed of their Internet connection, but by the difficulty of adjusting to this new way of thinking about music ownership.

When you conceive of music as files, you are liberated from a cumbersome reliance on discs and CD players to hear music. Of course, hardware is always needed. The CD player is merely replaced by the computer hard drive or the portable MP3 player. But flexibility is key. Whereas in the CD era disc-trapped music could function only when placed in an industry-sanctioned playback machine, in the file era music is far more transferable, portable, and programmable. In can be stored in your home or online, in your computer or on a blank CD, in a portable player or in a shelftop music server. Files can be infinitely recombined with other files.

The new view of music can be counterintuitive; we are all keyed to expect products to be tangible. But music itself, as separate from its delivery mechanisms, has always been intangible—software, not hardware. The digital music revolution asserts the essential sublimity of music by rendering its product immaterial and instantly communicable. Music can still be packaged, but the consumer now has far more control over the method and configuration of the packaging. Music is no longer defined by the disc-player alliance. Companies in the disc and player businesses bridle at this new reality, but technology-enabled consumers are setting the evolutionary direction of the marketplace.

Digital Music in the Post-Napster Universe

The downfall of Napster as a free service is no more the end of digital music than file-sharing is the only way to enjoy MP3. Free song-trading through Napster's offspring has remained quite the rage. But even putting file-trading aside, the digital music universe is more vibrant and varied than ever. The streaming music scene by itself is so astonishingly fertile as to make anybody sit up and take notice. Semiestablished new-music companies providing music by subscription, or stocked with talented indie artists eager to be heard, are maturing into solid alternatives to the staid programming furnished by record labels and the pat playlists of consolidated radio station chains.

The post-Napster digital music landscape is marked by increasing commercialization, as the offline corporate forces move begrudgingly into the virtual space with subscription services designed to legally deliver top music acts in streaming and downloadable formats. Whether these new services are, in the long run, a hit or a bust among spoiled online consumers remains to be determined. One aspect of the current trend is immediately apparent, though: intensely branded media consolidation leads to fewer apparent choices. That consolidation is conspicuous from the top to the bottom of the hit-music industry, from outrageously hyped CD releases to cookie-cutter radio stations.

Even the Internet, once so individual, has not escaped corporate homogenization. The variety of online music selections grows every day. But the Internet's growth across the board has been characterized by more people visiting fewer destinations, as if the virtual universe were pockmarked by black holes (Yahoo!, AOL, MSN, Lycos, eBay, Amazon, and so on) from which online traffic cannot escape once sucked in. As MusicNet, Pressplay, Windows Media Player, RealJukebox, and other powerfully branded music services establish massive footprints on the Net, consumers might forget how to search, find, explore, discover, and thrill to the depth and scope of digital music.

This book is about enabling that thrill. Greater choice requires more tools and better understanding of how to use them. These pages seek to organize an immense universe of possibility, identify its mysteries, illuminate its solutions, and help keep the digital songstream playing for a long, long time.

1

The Household Digital Music Center

Consumers must develop some new ways of thinking about music and music ownership. They include realizing that the essential music product is not the compact disc, but the files on that disc. The codependency of music, the disc, and the CD player is shattered in the new era of digital music. This liberation takes some getting used to, and is consolidated by the single device that is absolutely central to the new musical household: the computer.

In the scheme of this book, the computer is the home's central music appliance. It acquires, plays, stores, and manages the distribution of music to other devices. The computer dominates the home stereo system. That doesn't mean you should put your receiver and speakers out by the curb. But it does mean that their power has been usurped, and you might find that you rely on them far less as time goes on. Certainly, if you follow the empowerment paths outlined in this book, your traditional components will fall in line behind the computer in the musical food chain. As the store-bought CD diminishes in importance, so do the home systems dedicated to its importance.

The CD is hardly dead, and will continue to exist for some time. It took six years for the CD to outsell vinyl albums, and for years after that (even now) LPs continued to be manufactured and sold. (In the first three months of 2002, music on vinyl outsold music on cassettes in Britain, reversing a seventeen-year trend.) In the most resolute digital music household, music

The Music Appliance of the Future

A battle is afoot between computer advocates and those who favor alternative music managers. At stake is the control of a household's current of music, flowing from online sources to in-house storage to the ears of its owners.

The computer can currently do it all, but it is the perennial dream of the convergence industry to eventually eliminate it. Convergence is all about combining the specialties of two (or more) devices into a single unique task-solving piece of consumer electronics. The computer is a powerful, but still rather unfriendly, musical platform. Traditional music components are much easier to operate but cannot go online, rip CDs, burn CDs, or play back compressed files. So, the reasoning goes, consumers need a hybrid device that incorporates the ease of a stereo component with the task-oriented power and online capabilities of a computer. Several such devices are in development, as described a bit in this chapter and in chapter 10.

The other approach is to simplify the computer and fashion it more specifically as a music machine. That is the tactic of Steve Jobs, the visionary force behind Apple computers. He is philosophically opposed by Steve Perlman, the inventor of WebTV and a newer set-top product called Moxi, a dedicated home entertainment system with strong music-management features. Many other companies, for whom it is easier to introduce a dedicated digital music device than a new computer platform, are pitching their tents against the PC to some degree.

The resolution of this struggle lies in the future. For now, the computer is the most evolved, complete provider of the digital music experience in all its facets.

CDs serve the same function as software CDs: they are archival discs, stored on the shelf against the day that their copied files are lost or damaged. The first thing such a household does with a purchased music CD is "install" it in the computer, which means ripping the files from the disc to the hard drive, usually in MP3 format, for integration into the master collection. (Enhanced CDs offer extra interactive features that add value to the disc, but these products have not taken off as planned.)

Of course, music CDs can be played in a traditional CD player just as always. For many people, though, this increasingly means sliding the disc into the computer's CD drive. And once the album is ripped, there's really no point in bothering with the disc when listening via the computer. When it comes to off-computer listening, alternative MP3–enabled players (which can often handle other compressed formats too) further push the original disc out of the picture.

Overall, the computer grows in importance as ripped and burned files reduce the music CD to a one-step delivery mechanism, just like any other software disc. Music *is* software. And the computer is the household's central clearinghouse for its acquisition, storage, and (frequently) playback. As such, a well-equipped computer dramatically magnifies the home's capacity for manipulating its musical environment. The balance of this chapter is devoted to breaking down the components of an ideally outfitted music household in the digital music era.

I want to emphasize that fancy gear is by no means a requirement. The chapter's final section discusses the least you need to dive into the realms of downloading, ripping, burning, and managing a collection. Much of the required software is free. While the physical devices can add up in cost, nobody needs everything at once, and this chapter matches your musical priorities to computer components and peripherals.

The Music Machine and Its Peripherals

Almost any new computer purchased since mid-2001 has everything you need to accomplish basic ripping, burning, and storing of music, with plenty of processing power and enough hard drive space to accommodate a substantial, growing collection. For people disinclined toward upgrades and add-ons, the easiest way to equip a musical household is to simply own a new computer with an internal CD burner (CD-R drive). A modern, off-the-shelf computer, combined with an Internet account, puts you in the game.

The beauty of most computers is their modular nature, which allows them to be upgraded and added to when special needs arise. So, if you have an older computer and are frustrated by some of its limitations, you can turn it into a power music machine with a few targeted alterations. Upgrading requires either a do-it-yourself penchant for connecting electronic components, or a willingness to take the computer to a repair shop for installation of new features. This chapter is not an upgrade manual; it assumes that you can get the job done somehow and concentrates on the musical value of a computer's parts.

The Platform

The Mac versus PC debate rages in the digital music realm as everywhere else, all the more because of Apple's bundling of music software into the Mac operating system—not to mention Apple's "Rip. Mix. Burn." advertising slogan that created something of a public relations furor. There is also the Apple-created iPod portable MP3 player, one of the seminal gadgets in the promotion of digital music. Nevertheless, though the Mac can accomplish basic digital music tasks, the product and development deficit between the Mac and Windows platforms is just as glaring in this field as in any other. This book is written from the perspective of a Windows/PC user. As of this writing, most subscription services and desktop software are developed for Windows computers, and do not bother making counterparts for the Macintosh.

For Windows users, the platform issue becomes: Which version of Windows is best for digital music?

It's important to be running Windows 95, at least. Windows 98 offers incremental improvements. One of the benefits of upgrading to Windows 2000 is its more sophisticated use of the computer's infamous resources. When programs are run, Windows stores bits of information and graphics that pertain to those software applications. The resources are not necessarily purged from memory when the programs are closed, however, which leads to the dwindling of available resources over time that inevitably leads, in Windows 95 and 98, to a need to reboot. This fact of daily life is addressed in Windows 2000 (and XP), in which resources are handled more intelligently. The result is better, fuller use of RAM memory, and the capacity to run more programs simultaneously. I find this improvement important because of the parallel nature of managing a collection: I like to rip, download, organize, and play back music all at once, and doing so requires the use of several programs in addition to basic e-mail and Web browsing, which are always running.

 Pro & Con Windows XP incorporates the secure audio path (SAP), a kind of software roadblock for unauthorized copies of media. SAP was designed to work behind the scenes, invisibly detecting and disabling music and other media that was copied without authorization. If such automated safeguards are important to you and your family's computer use, Windows XP is attractive on that basis alone. Privacy advocates and Internet libertarians generally frown on such protections implemented at the operating-system level, and I know some observers of the digital music scene who avoid XP out of fear of its potential intrusiveness.

RAM Memory

Random access memory (RAM), the storage space that holds program elements needed for ongoing tasks, is always important. Generally, the more you have the better, especially now when memory chips have become so inexpensive. RAM is measured in megabytes (MB); a large amount of RAM makes Windows run smoother and enables simultaneous opening and use of many programs (especially in Windows 2000 and XP). RAM does nothing for the speed of your Internet connection or the inherent processing speed of your computer. But ample RAM does quicken daily tasks by relieving your computer of stress and data-swapping to the hard drive.

Reminder Don't confuse RAM with hard drive space, both of which are types of memory. You don't store your music collection in RAM. You never manually move files in and out of computer RAM; rather, that memory is used automatically and invisibly by the computer for its own needs.

The bottom line for RAM capacity in a Windows 98, 2000, or XP machine is 128MB. At the time of publication, many off-the-shelf computers contained just the minimal 128MB, leaving any desired upgrade to you. That amount causes bottlenecks when running a few programs. Adding RAM is a fairly easy upgrade, but still involves opening the computer's case, finding the proper slots, plugging in the rectangular memory chips, and closing up the computer. If you're buying a computer online from a company that builds the machine to your specifications, it's worth bumping the price slightly to load up on RAM. Multiply the 128MB by four to get a half *gigabyte* or go for the whole gigabyte (1,024 megabytes). Even doubling to 256MB makes an appropriate difference in Windows 2000 and XP.

Alert Not all RAM chips are the same. Be sure to look in your computer manual, or an online technical help site, to ensure that you get chips of the correct type for your machine.

Hard Drive

The storage area of a computer, the hard drive, is an obviously important component to a music collector. MP3 and other compressed file formats are small, but they add up fast when ripping a CD collection or downloading intensively from an all-you-can-eat subscription service. Serious collectors invest in massive hard drives. The alternative is archiving a large MP3 collection on CDs: it can be a good idea, no matter what, to back up portions of your collection that would be difficult to reconstruct if lost. But centralization is the key to ultimate flexibility and home programming, so ample hard drive space is worth some investment.

Most new computers have fairly substantial drives of at least 20 to 40 gigabytes. Those basic drives provide a good start, and might be sufficient for quite some time. Remember, though, that all your applications, the operating system, and nonmusic content files must find room also.

Power User If you're starting with, or upgrading to, a new hard drive, consider partitioning it and dedicating one partition (sometimes called a virtual drive) to music, or music plus other entertainment media. Partitioning makes organization easy, and also helps you track remaining space. Commercial programs (Partition Magic is one) help with the process. After partitioning, each newly created portion of the hard drive has its own letter assignment: C drive, D drive, E drive, and so on. Conceptually, and in Windows Explorer, they appear to be physically distinct drives.

Upgrading the hard drive is generally accomplished in one of three ways:

- **Replacing the current drive.** The difficulty here is transferring everything (or at least what you wish to keep) from the old drive to the new one. You might even need to acquire a new operating system. Even the best-case scenario involves much copying. Repair shops can do it all for you, creating an exact copy of the old hard drive on the new drive.
- **Adding a second internal hard drive.** A medium-hassle upgrade for the do-it-yourselfer, adding a drive eliminates the need to copy gigabytes of files from the original drive. Be sure that there is room and necessary cabling inside your computer's tower for another drive (it's not a problem in most newer computers), or take the box into a repair shop for guidance. If everything checks out, you can dedicate one drive to music and other media files, leaving your programs and operating system on the first drive.
- **Adding an external hard drive.** External, stackable drives are possibly the best solution if you don't mind paying a little more than for an internal. These units sit near the computer tower, and are connected either wirelessly (through the Firewire standard) or via the computer's USB port. The stackable models allow you to continue adding drives as you need them, setting up a memory chain. Prices are falling, and as

this book neared publication you could find 100–gigabyte drives in the neighborhood of $300. These potential music warehouses can be plugged into any computer, making them deliciously appealing for carrying to a party, or even just to another room in the home in which there's a computer.

Huge hard drive capacity is appealing when paired with high-speed Internet. You might be amazed at how quickly the gigabytes get eaten up if you're downloading every night from all-you-can-eat sites like EMusic.

Sound Card and Speakers

These two components are naturally paired, but good speakers are far more important than a fancy sound card. Playing an MP3 is a relatively simple task for the computer, requiring less processing muscle and dedicated sound card memory than dealing with interactive gaming soundtracks. Gamers put great emphasis on upgrading the sound card, but if your interest is primarily the simple playback of song files, chances are the original sound card of any reasonably modern computer delivers perfectly adequate performance.

Speakers, though, represent an entirely different level of consideration. The importance you place on excellent speakers should correspond to the importance of the home-base computer as a playback component. If your inclination is to get the music out of the computer quickly, listening mostly to burned CDs playing in a traditional stereo, or to MP3s through a shirt-pocket player, then window-rattling speakers attached to the computer are unimportant. Still, *some* listening always happens at the computer itself. Very few computers are sold off the shelf without speakers. Speaker excellence has reduced in price to the point at which enjoying fine sound through your main downloading source is affordable for most reasonably serious hobbyists. To put a rough number to it, you can easily drive your neighbors to relocation for under a hundred dollars.

The one speaker item that upgrades sound dramatically and with little effort is the subwoofer (sometimes called a woofer). A subwoofer is a boxy speaker that usually sits on the floor, adding low- and midfrequency sound to the mix. Traditional desktop computer speakers concentrate on mid- and high-frequency sound. Subwoofers anchor the sound with depth—what sound engineers call "bottom."

Subwoofers can be purchased separately, but the better choice is to get an integrated three-speaker set that includes two desktops and a subwoofer. These speaker sets are amplified, and require a single plug on your power strip. The sonic benefit of integrated sets lies in coordinated crossover points for the frequencies handled by each of the two components (the subwoofer, and the two desktops). Throwing an independent subwoofer into the mix certainly adds a bassy low end, but the acoustics are not as smooth across the entire frequency range. The result might be that some recordings come across worse than others.

♪ **Reminder** Of all computer components, speakers demand the most in-store shopping time. Buying speakers online without having heard them should be the last resort of those living far from an electronics retailer.

CD Drives

This essential component enables ripping, burning (if it's a CD-RW drive), and playback of audio and MP3 CDs. It's difficult to find a computer without a basic CD drive. In such instances, though, internal and external drives can be added, keeping in mind the same set of considerations discussed in relation to hard drives. Most new computers are sold with recordable CD drives (called CD-R and CD-RW) drives. There is no difference between a CD-R and CD-RW drive; they are both commonly referred to as CD burners. The difference between once-recordable CDs (CD-Rs) and re-recordable CDs (CD-RWs) lies in the disc, not the drive. The distinction is explored later in this chapter.

When choosing a CD-RW drive, whether internal or external, speed is the important specification to look at. Three speed categories for each drive are listed in catalogs and online stores: write, rewrite, and read. They are usually listed in that order, as in:

32	x	12	x	40
Write		Rewrite		Read

The speed multiples in CD-RW specs are founded on a base speed of 150 kilobytes per second (150KBps). It might be tempting to think of "32x" as meaning thirty-two times the real-time duration of a piece of music, but that logic breaks down when you consider that a single piece of music can be uncompressed or compressed, and these two files would burn in two very different amounts of time. The important fact is that faster multiples mean faster burning. The middle number (rewrite speed) is the least important if you concentrate on CD-R discs, not CD-RWs (which I generally recommend). The last number (read speed, or the speed at which the drive can grab a disc's file in preparation for doing something with it) is almost higher than you need for simple music playback.

Some media-oriented computers contain both a CD-RW drive and a DVD drive. DVD is currently used primarily for movies, but its future probably includes music. DVD drives have always been able to play music CDs as well as movie discs, so are useful in copying albums for personal use. The original album is placed in the DVD drive, and the computer copies to a blank disc placed in the CD-RW drive.

USB Port

Portable MP3 players, external storage drives, and other peripheral gadgets need an on-ramp to your main computer. That connection is most often (for the time being) provided by the USB port. Just about any computer built in the past three years is equipped with a USB port, which is often located on the front panel of the tower. If your machine lacks one, USB ports are available as card-based add-ons that put the port on the back of the tower, clustered with the serial, parallel, sound card, and modem ports.

The USB 2.0 standard offers a quantum leap in transfer speed. New computers have USB 2.0 built in; older machines can be upgraded. The speed difference is profound, but not necessarily a priority. Loading up a portable MP3 player with an hour's worth of music doesn't take long even with the original USB interface. But if you're constantly swapping gigabytes of files in and out of a portable jukebox or external hard drive, the upgrade might be alluring.

Extras

Basic accessories are important to busy music collectors, especially:

- **Blank CDs.** Sales of blank CDs are rising faster than sales of prerecorded music CDs, thanks to cheap prices and the desire to burn MP3 collections to disc (see chapter 2). Burned data CDs archive a collection, and burned audio CDs create playable discs for the car or any CD player unattached to the computer. For serious archiving and cost-effective pricing, purchase blank discs on fifty-disc or one-hundred-disc spindles. The most common CD format accommodates 700 megabytes of data, or eighty minutes of audio.
- **CD cases and labels.** Although you can buy blank CDs wrapped with cases and paper inserts, those packages are far more expensive than

About Blank CDs "for Music"

If you've shopped around, you might have noticed certain packages of blanks CDs specially formulated for music. This product category is primarily a marketing and copy-protection distinction. "For Music" CDs do not offer higher-grade burning of either data or audio when used in a computer. These specialty products are required when burning in shelftop, stand-alone CD burning units connected to a home stereo system. Those devices check for certain authentication data coded onto the discs, without which the burner does not proceed with recording. A royalty on the sale of these discs is collected by ASCAP (American Society of Composers, Authors, and Publishers) and distributed to its members. None of this applies to computer burning, though, whether you're burning audio formats or not. So avoid these uniquely marketed discs and their high prices.

buying each accessory—blank discs, cases, labels—separately and in bulk. I like multicolored CD cases (though burning hipsters scorn them) because I like to separate portions of my archived collection by hue. As to labels, coordinate your choice with both your printer (inkjet or laser?) and favorite labeling program. (Some burning software, such as the burning module of Musicmatch Jukebox Plus, incorporates label-printing software.) Most labeling software recognizes standard label configurations issued by many manufacturers. Personally, I write most of my labels by hand (and sometimes forgo the label entirely, marking up the disc directly).

- **USB hub.** That USB port in the front of your computer is in high demand by all kinds of media appliances, from MP3 players to external hard drives, from scanners to digital cameras. Whatever you're plugging into it now, taking up digital music only stresses the situation more. USB hubs effectively increase your computer's (simultaneous) USB capacity. USB hubs are available in internal configurations that require opening up the computer for installation—the result is additional USB ports on the back of the tower—and external versions that plug into your original USB port.
- **External players.** A range of portable and shelftop devices move the music out of the computer and into your walking-around life. See chapter 10 for more information about MP3–enabled portable players, car players, and stereo components.

- **More computers!** Don't laugh. One of the best single-room music solutions is a cheap laptop running basic jukebox software (see chapter 9), connected to an under-$100 set of great speakers. There is a race proceeding between the computer industry and the hi-fi industry to equip noncomputer rooms of the house with digital music. The computer industry is winning this race, and putting old computers to service as simple playback machines fits the bill. Do your heavy lifting (ripping, burning, downloading, archiving) at the home's main computer, then distribute your collection via burned CDs or home networking.

The Internet Connection

An undeniable truism holds that high-speed Internet connections encourage digital music consumption, and, conversely, digital music drives adoption of high-speed home connections. There's no question that a broadband connection liquifies the digital music experience. Both downloading and streaming are rendered dynamic with fluid online connections that transfer content quickly. You don't *need* a high-speed connection to reap benefits of the MP3 phenomenon—in fact, you don't need to go online at all to rip CDs and enjoy flexible home programming and increased portability. File compression is at the heart of this revolution, not fast Internet performance.

Nevertheless, being connected to the Net is an indivisible part of immersion in the digital music lifestyle, and faster connections open bottlenecks and ease frustrations. Collecting music through subscription plans is transformed from a tasty meal to a gluttonous feast through a broadband connection.

Residential Internet connections achieve broadband status in one of three ways:

- **Cable.** Many (but not all) cable-TV companies provide Internet service through the same wires that deliver cable channels. The cost is usually about $40 per month for unlimited use. Service quality varies; at its best, speeds greater than corporate T1 connections are attained. The cable company normally supplies a specialized modem to replace the computer's telephone modem (it's called a cable modem), but does not supply the necessary ethernet card that the modem must plug into. (You can buy and install an ethernet card yourself, or get a repair shop to do the job.) Two types of cable Internet service exist: one-way (which uses a regular telephone modem to slowly send information *to* the Internet), and two-way (which employs cable lines at very high speed in both directions).

- **DSL.** A technology deployed by telecom and phone companies through preexisting phone lines, DSL is limited by a couple of restrictions. First, the residence must be located within a short distance of a telephone switching station; the service range is expanding as telecom companies build out their switching networks. Second, pricing policies sometimes offer different tiers of service in which lightning-fast service costs more than merely fast service. Even the lower tiers can be pricier than cable service.
- **Satellite.** By far the least common solution, satellite service provides high-speed connection for some people in locales unserved by cable-Internet and DSL. Satellite broadband is generally more expensive then either cable or DSL.

When considering upgrading to high-speed Internet (assuming it's available—check with your cable and phone companies), you must of course grapple with the higher price. For most people, broadband costs about twice as much, per month, as operating a phone modem. The benefits include freeing up a phone line in some cases, and much better streaming and downloading performance in all cases. Full-bore engagement with digital music can include a shift in music expenses that you might wish to consider. If you're a heavy CD buyer, you could actually save money by subscribing to a few online music services with a high-speed connection, if those services replace many disc purchases.

The Least You Need

Reducing fancy gear to the most basic necessities, there are three components you need to get started satisfactorily with digital music:

- a computer;
- a CD burner; and
- an Internet connection.

Fundamentally equipped with these three essentials, you can rip CDs, burn CDs, and download music. How quickly this all transpires depends on the quality of the CD burner and the nature of the Internet connection—but it doesn't really matter at the beginning. The point is to discover the profound usefulness of removing tracks from their discs, and of compressed music files in general. From there, you can upgrade as your appetites sharpen.

2

Ripping and Burning

When you buy a music CD, you're purchasing a platter with digital files stored on it. In the past, that platter "worked" only when placed into a CD player. The digital music revolution has made the files more important than the disc, and enables us to use our computers to remove, shrink, manipulate, and store those files.

This chapter is all about the advantages and methods of treating your purchased CDs as files instead of platters, in two important ways:

- *Ripping* those files off the CD and turning them into more flexible, portable files. In this way the song is untethered from the disc, and the disc is untethered from the CD player.
- *Burning* (recording) files back onto blank discs in your choice of format.

Ripping and burning result in liberation for the music collector.

Ripping is perhaps an unfortunate term for copying a song from a CD to a storage drive, even if does stylishly evoke an image of tearing songs forcibly from their platters. All too easily, ripping music can be equated with *ripping off* music. Certainly, the recording industry has used "ripping and burning" to describe what they view as evil music pirates depriving artists and companies of their well-deserved compensation. The most visible file-management programs shy away from the word *ripping*, although they all incorporate the actual function: RealOne calls the dreaded task "saving," Windows Media Player "copying," Media Jukebox "encoding," and Musicmatch "recording."

Euphemisms aside, ripping purchased music for personal use is solidly protected by copyright law (see chapter 11). Not to be naive, everyone knows how common it is to take the process a step further by copying CDs for friends, exposing copied songs to file-sharing networks for downloading by strangers, and infringing copyright by other methods. Still, ripping by itself is sanctioned by law, it's fun and easy, and it has many benefits.

This chapter is devoted to ripping and burning for convenience and flexibility. Ripping to MP3 format shrinks the files to about one-tenth their original size, making them far more portable. When I travel I carry three or four burned CDs, each one holding ten to twelve albums ripped into MP3 format. Those three discs replace at least thirty original CDs. In the flexi-bility department, a centralized MP3 collection can be programmed and playlisted in ways that support any soundtrack your life demands. (Chapter 9 touches on that issue, and chapter 8 delves deeply into the nuts and bolts of managing a large centralized collection.) Keeping your music collection on your computer's hard drive empowers you to build a soundtrack for your home life with unprecedented precision and variety.

A question naturally arises concerning the value of the CD, as a prod-uct, in a marketplace that increasingly rips the files and discards the platter. The original CD might not actually be thrown in the trash, but I know that in my case my collection of original CDs has become mostly decorative. The first thing I do with a purchased CD (and yes, this anti-CD curmudg-eon still buys a lot of them) is put it in the computer, before even listening to it, and rip its files into my hard drive collection.

My habits notwithstanding, original CDs still fulfill some important functions, even in a ripped world:

- Your collection of original discs is your highest-quality archive of your music. Lose your MP3 collection somehow, and you can start fresh.
- The packaging often contains artwork, information, and lyrics.
- Enhanced CDs are bundled with multimedia extras and Web links.

Ripping CDs and Copying CDs

Ripping is copying, but not all copying is ripping. In popular articles about the digital revolution, there is some confusion concerning the difference between ripping a CD's tracks to a hard drive (the most common type of ripping) and copying a whole CD to a blank compact disc (known as CD copying). Both activities are popular, but CD copying requires a better-equipped computer with two CD drives, one of which is a CD burner (see chapter 1). One of those two CD drives can be a DVD drive, because they can play music CDs as well as movie discs.

CD copying is as legal as ripping when practiced for personal use. For example, making a second copy of a purchased CD for playing in your car is convenient and protected by U.S. regulations. Both ripping and CD copying cross the legal line when the copy is given to another person, either through online file-sharing (of ripped files) or informal giveaways of CD copies.

The Basic Ripping Process

Technically, *ripping* refers to any digital copying of a complete work, usually a song and often an entire album. You can rip a CD track, an entire CD, a streamed song, an ongoing Webcast, and even a previously ripped file that you wish to encode in a different format. It's all ripping, but this chapter concentrates on ripping CD tracks and entire CDs, the most common, easy, and useful ripping function.

Many programs enable ripping, and several of them make the process ridiculously easy. A basic method has become more standardized than it was a few years ago, when you needed to know more about the nuts and bolts of ripping. Following is a checklist of the essential tasks that comprise the entire rip:

- **Placing the source CD in the computer's CD drive.** If you have two or more CD drives attached to the computer, it doesn't matter which you use. You do not need a CD burner.
- **Opening a ripping program.** Several programs are detailed later in this chapter. Many are free. Some might already reside in your computer.
- **Getting track information.** It might seem surprising, but the track information your ripping program needs (in order to assign filenames) doesn't usually come from the CD. It must be imported from one of a

few specialized online sources, and your computer must be connected to the Internet in order to get the album and track names. This is one considerable inconvenience to the ripping process. It's not that you can't rip without the album and track information—you can—but the program cannot create intelligent filenames for the tracks without it. Active ripping assumes an always-online lifestyle. When you rip while offline, you usually must rename your ripped files manually.

- **Selecting tracks.** You always have the option of burning one, any combination of, or all tracks. One great benefit of ripping is the ability to extract favorite songs from an album.
- **Choosing a file location and file-naming standard.** Ripping programs must put the ripped files somewhere on your hard drive, and they will select a default location for you, but you save yourself trouble by picking out your own location. In most cases you may also choose the kind of folder structure the program will put onto your hard drive to house the ripped files. Finally, most programs let you opt to include certain information—song title, album name, artist name, track number—in the filename, and in what order the information categories appear. These choices are stored for future ripping sessions, but can always be altered.
- **Choosing a bit rate.** This selection influences the sound fidelity of the ripped files; in other words, how closely they correspond to the sound quality of the source CD. You can pretty much equal the CD's quality, but you cannot exceed it. This selection is stored for the future, but can be changed at any time.
- **Choosing various other settings.** Programs vary in this department. Many allow ripping to non-MP3 formats. Some allow analog copying in addition to the more common digital copying. Other options apply to the type of CD drive you're using. With the exception of format type, many of these choices are more abstruse than necessary, and can be safely disregarded. I discuss important exceptions in the individual reviews of ripping programs later in this chapter.
- **Letting it rip.** Finally! The program rips through the CD, placing compressed copies of each selected track on your hard drive. Ripping usually transpires at some multiple of real time, which is to say that it doesn't take as long as it would to listen to the CD. The exact speed depends on the encoder built into the ripping program, your computer's processing power, your selected rip settings, and the type of CD drive you have.

- **Cleaning up filenames and moving the files.** It makes sense to rip to a directory apart from the tracks' permanent home on your hard drive (see chapter 8 for suggestions about managing your music library). If the automatic file-naming settings are correct, renaming isn't necessary. But if you ripped without track information, then you need to rename the files before moving them.

The next sections discuss four of these steps—getting track information, automatic file naming, folder assignments, and bit rates—in more detail. Although it might seem unglamorous and hardly musical, mastering the settings that control these functions will serve you well in the long run.

Getting Track Information

Any good ripper employs a built-in connection to one of the online databases of CD and track information. These warehouses use "hashing" technology to identify CDs from small chunks of music data sampled by the ripping program and sent to the database. Within seconds, the ripper has the information needed to display your CD's title, all the song names, track timings, artist name, year of release, and genre. In other words, all the information needed to fill in the ID3v1 tags for each track. ID3 tags (which come in two versions) are used by MP3 players to identify and sort songs (please see chapter 8 for everything you ever wanted to know about ID3 tags).

Reminder The process of obtaining track information is crucial to effortless ripping. The program uses the data to create filenames, saving you tons of work, and to insert the ID3 tags, saving you even more heavy lifting down the road. Because your computer needs to have an open Internet connection to get the track information, try to arrange for most of your ripping to occur on a connected machine, or one that can get connected without hassle.

Most rippers use the Gracenote/CDDB database, which used to be called, simply, CDDB (an acronym for CD database). Many programs still refer to the service as CDDB. Another data source is the All Music Guide, sometimes abbreviated as AMG.

Ripping programs differ in how the information-gathering process is started. Some retrieve it even if you don't ask. This can be a problem with noncommercial discs that aren't represented in Gracenote and AMG. For example, a friend recently sent me a CD containing several of his informally recorded concert appearances during the 1970s. I couldn't play the disc in Winamp because the program kept tying up my resources in futile attempts to find track information; playback would stall with each new track. Automatic retrieval is handy with commercial discs, though, and is usually so fast that if your computer is already online you might not realize that a data transfer has occurred. When the track information does not zip in automatically, look for an onscreen button that says something like "Get CD Info" or is simply emblazoned with the CDDB acronym.

Assigning Filenames and Folders

The ripping process is eased by automatic file naming and folder assignment. Using these two features in combination, you can end up with perfectly labeled files that are either in their permanent spot on your hard drive or are one move away.

If you keep a music library distributed over several file folders—for example, with folders for different genres, as described in chapter 8—it makes sense to direct all your fresh rips to a dedicated "Rip" folder. From there you can drag the files to the appropriate final folder. If you keep all your music in a single master "Music" folder (which I don't recommend), you might as well rip directly to that folder.

Many ripping programs offer two basic choices in folder assignment: ripping everything to one folder, or letting the program create a new folder for each artist, and a nested folder within it for each of that artist's albums. The latter approach is admirable in its fastidiousness (see figure 2.1), but the result, when spread out over a large ripped collection, is an overly complicated system of folders. Because you can easily group your songs into their original albums through judicious file-naming (which I'll get to shortly), there's no reason to dedicate a folder to each album, or even to each artist. Still, the choice ultimately depends on your own organizational style.

 Reminder Remember that if you access your collection mostly through a jukebox program such as Media Jukebox that relies on ID3 tags to sort and present your files, then the folder structure doesn't matter as much as when you identify your music files directly through Windows Explorer. Because I use both methods, I prefer a modest folder structure of my own design, and I decline the subfolder option found in most ripping programs.

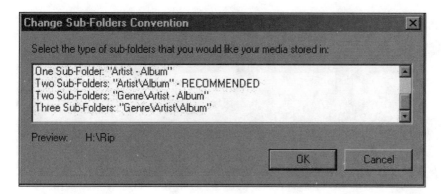

Figure 2.1. Many ripping programs offer to create dedicated folders for each artist and album.

When it comes to naming files, the ripping programs assume that you want some combination of the basic artist/album/track title/track number information pieces in your filename. File naming is crucial for easy access and sorting of your collection outside of a jukebox program. When burning your files to CD, for example, you might (depending on the program used) identify them by filename, not ID3 tags. Automatic file naming, provided by most ripping programs, emits perfect—and perfectly consistent—filenames.

In most cases you have a choice of several file-naming conventions, each of which puts the basic information pieces in a different order. This choice is largely a matter of taste, but I find two rules useful:

- **Always include the track number as one of the information pieces, even though it exists in the ID3 tags.** If you don't, Windows Explorer lists album files in alphabetical order. In fact, Windows Explorer *always* defaults to listing tracks alphabetically, and positioning the track number correctly assures that the alphabetical list is the same as the album's song order.
- **Place the track number somewhere before the track name.** You want the number to take precedence over the song titles, which can throw the alphabetical list out of album order.

Reminder Keeping these rules in mind, it's best to start the filename with one of the unchanging information pieces (artist name or album title), or the track number. I prefer organizing my folders by artist, so I always start with the artist name.

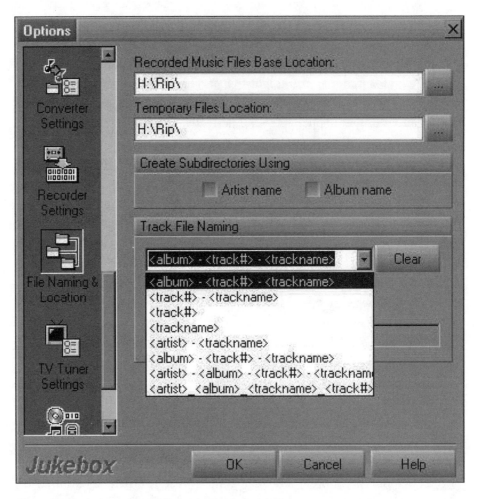

Figure 2.2. Automatic file naming saves work and results in cleanly labeled rips.

Figure 2.3. Assigning automatic file naming in Media Jukebox.

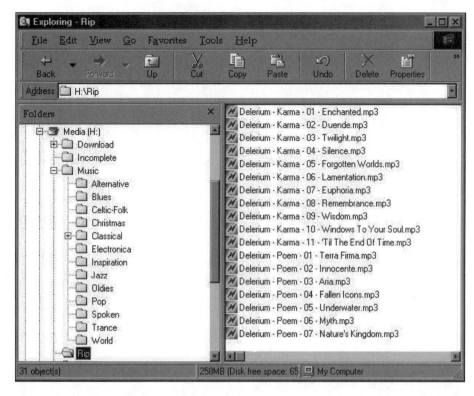

Figure 2.4. *Auto-named files of newly ripped albums.*

Figure 2.2 illustrates the automatic file-naming setup panel in RealOne, which allows you to set the position of each information piece using drop-down menus. As you make choices, a sample filename appears beneath. Figure 2.3 illustrates how the setting is made in Media Jukebox, with a single drop-down menu.

As you can see in Figure 2.4, automatic file naming makes a tidy collection of tracks, ready to be moved to their permanent folder. Proper positioning of the track numbers before the song titles keeps the alphabetical list identical to the song order of the albums.

Choosing the Bit Rate

Now it might seem as if we're moving into deeply technical territory, but all you really need to remember is this formula: Higher = Better + Bigger. Higher-numbered bit rates create better-sounding files, and larger files. The industry standard for MP3 ripping, employed by EMusic's subscription service, MP3.com's free downloads, and virtually all online music distributors that deliver MP3 files, is 128k. (The "k" stands for *kilobit*, and the full acronym "kbps" stands for *kilobits per second*. The bit rate represents the average number of data bits used by the song file each second.) CDs are recorded with a whopping 1411.2kbps, so you might wonder how a paltry 128k MP3 file can sound like anything. That's exactly why the MP3 compression scheme was a blockbuster invention: it reduces the file size drastically without a great reduction in fidelity.

Most people are satisfied with the sound of a 128k MP3 file, and unsatisfied with lower bit rates. Accordingly, 128k creates the smallest possible nice-sounding file. Going up to the next common rate, 160k, makes an important difference to some people; in fact, 160k is my default setting for most rips. The next common level, 192k, sounds quite excellent to my ears, and I sometimes use it, but I've never had the urge to push upward any higher. The option exists to go as high as 320k (see figure 2.5), and such high-quality encodings are becoming more common in the file-sharing networks.

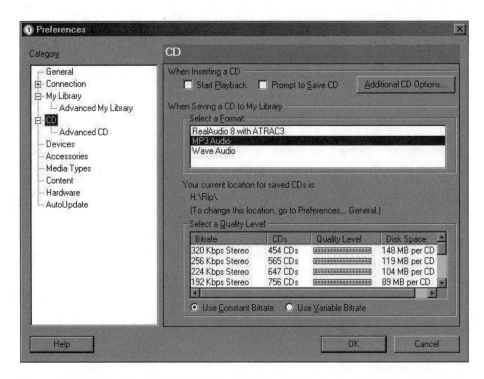

Figure 2.5. *Assigning bit rates in RealOne. The higher the bit rate, the more closely your ripped files sound like the CD.*

WMA Bit Rates

Some rippers enable WMA ripping, through which CD tracks are copied as Windows Media files. WMA bit rates are generally lower than MP3 bit rates because the WMA format is more efficient. A 64k bit rate sounds far better in WMA format than it does in MP3 format. The upshot of this discrepancy is that good-sounding WMA files are smaller than good-sounding MP3 files. Not a bad deal, but keep in mind that WMA files are not recognized universally by software players and portable devices to the same extent that MP3 files are. So by ripping to WMA you trade universality for encoding efficiency.

Reminder Increasing the bit rate from 128k to 160k adds about 15 megabytes to the size of an entire album (the exact amount depends on the length of the album, of course).

Alert Ripping with high bit rates slows down the copying, and increases the load on your computer's processor. Neither of these factors is necessarily a problem if you're not in a hurry. But increasing from 128k to 160k increases rip time by about a third, and high bit rates also bogs down the rest of your simultaneous computing (browsing the Web, playing music files, and so on). The more powerful the computer, the less these factors impact it.

If both quality and storage space are issues, some ripping programs let you opt for variable bit rate (VBR), as opposed to the constant bit rate (CBR) already discussed. Variable bit rate encoding lets the ripping program determine exactly when in the songs a higher bit rate is required to replicate the music with good fidelity. If you watch the bit-rate gauge of an MP3 player during the playback of a VBR file, you can see the rate jumping around quickly—sometimes several times a second. Programs that offer this feature use descriptors such as "Normal" or "Very Good" to describe the VBR quality, because it cannot be quantified with a single bit rate. (Musicmatch uses a unique slider mechanism for very fine control, as you can see in figure 2.6.) "Normal" generally corresponds in sound quality to a 128k CBR file, and is a little smaller. Most people use variable bit rate to get higher quality than that while squeezing the size down somewhat. If you

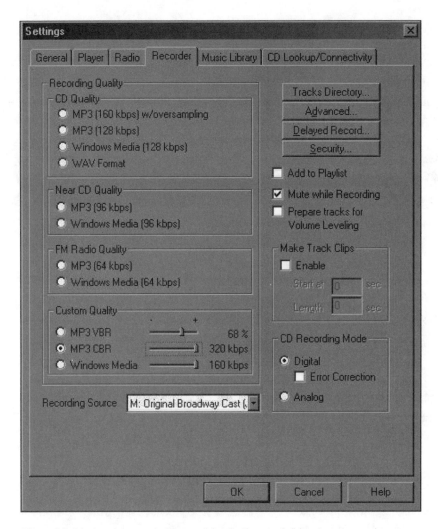

Figure 2.6. Musicmatch uses both one-click selections and sliders to set a precise bit rate for ripping.

have lots of storage space for your ripped albums, forget VBR and go for the higher constant rates.

Choosing a Ripping Program

I bounce around among several ripping programs, but I'm a software junkie. Most people settle on one solution to simplify the ripping lifestyle. When all the settings are in place, ripping becomes a simple matter of inserting the CD, opening the program, and clicking the Rip (or Save, or Copy, or Encode, or Record) button.

A number of dedicated ripping/encoding programs are available, and one of them (AudioCatalyst) is described in this chapter. Integrated media players also offer ripping options, and I will describe four major integrated desktop media programs. There is some convenience to ripping with an integrated program that you might already be using for burning, library organizing, Internet radio streaming, and playlist creation. The advantage to using a dedicated program is that its features might be more sophisticated.

Reminder Don't confuse ripping with CD management. Ripping is a form of CD management, in that it compresses CD tracks and stores them on a single source: your computer's hard drive. But rippers/encoders are in a different class of software than so-called CD managers. The latter group includes what are essentially database programs for managing the information of your CD collection, not the music itself. The programs act as desktop CD players, replacing the built-in Windows CD Player and media jukeboxes that are described in chapter 9. They also store track information and playback preferences for each album. Because CD management programs place emphasis on the disc, not the removable files, they fall outside the main focus of this book and aren't reviewed in any detail.

Assigning CD Playback to Your Ripper

Almost every media player can recognize a music CD in the drive and play it. Furthermore, Windows provides its own little CD Player that is dedicated to the task. Most computers arrive off the shelf with Windows CD Player assigned as the default CD player, which means that it springs to life automatically when you put a CD in the drive. However, almost any media player can steal that task away from Windows CD Player, and it is most convenient to direct it to your preferred ripping program. That way, whenever you slide a CD into your drive, your favorite ripper appears on the screen to make a copy if you wish.

The CD-playing assignment (and all other file assignments) is selected somewhere in the Preferences or Options panel of your preferred program. You might find an explicit selection for audio CDs, or the assignment might be buried among all the other possible file types. In the latter case, look for the CDA file type, as CDA is the native file type for music CDs. Don't confuse CDA with WAV, which many people think is equivalent. Assigning WAV playback to the program does not make it open for CDs.

Ripping and Encoding

A little software browsing online might lead to confusion between the terms *ripping* and *encoding*. All ripping is encoding because it copies CD tracks in a different format code. Technically, all encoding is ripping, but is not typically referred to as ripping. For example, changing a downloaded WAV file to an MP3 file is colloquially a rip, but is more officially known as encoding. Adding to the confusion, some download sites refer to rippers as encoders. The problem is that not all encoders can reach into a CD and copy its files: the files need to already reside on your hard drive for them to work.

This problem is quickly disappearing as programs become more integrated. If you don't search pretty deeply for out-of-the-way programs, chances are you won't encounter any confusion. Remember that most rippers deal primarily with CDs, and most encoders deal primarily with files already on the hard drive. When in doubt, read carefully about the program before downloading.

RealOne

Whatever shortcomings hinder the RealOne subscription service (described in chapter 4) and the RealOne jukebox program generally (see chapter 9), those complaints don't extend to ripping, which is implemented in superb style. Of the four major media players covered here, RealOne is my choice for ripping, and I turn to it often.

Sorting out the RealNetworks brands can be a bit confusing. RealOne is the name of both a subscription service and a stand-alone media program that delivers the service, and also performs basic desktop music functions for the subscribed and unsubscribed alike. The RealNetworks site (www.real.com) cements the service to the program so relentlessly that you might think, on first perusal, that you can't get the program without shelling out the dough for the service. Not true. Go to the site and scour the home page for the "Free RealOne Player" link. As of this writing, you may download the player without committing to the RealOne subscription trial period.

Once you download the free RealOne Player (assuming that for now you don't choose to subscribe to the service) and install it, you might notice that the application files refer to programs called RealPlayer and RealJukebox, and the download folder contains nothing resembling "RealOne." Yet, opening the program displays the RealOne Player logo.

This trademark tangle resulted from the consolidation of previously separate programs (RealPlayer and RealJukebox among others) into the integrated RealOne program. If you subscribe to the streaming/downloading service that includes MusicNet (see chapter 4), you may update your program to RealOne Plus, which delivers higher-quality video streaming.

RealOne's excellent ripping features are somewhat undermined by the bandwidth-clogging pushiness of the program. Video ads and a graphics-heavy directory page are pushed onto your screen when connected to the Internet, which is a nuisance when your only desire is to perform a quick rip of a new CD. Setting the program to open to the CD screen, not the Web screen, helps streamline its performance. Follow these steps:

1. **After RealOne is open, click the Tools menu.** A drop-down menu appears.
2. **Click the Preferences selection.** The Preferences panel appears.
3. **In the left-hand pane, click General.**
4. **In the right-hand pane, click the drop-down menu in the RealOne Player Options section.** (See figure 2.7.)
5. **Select the CD option.**
6. **Click the OK button.**

Figure 2.8 shows RealOne in CD mode, and this is where ripping transpires. First, though, you need to assign your bit rate, folder designation, filename convention, and format type. Doing so requires visiting four sections of the Preferences panel. Click the Preferences button at the bottom of the CD screen in RealOne, then follow these steps:

1. **In the left-hand pane, click CD.** The right-hand pane displays file formats and bit rates (see figure 2.5). Assuming you wish to rip your CDs to MP3 files, select MP3 Audio. In the bottom portion of the pane, select your preferred constant or variable bit rate. (The numbers in the Disk Space column are estimates.) Clicking the Additional CD Options button lets you instruct the program to automatically get track information (good idea), play the CD while ripping (I prefer not to stress my computer's resources when ripping), and a few others.
2. **In the left-hand pane, click General.** In the File Locations section, use the Browse button to assign the folder location for ripped files. You can set the Default Download location too, if you plan to use

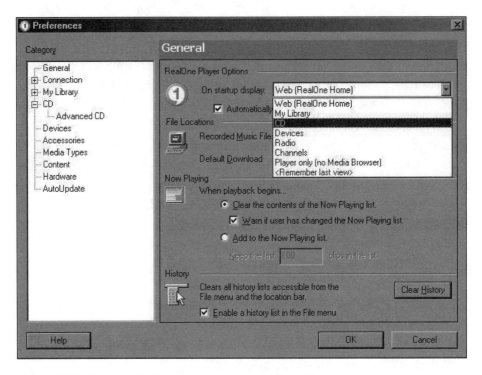

Figure 2.7. Set RealOne's Preferences to open the program in CD mode.

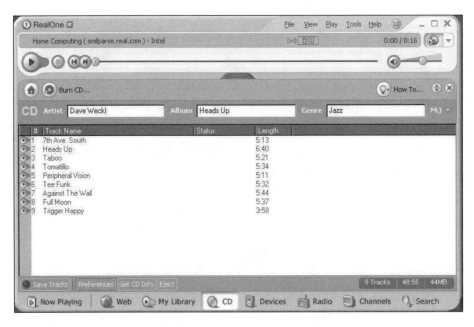

Figure 2.8. The ripping panel in RealOne.

RealOne for downloading. I routinely make every possible setting for all the programs I use so that I never have to search for a missing file.

3. **In the left-hand pane, click Advanced My Library.** Click the small plus sign next to My Library to reveal Advanced My Library (see figure 2.9). Use the options under the Change Sub-folder… and Change Filenames… buttons to set these crucial automatic features. Although RealOne recommends a system wherein each ripped album creates two subfolders, my preference is for no subfolders at all, using explicit filenames to distinguish artists and albums. (See chapter 8 for more on the fascinating topic of naming song files.)

4. **In the left-hand pane, click Advanced CD.** Click the small plus sign next to CD to reveal Advanced CD. Here, you set digital or analog recording; the digital default should be left alone in nearly all cases. In fact, almost everything in this section can remain unchanged, but you might want to look at the Advanced CPU Options… button. Clicking it reveals a slider that determines how your computer prioritizes ripping among your other simultaneous tasks. Dragged all the way to the right, the slider tells your computer to make ripping a top priority,

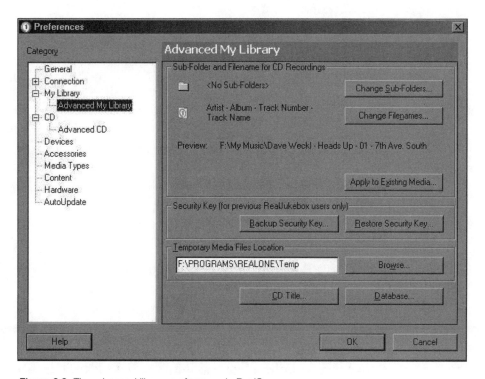

Figure 2.9. *The advanced library preferences in RealOne.*

slowing down other functions to maintain ripping speed. If you're rip-ping CDs in the background while listening to music and otherwise making demands on your computer's CPU (the central processing chip), try a central or far-left setting.

After setting your default choices (which can be adjusted at any time), simply click on Save Tracks on RealOne's CD screen to rip whatever CD is in your drive.

RealOne shines in the bit-rate and file-naming departments, making it easy to choose from a splendid variety of choices. But, even better, the pro-gram is equipped with one of the best ripping engines in the business. (RealNetworks owns Xing, the company responsible for developing the excellent AudioCatalyst.) Additionally, the interface keeps you informed of what's going on: the progress and speed of the rip.

Windows Media Player

Windows Media Player probably exists on your computer already, making it the easiest program, of those covered in this chapter, to start using. The sad truth, though, is that Windows Media Player is probably the least effec-tive ripper in the roundup.

First of all, the program does not rip to MP3 at all, which might push it straight off your radar. Naturally enough, Windows Media Player encodes to WMA (Windows Media) format—and that format alone. Also, there is no way to change the default folder-creating system of artist or album sub-folders beneath your assigned "Rip" folder. That's enough to put it off *my* radar, even when I do want to rip WMA files.

But if all this is exactly your cup of tea, Windows Media Player is the perfect ripper, and setting it up could hardly be simpler:

1. **With the program running, click the Tools menu.**
2. **Click the Options... selection.** The Options panel appears.
3. **Click the CD Audio tab.**
4. **Set the bit rate using the Smallest Size–Best Quality slider.**
5. **Use the Change... button to set your destination folder.** Remember that the program creates two subfolders beneath it.

With no automatic file naming and no personalized folder manage-ment, you're ready to rip with these few basic settings. But the truth is that

Windows Media Player shouldn't play much part in the ripping life of most digital music enthusiasts.

Media Jukebox

Media Jukebox, which enjoys a high recommendation among integrated desktop players and library organizers described in chapter 9, performs serviceably as a ripper. Its strongest asset is the format neutrality that serves the program so well as a desktop organizer. Media Jukebox rips to MP3 (naturally), WMA, WAV, and even the newer Ogg Vorbis (OGG) format. Although Media Jukebox doesn't offer the degree of flexibility of file naming found in RealOne, the basic choices are ready to go. And the Options panel is easier to navigate than RealOne's Preferences panel.

The following steps let you make basic rip settings:

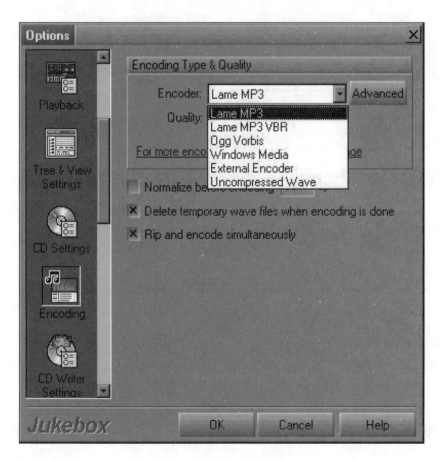

Figure 2.10. *Choosing a ripped format in Media Jukebox.*

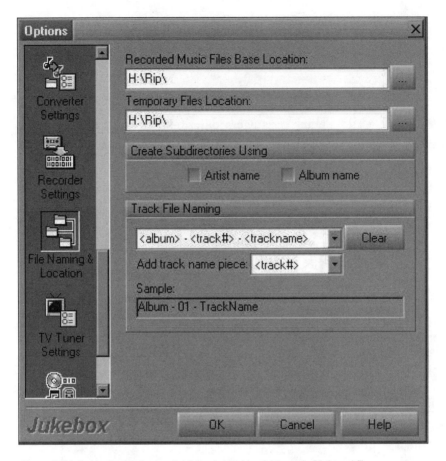

Figure 2.11. In Media Jukebox, establish a hard drive folder to hold ripped files.

1. **With Media Jukebox open, click the Settings menu.**
2. **Click the Options… selection.** The Options panel appears.
3. **Scroll down the left-hand icon menu and click Encoding.**
4. **Click the drop-down menu and choose a format.** Don't be thrown by the "Lame" designation next to the MP3 encoder options (see figure 2.10): Lame is a type of ripping engine, not a indication of quality. The 'Lame MP3' selection leads to constant bit rates, and the 'Lame MP3 VBR' selection leads to variable bit rates. The 'External Encoder' option allows you to assign another program to the ripping process; Media Jukebox automatically opens that other program when you begin a rip.
5. **Scroll down the left-hand menu and click File Naming & Location.** Here, use the Recorded Music Files Base Location (see figure 2.11) to

direct rips to a main "Rip" folder. The Temporary Files Location is where the program does its encoding work; I keep that folder the same as the "Rip" folder. Use the drop-down menu in the Track File Naming section to assign a filename convention from the list. The check-boxes above that menu let you assign subfolders if you wish.

With your settings complete, click CD & DVD from the left-hand menu in Media Jukebox to see the CD's tracks. Click the Copy from CD button in the toolbar to begin your rip.

Musicmatch

Musicmatch provides a thoroughgoing set of ripping tools for turning CD tracks into MP3, WMA, or WAV files. While the interface is on the thorny side and a bit rigid, the silver lining is extreme precision in user settings. When reading this section, you might refer to chapter 9, where Musicmatch Plus is described in detail.

Before ripping any albums, you have to make sure your settings are in order. Press the Control + Shift + S keyboard combination to see the Settings pane, then click the Recorder tab (see figure 2.6). Now follow these steps to make your bit-rate, folder, and other miscellaneous settings:

1. **Choose a format and encoding rate.** The assumption here is that you're ripping to MP3. Musicmatch breaks down the MP3 encoding rates uniquely, offering preset choices for CD Quality, Near CD Quality, and FM Radio Quality, in order of deteriorating fidelity. Farther down, you can try the sliders in the Custom Quality section for setting a constant or variable bit rate.

2. **Click the Tracks Directory… button to set folder assignments.** The New Tracks Directory Options panel opens (see figure 2.12). In typical ripper fashion, Musicmatch allows you to assign a main destination folder, and create artist and album subfolders. I always rip to a dedicated folder, then move the files to their final destination, and never check the Make Sub-Path boxes. In the Name Track File portion, you can determine how the track files will be named. Remember to always put the Track Number before the Track Name. Use the arrow buttons to juggle the order of information pieces in the filename. The final filename format changes at the bottom of the panel, reflecting your manipulation of the settings.

3. Click the OK button in the New Tracks Directory Options panel.
4. Back in the Settings panel, check Add to Playlist if you'd like to listen to the newly ripped MP3s.
5. Uncheck the Mute while Recording box if you wish to rip at high speed. Checking that box tells Musicmatch that you want to hear the album as you're ripping it, and the program accommodates by ripping in real time.
6. Click the OK button. You're ready to rip.

Puzzling through the settings is the hard part, and Musicmatch makes it harder by giving you such detailed control over the operation. In most cases you can leave the Prepare Tracks for Volume Leveling option unchecked; that feature is best used when ripping compilation albums in which some tracks are louder than others.

Figure 2.12. Set the destination folder for ripped tracks in Musicmatch, and set the file-naming plan.

Guilt-Free Music The Make Track Clips is an interesting and unusual feature that invites you to clip some portion of each CD track by setting the start and length of the clip. Making short clips (under thirty seconds) is one way to share tracks in compliance with fair use regulations. You can use short clips as background music to a Web page, or e-mail them to a friend. You could upload them to a file-sharing service, for that matter, and, who knows, maybe you'll start a trend of legal clip-sharing. Just make sure the clip is shorter than thirty seconds (the Length setting). Although the fair use concept is supported by law, exact durations of copyrighted works are not specified. In music, thirty seconds is the recommended fair use ceiling.

The actual ripping in Musicmatch is simple:

1. **Place a CD in the computer's CD drive.**
2. **In the Playlist window, click the CD button.** This space displays the CD tracks.
3. **In the Player window, click the red Record button.** The Recorder window pops open (see figure 2.13).
4. **In the Recorder window, click the ALL button.** Doing so selects all tracks for ripping. Use the check-boxes to exclude any tracks you don't want. Mysteriously, this window cannot be resized vertically, forcing you to scroll down to see all the tracks.
5. **In the Recorder window, click the Record button.** This is the second time you've clicked a Record button, and this time a recording will actually ensue.

You now own ripped files sitting in your specified directory, ready for filename checking, importing into your preferred jukebox (see chapter 9), and ID3 tagging. Oh—and listening!

AudioCatalyst

Owned by RealNetworks, XingTechnology produces AudioCatalyst, an exemplary dedicated ripping program. Of the many stand-alone rippers you can find at Download.com, AudioCatalyst receives an enthusiastic recommendation from this book.

Ripping is called "grabbing" in AudioCatalyst, and the interface (see figure 2.14) makes copying a button-push affair, once you've established your settings. As in other programs, you can choose a bit rate, file-naming

Figure 2.13. The Recorder window in Musicmatch, where ripping transpires.

Track name	Time	Filesize	Information
☑ Still Rainin'	04:49	48.74 Mb	
☑ Second Guessing	05:10	52.20 Mb	
☑ I Am	05:05	51.33 Mb	
☑ Breakin' Me	04:32	45.82 Mb	
☑ Wander This World	04:50	48.92 Mb	
☑ Walking Away	04:14	42.87 Mb	
☑ The Levee	03:42	37.49 Mb	
☑ Angel of Mercy	04:31	45.68 Mb	
☑ Right Back	03:55	39.61 Mb	
☑ Leaving to Stay	04:35	46.29 Mb	
☑ Before You Hit the Ground	03:54	39.44 Mb	
☑ Cherry Red Wine	03:30	35.49 Mb	

12 Tracks, Playtime: 52:53 | Total time left: 00:16:25 | Disk: needed: 98.33 Mb, free: 61274.69 Mb

Figure 2.14. The main display panel of AudioCatalyst.

protocol, and even set ID3 tags in advance. You must visit two Settings panels to accomplish the basic setup.

First, pull down the Settings menu and click the General… option. As shown in figure 2.15, settings in the CD-ROM Access Method portion are filled in automatically. Click the Detect button if for some reason the program leaves those fields blank. Beneath that information, click the Naming

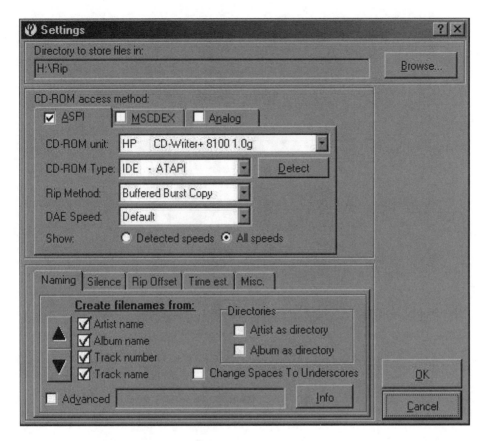

Figure 2.15. *Making rip settings in AudioCatalyst.*

tag to set the file-naming method. Be sure to put the track number before the track name. Leave the *Artist as Directory* and *Album as Directory* boxes unchecked if you don't want the program to create nested folders within your main ripping folder. (The main folder location is set at the top of the panel.) The Silence tab is great for eliminating annoying silences at the beginning and end of some recorded tracks.

When you're done with the General Settings, open the XingMP3 Encoder Settings (also in the Settings menu), as shown in figure 2.16. In this panel you choose a format (MP3 or WAV, or both) and decide whether to set ID3 tags in advance. The program can insert basic ID3v1 tags (see chapter 8 for more about tagging); click the Edit ID3 Tag button to create the tags. (Notice that the Title field, corresponding to the track name, is unavailable, because the available tags are applied to every ripped track of the album.) Then set your preferred bit rate (variable or constant), click OK, and you're ready to rip.

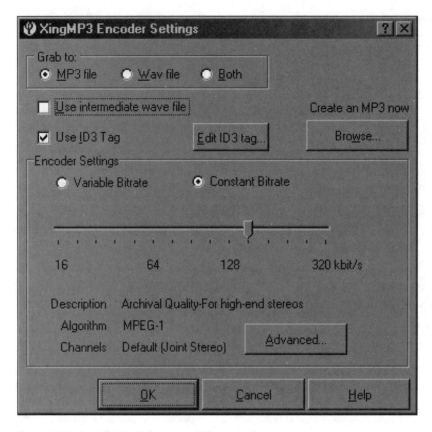

Figure 2.16. AudioCatalyst's format and bit-rate settings.

With your settings finalized (of course, they can be altered at any time), ripping through AudioCatalyst is simple:

1. **Place a CD in the computer's drive.**
2. **Open the AudioCatalyst program.**
3. **Click the CDDB button to retrieve album and track information.** You must be online for this step to work.
4. **Select which tracks you wish to copy.** Right-click any track to Select All or Select None.
5. **Click the Grab! button.**

The AudioCatalyst ripping engine is fast, accurate, and trouble-free in my experience. The streamlined program size can be more appealing than opening one of the bloated multipurpose jukeboxes just to rip a CD.

Burning CDs

Of all the digital music activities (ripping, burning, downloading, maintaining a collection), burning is the simplest. The flip side of ripping, which extricates tracks from audio CDs and copies them in MP3 format, burning makes copies of MP3s (and other compressed formats) to blank CDs. There are two basic types of burning:

• audio burning; and
• data burning.

Audio burning creates so-called Redbook CDs, referring to the standard disc formatting understood by consumer CD players. Data burning creates MP3 CDs (other formats are possible, but MP3 is by far the most common) that can be played on computers with MP3 software, and in portable MP3 CD players (see chapter 10). Data burning merely transfers compressed files from a computer's hard drive to a blank CD.

There are advantages to both types of burning. Audio CDs can be played without regard to computing equipment and software: you just pop them into any CD player. They are easily transportable, and can be played in almost any household. The convenience of MP3 CDs lies in their music capacity; since MP3 files are so small, you can fit a lot of them on a blank disc. A 700–megabyte blank CD holds about 150 or 200 MP3 songs (depending on the size of the files, which in turn depends on both the length of the songs and the bit rate at which they were encoded). So, a single data CD might accommodate ten or twelve music albums in compressed format.

Burning with Speed

The alacrity with which a CD burns depends on two factors: the amount of material being copied, and the writing speed of the CD burner (see chapter 1). Software has little to do with it, so there's no need to jump from program to program hoping to speed up your burns. If archiving your collection to CD is a priority, consider upgrading to the latest CD-burning machines that can flash through the process relatively quickly.

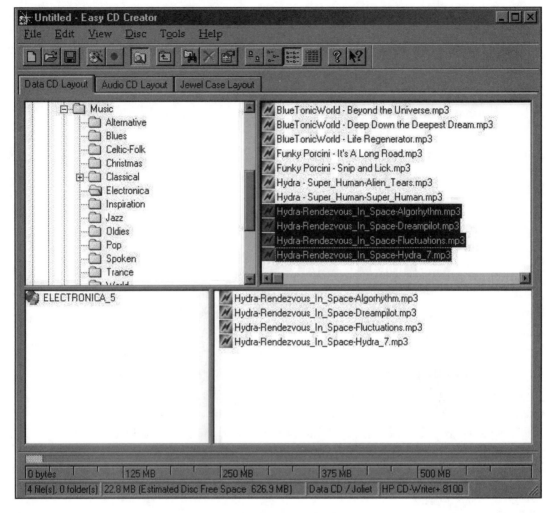

Figure 2.17. The drag-and-drop burning interface of Roxio's Easy CD Creator.

Both audio and data burning are simpler than ripping, because you don't need to decide on bit rates or storage locations, both of which considerations require planning, setting, and occasional adjustment. Instead, burning demands only that you choose which tracks you wish to burn. For this reason it would be a waste of space to fastidiously document the burning process in each of the many programs that implement it. CD burners—and computers equipped with them—come with software that provides an easy, drag-and-drop method of selecting tracks, ordering them, and starting the recording process. (Figure 2.17 illustrates the selection window in Easy CD Creator version 3.5, a program by Roxio that is bundled in many computers.) The operation is not essentially different than backing up data to a CD, which many people are familiar with when they burn their first music CD.

In jukebox programs like Media Jukebox (whose library management features are described in chapter 9), the playlist and burning features are integrated, making burning a three-step process of clicking a button, inserting a blank CD, and clicking another button. There aren't many options to decide on (after the crucial decision of burning an audio or data CD), though many programs give you a choice of trivialities such as whether to eject the CD when the burn is complete. Figure 2.18 shows the CD Writer panel of Media Jukebox. Notice that with the Create Folders selection checked, the program automatically creates an album-based folder system on the blank CD, pulling the necessary information from your ID3 tags.

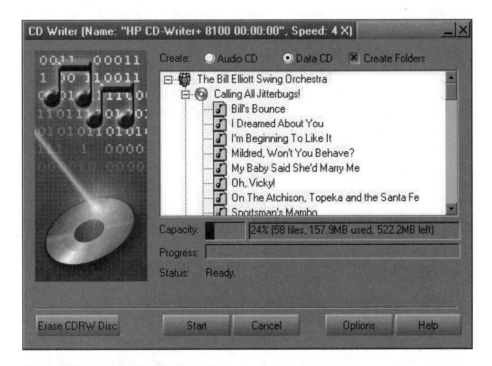

Figure 2.18. Burning a CD in Media Jukebox.

Burning through Bad CDs

Burning normally proceeds smoothly, but every now and again a disc is ejected from the drive incomplete, with some error message appearing on the screen. In most cases, the fault lies with the disc, not with the software or with you. Just pop in a fresh blank disc (thank goodness they're cheap) and try again.

 Power User Musicmatch contains an adequate burning function, as do most desktop jukeboxes, and it really shines when it comes to label and insert printing. If you like designing and printing CD labels and jewel case inserts with graphics and track listings, Musicmatch integrates burning and printing into a single satisfying task.

 Pro & Con The difference between using a jukebox program for burning and using built-in software that came with your computer is the interface layer that jukeboxes place between you and your files. If you are accustomed to this interface, and use one of the jukeboxes described in chapter 9 for most of your listening, organizing, and playlisting, then burning within that familiar environment is the way to go. If you prefer working directly with your files in a screen environment resembling Windows Explorer, then using a generic data-backup program as supplied with your CD burner or computer is preferable.

3

Choosing an Online Music Subscription

Paying a periodic subscription fee for entertainment isn't a new concept: think of your cable bill or any magazine subscriptions you might have. But the idea of paying a monthly or yearly bill for delivery of music *is* rather new. Some precedent has been set by cable music systems, which deliver full-time, genre-based "stations" of music programming without talk or commercials. These plans, which have never taken off in a big way, are attached to the cable-TV service and added onto that bill.

Although some people are devoted to cable music, the system's downfall is lack of programmability; like traditional radio, you take what's given to you (although that might be changing with new, more programmable systems). That's one reason the music industry has for decades been primarily a product industry (CDs), not a service industry. Traditional radio is free to the listener, and primarily a promotional outlet for record labels. Paying for commercial radio is out of the question. But paying a subscription fee for music delivery (streamed and/or downloaded) is an idea whose time has come—or, to be more precise, whose time has been forced down the throats of a reluctant music industry.

Who is doing the forcing? Napster was the strongest catalyst for new music services. During Napster's heyday, when about 50 million registered users downloaded the music-sharing program, surveys indicated that many

Legal Napsters?

Because the original version of Napster was the motivating force behind the entire fledgling music subscription industry, it's fair to ask whether the current crop of pay-by-month music services represent a copyright-friendly alternative to the gray-market Napster that so many people loved. The music industry would have you believe so, but the truer technical answer is: no; the differences between Napster and its authorized descendants are too severe.

This conclusion is not based on the fact that Napster was free and the subscription plans are not. The real difference lies in the nuts and bolts of the two types of service. Napster connected users to each other; the new services connect users to a central inventory of licensed music. Not that there's anything wrong with that in theory, but the result is an unpredictable selection and much less music overall. Napster's delight wasn't its lack of cost; it was the astonishing availability and variety of music stored on millions of personal hard drives.

Napster is out of the picture. After ceasing operations in mid-2001 in compliance with court injunctions, the company was supported by Bertelsmann Music Group (BMG), one of the big five record labels. Almost a year later BMG purchased Napster outright and pushed it into Chapter 11 bankruptcy reorganization. At the time of publication, nobody knows whether the service will ever resurface, but is appears unlikely.

of them would be willing to pay a monthly fee for its vast selection and easy access to songs. The record labels whose material was being traded freely were compelled to dream up legitimate services with advantages that might lure music-lovers away from the chaotic and inconsistent realm of bootleg swapping.

As of this writing, the experiment has not worked to any great extent, but that's not to say there isn't solid value in the label-sanctioned services currently available, and even sheer joy. I have strong recommendations and dissuasions to make on the subject, and that's partly what this chapter is about. More than just nudging you toward better services, this chapter gives a thorough grounding in the issues, advantages, disadvantages, selling points, and drawbacks of music subscriptions in general, so that as new plans are launched you can ask the right questions and make the best choices for your needs and tastes.

Music subscriptions, even in the nascent stage of their evolution, fill a niche left gaping by the partially intersecting features of CDs, radio, cable music, and unauthorized MP3 downloads. CDs let you choose your artist or band, but are difficult to audition completely before buying, which sometimes leads to disappointment. Radio is passive entertainment that doesn't allow you to program your listening beyond selecting a station type. Cable music suffers the same drawbacks as broadcast radio, helpfully removing the commercials and talk but charging a fee for an unconfigurable experience. Unauthorized downloads don't cost anything, but are a mixed bag in every way, providing inconsistent labeling, audio quality, and selection.

Enter music subscriptions, which at their best provide tantalizing new ways of acquiring music, and at their worst offend users with unwieldy restrictions and stingy selection. The remainder of this chapter describes how these plans work; then, in chapter 4, several specific services are highlighted.

The What and How of Music Subscriptions

The essential characteristic of a music subscription is that you pay for a period of time, not for a product. During that time you have *access* to

Legitimacy behind the Scenes

What makes a music service legit? Well, the up-front giveaway is the subscription fee, although I hasten to add that many free download and streaming destinations are perfectly legal and aboveboard. The subscription services covered in this chapter, which charge the user by the month or by the year for either unlimited or limited-bulk music access, all have one thing in common: they *license* music from its copyright owners. In the case of a service operated by a group of major labels, some or all of that licensing is free. Independent service providers must negotiate with the labels for the right to stream and/or download the label's songs to users.

As far as those users are concerned, paying for a legit service has several technical and quality advantages. Beyond smoothness of operation and quality-of-service issues, legit subscribers have the satisfaction of knowing they are contributing to a new era in music distribution without running afoul of copyright law or possibly damaging the music-biz food chain. All the same, many digital music hobbyists refuse to participate in some legit subscription plans for a variety of reasons, which are discussed both here and in Chapter 11.

music—either as a listenable stream, a capturable download, or both. Most plans extract payment by the month, with discounts offered for longer (quarterly or yearly) sign-ups.

Online music subscriptions all point to the computer (and, in the future, perhaps to alternative devices like PDAs, Net-connected MP3 players, music-enabled cell phones, or tablet computers) as the central music machine in the household. You either listen to the music through the computer, acquire songs by means of the computer, or both. So is the computer being turned into a pricey radio? It might seem so, especially with plans like Rhapsody and Radio MX, which offer only listening with no downloading. But these services take a big step beyond radio in their programmability—the degree to which you can choose what to hear—which might be worth the price to you.

One thing's for sure: having a fine set of speakers attached to your computer becomes all the more important if you get into online delivery of subscription music (see chapter 1). Even if you eventually transport all your music to other playback devices, you'll be auditioning so much material before downloading that the computer itself must sound good.

Owning versus Renting Songs

Music subscriptions have introduced a novel concept to music consumption, and that is song rental. The services themselves do not, and would never, refer to their plans as rental services, but in some cases that's what they are.

Song rental comes into play when a service allows you to download songs "wrapped" with code that determines under what conditions they can be played. One condition might be that your computer be logged onto the Internet, thus enabling the service to check to make sure that your subscription account is in good standing. In that case, you rent the songs for as long as you subscribe to the plan. Another condition might be that the songs are playable whether you're connected to the Internet or not, for a certain duration of time, such as one month. At the end of the viable period your song expires (more accurately, your license to play the song expires). In both scenarios you don't really own the music, and don't get to keep it if you end the subscription.

From the viewpoint of music owners who license songs to subscription services, this quasi-rental arrangement makes perfect sense, because the plans are so inexpensive in light of the selection of available music. If the subscription allows fifty downloads per month, for example (yes, some plans limit the number of downloads; others are unlimited), and charges $10 per month, the labels are selling songs for twenty cents each. A CD priced on that scale would cost about $2.50.

Plans that place any constraints on how you play your downloads have taken considerable heat from free-music loyalists. Even some people happy to fork over a subscription fee for the right to download music heap derision upon services whose terms of use erode a sense of true ownership. Other users don't mind so much, considering limited-listen subscription plans to be excellent audition services, rather like huge jukeboxes, enabling them to discover new music that they then acquire on CD.

The Copy Controversy

The distinction between owning music and renting it through subscription plans is reflected in the ability (or lack of ability) to make copies of songs downloaded through such services. Burning, a dirty word in the record industry, is sometimes limited in various ways by the subscription services. When it is limited, burning can be constrained in some combination of the following ways:

- No burning whatsoever is allowed.
- A certain number of burns are allowed.
- Audio burning is permitted, but not data burning.
- Certain types of copying are disallowed, such as burning to CD or transferring to a portable player.
- Limited burning of any single artist is enforced.
- Burning is permitted, but at extra charge.

Even more than with issues of music rental, many music lovers feel their rights are impinged by limitations on burning. Making copies of music for personal use, after all, is a protected right under current U.S. copyright law. However, personal-use copying is not *mandated* by law—that is to say, it's up to the copyright holder to decide whether to offer products and services that allow personal copying, and under what conditions.

The inability to copy music that has, in some sense at least, been purchased, definitely goes against the trend and convenience of digital music, and is a big part of why some online subscriptions didn't take off in 2002, when first introduced. At the same time, it should be noted that even those plans offering unrestricted downloading, burning, and transporting haven't exactly taken the world by storm. Still, online message boards populated by the most ardent early adopters of music subscriptions make it clear that post-download restrictions comprise one of the main reasons that users defect from these services.

Limiting the Music Feast

Like a bartender cutting off the drinks, or a restaurant limiting trips to the salad bar, some subscriptions keep track of how much music you're accessing, and stop you from overindulging. The difference between a limited service and an unlimited one is one of the primary value distinctions. At this writing, the download services created by alliances of major labels offer subscription packages that tabulate the number of streams and downloads you listen to and acquire, providing tiered levels of service that correspond to your musical appetite. For example, $10 a month might get you a few hundred streams and fifty downloads, while $15 a month allows double the number of both. (Exact subscription terms are subject to continual change.) At publication time, the trend is toward unlimited streams and downloads, with limitations on burning.

Generally, you pay for limitations when it comes to contemporary hit music, while more quirky subscription catalogs are unlimited. This tendency simply reflects market supply and demand, and is very good news for those with unusual tastes, or anyone with a sense of musical adventure and a big hard drive. The technology trend is always toward dropping prices and greater availability, so we might see relaxed limitations as time goes on—but don't be too impatient. The record industry exists in such a severe spasm of uneasiness about online distribution that it won't relax easily. The future appearance of music subscriptions depends to some extent on how successfully the industry can litigate against—and shut down—unauthorized song downloading. Keep an eye on this book's site (www.digitalsongstream.com) for progress reports and industry bulletins.

Subscription Streaming and Downloading

The distinction between streaming and downloading is crucial. Two major services at the time of this writing (Rhapsody and Musicmatch) don't allow any sort of downloading, which means you really don't own the music you're paying for. Those services bring a listen-only type of music access to the table, including features that allow much more personalization than free radio, and that's what you're paying for: the ability to program your own streams to some extent. Rhapsody and Musicmatch are by no means the only no-download subscription plans around, but they are two of the most prominent.

Most streaming-only plans are nonportable in one sense: you can't remove the music from the computer onto a CD or transfer it to an MP3 player and take your listening elsewhere. (Actually, software does exist to record streams, but using such software to rip streams into captured MP3s violates your plan's terms of service. Furthermore, some of those stream-recording programs themselves operate in gray areas of copyright law and have, in some cases, been weakened or removed from the market through litigation.) In another sense, though, the plans are portable in that they can be accessed from any computer onto which the plan's software has been installed. And at least one streaming service, Rhapsody, was (at the end of 2002) working on wireless delivery of its music streams to cell phones and PDAs.

Streaming subscription plans work like any other online service that requires a log-in, and you need to be online to use them. Getting started involves the same basic steps required of any new online account:

1. Sign up (by making your first payment).
2. Download the necessary software (if any is required).
3. Establish a username and password.
4. Log on to the Internet, and then to the service, to hear music.

Bandwidth is an issue with streaming plans, even more than when downloading. Downloading through a telephone modem is slow, but at least sound quality doesn't suffer after you've finally got the music. With a stream, though, the bottleneck of a slow modem can easily affect listening pleasure, and is impossible to circumvent. Some subscription plans plainly recommend that people with low-speed Internet connections stay away; others offer a choice of speed options, like many Web radio stations (see chapter 7). A few leave you to discover on your own that the service does not stream smoothly through your connection. Ideally (and normally with a high-speed connection) subscription streams should sound close to the same quality as a CD, and certainly as good as MP3s encoded at 128k.

If your Internet connection cannot keep up with the streaming subscription service, you'll be forced to choose a low-bandwidth option, and the music's fidelity will be compromised to stream smoothly; if you have no bandwidth choice, the music will suffer interruptions while the stream pauses to rebuffer.

Alert Short of upgrading to a high-speed Internet connection, the solution to a poorly performing stream service is to get out of the plan, preferably during the trial period (if there is one). Don't forget to *use* that trial period, and, more important, don't forget to dump the service if it, or your modem, doesn't measure up. Bail out before your credit card is billed, and stay on top of the situation. Don't be surprised by difficulties: I've heard a few frustrating stories in which subscribers encounter roadblocks to leaving the service, and even one case of a customer who discontinued her music subscription for a few months and has never been allowed to rejoin. Obviously, some e-commerce kinks are part of these services' growing pains.

Some plans offer both streaming and downloading. This can work in three basic ways:

- You can click on streaming excerpts of songs that can be downloaded (as with EMusic).
- Whole-song streaming of music is available for downloading, in which case the streams and downloads might be counted against a monthly allowance.
- Unlimited whole-song streaming and downloading are available (as with the MP3.com Classical Channel).

Info.Update Music subscriptions are a new and evolving type of e-commerce, and these models have been established early. Doubtless, innovative ways of combining streaming and downloading will be developed. The *Digital Songstream* Web site (www.digitalsongstream.com) tracks this field closely and contains details of new and proposed services.

As to the download-only services, they of course provide simple acquisition of songs and, in some cases, whole albums. But the getting isn't necessarily so simple, actually, when you factor in a couple of wrinkles; namely, non-MP3 music formats and proprietary software players, both described in the next section.

Difficult and Easy Subscriptions

Downloading, streaming, buying music in virtual formats, burning it to CDs, and all the other relatively novel activities of the empowered digital music consumer, are tricky enough to master without subscription plans making life more complex. But some plans do complicate life, thanks to the insecurity of a recording industry that has moved online under duress. The result is a type of subscription download service, primarily offered by the major labels, that confounds simplicity by introducing non-MP3 files into the mix, and sometimes requires a certain program to play your downloaded songs.

Understandably but perhaps misguidedly, the labels wish to discourage copying and distribution of songs downloaded through their subscription services. They are willing to lease access to the music, but that access comes with anti-copying restrictions built into the music files themselves; it's the same principle as copy-protected CDs, discussed in chapters 11 and 12. The results in both cases are inconvenience and limited use. Inconvenient formats can be worth the hassle. Still, the presence of non-MP3 services creates a landscape divided into two portions: easy (unprotected) and difficult (copy-protected) download plans.

The difficulty of copy-protected downloads goes beyond burning and portability limitations. The non-MP3 formats used to package the protected song files sometimes need to be played in whatever program is provided by the service, and cannot be played in the generic players like Winamp and Media Jukebox. This inconvenience creates two related hassles:

- You must run an extra program (and maybe more than one) to access your entire music collection, wasting computer resources.
- You cannot use your favorite software to build playlists that mix MP3 files and copy-protected non-MP3 files, and custom playlisting is one of the major attractions of digital music.

If non-MP3 files from a subscription service don't play in your favorite desktop player, you can try lobbying for a change. You won't get the service to change its delivery format, so don't bang your head against that wall. But you can send e-mails to the provider of your favorite program, petitioning for an update that covers the specific security format used by the subscription service. (Read the Help files or contact the customer service department of the subscription company to determine exactly what format is being used.) You can also lobby from the other direction: ask the subscription company to solicit your favorite player's company for a licensed version of its program, although this tack is, frankly, likely to fail. Still, the point of complaining and asking for greater compatibility between services and players is to remind all sides of the digital music industry that customers want easy, universal formats and standards. Universal transparency, wherein all programs play all file formats, is an industry goal. But this goal is not likely to be reached very soon.

Reminder Given the headaches of dealing with non-MP3 formats, don't take anything for granted: even if your subscription service tells you that the provided program *must* be used to play back songs downloaded from that service, it doesn't hurt to try playing them in your normal program. Silence is the worst that can happen. And you might be pleasantly surprised to find that the supposed limitation isn't really in effect. An example is with the Pressplay plan, which delivers songs in a secured version of the Windows Media format. Pressplay wants you to use the service program (which is downloaded and installed when you first subscribe) to get and play your music, but at the time of this writing songs also play in the latest version of Windows Media Player and Winamp, although the files did not function in Media Jukebox and other programs.

The subscriptions I call "easy" deliver open, unencumbered MP3 files that can be freely copied for personal use and play in any desktop media player. For the most part, such services offer music slightly outside of the mainstream. Music that doesn't get heavy radio play and marketing muscle is produced and distributed by artists and labels that care more about being heard than protecting each copy made of the music. Services such as EMusic and EFolkMusic contain rich storehouses of great music, offered at bargain prices and delivered in nuisance-free standard files. So the tradeoff is clear at this stage in the evolution of online music subscriptions: A-list music in difficult formats, or B-list music in easy formats. Fortunately, to my ears, a lot of B-list music is more interesting and soulful than some A-list music. The best advice is to go for it all, and along those lines please see the section called "The Cost of Today's Music Smorgasbord" later in this chapter.

In Search of the Whole Enchilada
Since Thomas Edison started this mess, a whopping amount of music has been recorded. During the analog era you couldn't always find what you

wanted in local record stores, and local scarcity gave rise to superstores with gigantic inventories of music. Now we live in a digital era in which all sorts of entertainment are but a mouse-click away. Yet, even now, scarcity persists, and in fact is enforced by industry territorialism and the relative newness of distributing songs online.

You'd think that with the current state of technology and online access, universal music selection would exist. Technically possible though that ideal scenario is, business considerations prevent it from becoming reality as quickly as consumers would like. There is nothing forcing any record label or independent artist to make music available through online subscriptions. (Not yet, anyway; certain members of the U.S. Congress have flirted with the idea of mandating and regulating the online licensing of music; see chapter 12 for a discussion of how the future might shape up.) And the virtual realm remains a frighteningly unprofitable place for many companies to sell music.

However, the major labels, fearful of being left farther behind by their wired customers, have waded into the waters. Each of the big five record labels has contributed to at least one online subscription service. Even downplaying idealistic expectations, a reasonable music consumer might wonder why there can't be a full selection of mainstream music at any single subscription site. After all, any decent record store stocks (or can quickly get) any popular artist or band's CD and sell it to you. Why isn't that sort of unfenced selection available in an online service, which doesn't have to worry about storing physical products?

There are many answers to that question, none of them satisfactory, and most of them disparaging of the record industry. Suffice to say that in the early stage of the new music subscription business, the big labels prefer to compete rather than cooperate. In a spasm of *Survivor*-like alliances near the end of 2001, three of the major labels clumped together to form one service (MusicNet), and the other two pooled their catalogs into an opposing service (Pressplay). With the marketplace for mainstream music thus inconveniently fragmented, these giant media companies were finally ready to party.

For customers, of course, this fragmented arrangement is—to use the youthful dialect of those most likely to abhor and disregard it—bogus. At best, the competition compels you to subscribe to two services in order to access an undivided catalog of mainstream music. At worst, you're forced to keep track of which band works for which label, then know which label is

Where the Labels Lie

It should never be the music consumer's job to track which record company releases a favorite band's music. Imagine if, in order to choose other forms of entertainment, we were required to know which Hollywood studio produced a certain movie, or which publisher printed a book. Yet that is exactly the situation the major labels have forced upon us, in their belief that the label brand matters.

So, making the best of a bad situation, this is a quick rundown of label-service affiliations for the five "majors" as of this writing. An entire book could be devoted to artist-label affiliations, so I won't attempt such a thing. Look on any CD to discover a musician's label at the time of that recording.

Sony Music Entertainment (Pressplay, Rhapsody, Musicmatch). Japanese entertainment conglomerate Sony houses Columbia, Epic, Legacy, Sony Classical, and Sony Nashville.

BMG (MusicNet, Rhapsody, Musicmatch). BMG is part of the vast Bertelsmann music and publishing empire. Labels include Arista Records, RCA, Ariola, Buddha Records, BMG Classica, and Windham Hill—plus about two hundred others.

Warner Bros. Records (MusicNet, Rhapsody, Musicmatch). Warner Bros. Records is a division of AOL Time Warner, the only American parent company of the majors. The WB logo appears in front of many Warner genre labels, such as WB Nashville and WB Jazzspace. Reprise is also a Warner label.

Universal Music Group (Pressplay, Musicmatch, Rhapsody, EMusic). Part of the French megacorporation Vivendi Universal, this media behemoth releases music through a wide-ranging network of label brands, some of which are little parent companies for more label clusters, some of which likewise spawn more labels. Imprints to watch for include A&M Records, Dreamworks Records, Geffen, Interscope, Def Jam Records (including Murder Inc. and Roc-A-Fella), Island Records (including Lost Highway, Roadrunner Records, American Recordings, and Rounder Records), Mercury Nashville, MCA Records, Motown Records, Celtic Heartbeat, Verve (including GRP and Impulse!), and, of course, Universal Records.

EMI Records (MusicNet, Rhapsody, Musicmatch). This British company includes Chrysalis, Parlophone, EMI Gold, Liberty US, and Liberty UK.

> ♪ **Reminder** Four things to remember. First, a label's affiliation with a certain subscription service doesn't guarantee that all the label's artists will be placed in the service (for a variety of contractual reasons). Second, of the five services currently licensing from the majors, only three (Pressplay, MusicNow, and MusicNet) allow downloading; Rhapsody and Musicmatch's Radio MX are streaming-only plans. Third, artists sometimes change label affiliations, so don't assume that your favorite band's entire discography is released on the same label. Finally, the label-service alignments listed parenthetically below are subject to change.

affiliated with which service—an utterly hopeless boggle of confusion that serves to infuriate would-be users and drive them more resolutely to the shady province of unauthorized downloads. At least, that's where things stand at the end of 2002, with no sign of imminent change. (Check www.digitalsongstream.com for updates.)

Two bright possibilities exist. One is that the majors will get over themselves, realize that their imprint is no more important online than in a record store, and create more useful services. The other is that independent online services will succeed in licensing a broader catalog of mainstream music than the major labels are, themselves, willing to consolidate. (Rhapsody and Radio MX are two hope-inspiring examples, although both are streaming-only services with no downloading.) Time will tell whether the independent services will have the resources to sustain themselves through early growing pains, and whether any company will succeed in licensing a subscription music catalog that by any stretch can be called complete.

To be less gloomy, even partial catalogs can be huge, and tremendous fun to explore. All but one of the major subscription services are decent-to-excellent values in my opinion, and worth diving into. With so much content controlled by so few labels (plus the dozens of small labels also contributing to the services), even a fragmented catalog is rich with more outstanding music than any person can absorb.

Coping with Subscription Hype

The record labels providing copy-protected music in awkward non-MP3 formats are trying to prevent unauthorized copying and sharing that goes beyond personal use. That much is obvious. But the agenda runs deeper, for both the labels and the subscription service hosting the labels' music. In both cases, the hope is that you'll build a nest in the service and that the catalog of label-provided songs will become your personal universe of music. The ultimate hope (and the reason behind providing all-in-one software that downloads, organizes, and plays the service's music) is that "digital music" will become equated in your mind with one service's brand and its song catalog. You won't need to copy the music, because you'll never leave the program.

The problem with getting too cozy with any single service lies in the fragmented nature of all the subscription services. As of this writing, only one plan (Rhapsody) holds catalogs from each of the big five (the five giant record labels that control most recorded music). And even Rhapsody's music inventory has gaping holes. So the service brand—whether it be Pressplay, MusicNet, Rhapsody, Musicmatch, or whatever—should never become lodged in your mind as equivalent to the universe of online music generally. Becoming lulled into thinking that way limits your choices drastically, and encourages a type of music marketplace in which the service brand and the label brand seem more important than the artist's name—which is never true.

On the other side of the coin, the open-MP3 services value distribution over copy protection, and the labels providing content to these plans want their artists to get heard above all else. They want you to spend lots of time in the service, just as the copy-protected plans do, and they want you to download hard, long into the night, massive quantities of music. The business plan of the smaller labels involved in these services is based on high volume: because each download is worth mere pennies (or less), they need to accumulate tons of download credits for their artists and songs. Unlike many copy-protected plans that count your downloads and shut you off above a certain ceiling, the unprotected MP3 plans want you to feast.

The best way to handle such a push-pull marketplace is to diversify your downloading and the money you spend on music subscriptions. Don't build your online music home in any single place exclusively, and at all costs do not succumb to any hype trying to convince you that a single plan represents a universe of music. Think of each plan as a galaxy, and be an explorer among the stars. The digital music vista is threatened by obstructive control by the giant media companies that provide both music and online services. Every music-lover deserves unlimited choice in this digital age. Don't be penned in.

The Cost of Today's Music Smorgasbord

Digital music isn't about *free* music, it's about *available* music. In my years as an online music scavenger, I've ended up spending more money for music than I did before, and getting so much more music for the money spent that I don't mind a bit. My money goes into a mix of traditional CDs, paid downloads, personalized streaming, and equipment to maximize the experience (blank CDs, big hard drives, and high-speed Internet connections). A few truths to keep in mind:

- Music CDs represent digital music just as much as downloads do, and are definitely part of the feast.
- The cost of music CDs, by remaining roughly constant in dollar terms since their introduction in 1984, have cheapened through inflation over the years.
- Music subscriptions offer astounding value to the astute and well-equipped customer.

Knowing all this, the question becomes how to manage a music budget with so many choices. More particularly, the question is how to divide purchases between the physical (CDs) and the virtual (downloads and streams).

There's no question that download subscriptions deliver far more tunes for the buck than CDs do, and my music budget is skewed strongly in that direction. Weighting your budget in this way is best for those willing to spend time burning downloads to CD, transferring them to portable players, and organizing a big song collection. It's not necessarily the way to go if you are attached to the prepackaged album, because most downloading scenarios encourage song-by-song acquisition in which the original track order is sometimes lost and you don't usually get lyrics, album art, and other packaging bundled into the files. If you are committed to compressed formats and tend to rip your purchased CDs anyway (see chapter 2), then putting most of your money into subscriptions really makes sense.

When it's time to purchase a CD, I have two criteria:

- Get it as cheaply as possible.
- Benefit the musician as much as possible.

CDs still represent the best way to get the whole package: art, lyrics, and a durable platter with high-quality files that can be ripped into differ-

Subscribing with a Slow Modem

Digital music is one of the driving forces behind high-speed Internet connections being installed in residences, but DSL and cable modems aren't available everywhere. Even where they are available, the doubled (or more) monthly fee puts off many people. If you look carefully at your music budget in light of online music subscriptions, the expensive Internet connection might pay you back in saved CD purchases. Nevertheless, for whatever reason, many wired music-lovers are trudging along with sturdy but speed-challenged telephone modems.

The good news is that a little planning overcomes the speed deficit. The real advantage to a high-speed connection lies in getting music impulsively, whenever the mood strikes. But with a small sacrifice of instant gratification, you can still become a power collector with a 56k modem. Just follow these two principles:

- Use your computer's idle time.
- Use parallel downloading.

The first is self-evident, and is usually practiced by downloading overnight. Make your selections, start the ball in motion, go to bed, and wake up to a bunch of newly acquired music.

Parallel downloading simply means downloading several items at a time. Almost all song-downloading environments allow multiple simultaneous downloads. The real question is whether parallel downloading creates technical problems such as tying your modem in knots, and the happy answer is: generally, no. My experience is that piling up multiple concurrent downloads doesn't slow down any single download, but your mileage might vary. Pressplay, in particular, seems friendly to parallel song downloads. Some services, like EMusic, make it impossible to set up stacks of simultaneous downloads, but encourage long queues by which your computer can suck down one album after another on autopilot. It's nothing to select six new albums from EMusic before bed, and wake up to a day filled with fresh music. In that scenario, it matters very little whether you use a telephone modem or the fastest cable modem.

ent machines for personal use. (Assuming the CD isn't copy-protected.) In some cases, it's the only way to get an album that can't be found in a subscription catalog, short of scouring Gnutella and FastTrack (unauthorized file-sharing networks) to assemble the tracks one by one, then correcting the filenames, revising the ID3 tags, and tolerating uneven quality.

Other situations lend themselves to CD purchases. Independent musicians marketing their own work through various online destinations are appealing, if only because buying this way sends most of your money to the musician or band without a costly detour through a record label. Buying CDs at MP3.com gets you a disc with both standard files and MP3s ready to be easily transferred to the computer, and also delivers immediate download privileges of the album from the site. Another outstanding shopping destination for independent artists is CD Baby (www.cdbaby.com), which carries CDs only from independent musicians—no corporate labels or agents allowed—and provides a generous split of the money to the artist.

For mainstream CDs, I often use record clubs. Yes, anachronistic record clubs, even in this digital age, offer excellent values. The shipping and handling charges are fierce, no question about it, but the sale prices more than make up for them, and scooping up buckets of music during sales pays off hugely.

How does it all add up? In my case, online subscriptions represent about three-quarters of my music spending. Just remember that carrying several plans makes sense only if you take the time to use them often, downloading, burning, and streaming up to the plan's ceiling.

4

Sampling the Music Services

Chapter 3 gave guidelines for evaluating the current crop of online music subscription services; this chapter examines those services. It isn't always pretty. But while per-month subscriptions haven't garnered much favorable press, and their shortcomings are all too easily identified, they still offer a nice buzz and decent value if you know where to go. Some of the plans described in these pages are downright fun. All of them bear watching, to see what their more advanced versions will bring.

MusicNet and Pressplay

Two high-profile music subscription services, MusicNet and Pressplay, are almost always discussed together because of their diametric competition and similar heritage. That is to say, they are each a product of the big five record labels, and they are the only two services created by those labels. MusicNet and Pressplay exist as an industry response to Napster. Inadequate though they obviously are as Napster replacements, they are interesting and valuable alternatives to unauthorized file-sharing.

The two plans have similarities and differences, and on balance are more alike than dissimilar. Their shared characteristics include:

- monthly paid access to a song/album catalog rich with major-label content;
- whole-song streaming and downloads;
- restricted download formats that limit song-copying, burning to CD, and removing from the subscribing computer;
- tiered subscription plans for more and less extensive (and expensive) access; and
- dedicated clients (installed programs) for accessing the service, browsing and searching the catalog, downloading, streaming, organizing, and playing downloads.

These parameters constitute what the recording industry would like to see as the basic format for online music subscriptions. Restricted formats are sticking points for most would-be customers who entered the digital music scene using the P2P (peer-to-peer file-sharing) on-ramp—sharing an unlimited volume of unrestricted files. Still, in the opinion of this P2P veteran, MusicNet and Pressplay, when all is working correctly, offer distinct, powerful advantages:

- consistently fast transfer speeds when downloading;
- classy organization of their music catalogs, creating a satisfying browsing experience; and
- consistent file accuracy and sound quality.

MusicNet and Pressplay differ from each other in two crucial ways that affect the user's experience:

- The two music catalogs represented by the services are mostly nonoverlapping. MusicNet and Pressplay are like two music stores, each of which is boycotted by the other's record-label suppliers, an impossible situation in the physical world.
- Unlike Pressplay, MusicNet (as of this writing) includes its music content in a broad media service that is mostly a nonmusical source of streaming news and information. While Pressplay is purely a music service distributed through a handful of high-profile Web destinations, MusicNet's music is buried in the varied media catalog of a parent service called RealOne.

Info.Update The next two sections discuss the services individually. Remember that specific features might have changed somewhat by the time you read this; check this book's Web site (www.digitalsongstream.com) for news updates.

Pressplay (www.pressplay.com)

As with MusicNet, Pressplay's subscription terms are unsatisfactory, yet the service is so well designed and presented as to beguile even a jaded digital music junkie. The music selection comes from two major labels and a swarming gaggle of indies, creating a fairly intriguing catalog. Personalization features immediately enhance the service's usefulness, and fast server performance almost makes up for the copy-protected files.

The subscription deal is a standard stream-download hybrid that allows an unlimited number of both. (The first version of Pressplay counted and limited the number of streams and downloads per month; both ceilings were lifted in version 2.0.) The files are encrypted, and can be played only in approved desktop players. Limited burning is available through the service program. As this book went to production, Pressplay offered special burning privileges to owners of the Sony NetMD portable player, a device-specific strategy that rather goes against the brand-neutral nature of digital music.

Following are some tips for getting the most out of Pressplay.

- Completing the My Pressplay section (within the Home tab) is a good idea, as the lists and recommendations that result enhance the service. Note, though, that the Top Ten Downloads and Top Ten Streams usually repeat items in the Top Ten Artists list, so don't choose all three to appear in your My Pressplay page. (See figure 4.1.)
- To see complete Pressplay charts of most popular artists, streams, albums, and downloads, click the Find Music tab and select Browse Charts.
- You can select multiple songs for streaming or downloading by clicking one item, holding the Shift key, and clicking another item on the list. Use the right-click mouse button to select an action for those tracks—downloading, streaming, or adding to a playlist.
- Browsing by genre and subgenre is rewarding (see figure 4.2).
- Parents should note that a Parental Advisory symbol is displayed next to tracks with adult-rated lyrics. Often, a "clean" version of a PA album is presented immediately beneath the original version.

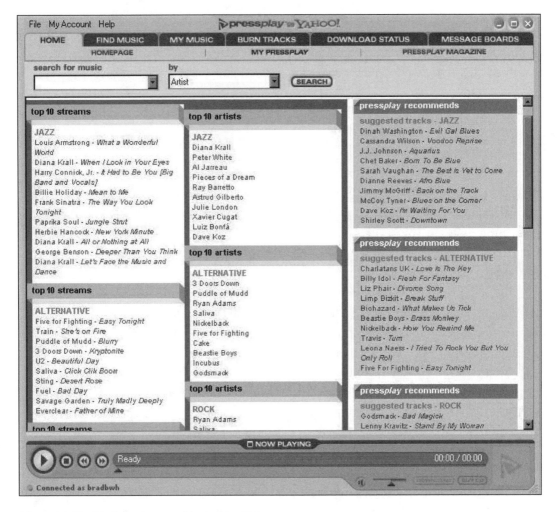

Figure 4.1. *The My Pressplay page lists download hits.*

- The My Music section (see figure 4.3) provides a complete music organizing and playlisting function for your downloaded tracks. You can quickly select all tracks to play in sequence by right-clicking All Tracks in the left-hand pane, and selecting Play Tracks.
- You can browse and listen to the playlists and downloaded tracks collected by other users in a method that other services should emulate. Go to the Find Music tab, then select Browse Top Playlists to see playlists. Use the drop-down menu to choose a genre, then examine the lists. Right-click any list and select Play Tracks to hear the whole list. Remember, when playing, that each song in the stream counts against your monthly allowance.

Figure 4.2. *Browsing for music by genre and sub-genre in Pressplay.*

Power User The neatest Pressplay trick involves finding new music by looking at the collections of members who share your taste. When browsing or searching for music in the Find Music panel, right-click on any track. Then select Find in Members' Collections. (The same selection appears when you right-click any artist name, too.) You are automatically switched to the Search for Member panel, and a list of member names appears. Click any name to see that person's entire Pressplay collection, which includes the track or artist you started with. This process closely resembles a feature in the KaZaA and Grokster file-sharing networks whereby you can scan the contents of another user's hard drive, and copy files from it. In Pressplay you

Figure 4.3. Pressplay manages your downloaded tracks, which cannot be played in most music programs.

are looking at lists of songs downloaded by other members, not peering into somebody else's computer. The result is even better than in the file-sharing programs, because the material is better organized, consistently tagged, quickly downloaded, and easily streamed.

 Pro & Con Perhaps Pressplay's most vexing shortcoming is its manic digital-rights management that often requires updating of the built-in media player. Sometimes this process, cumbersome at best, doesn't work properly and customer service must be called for help. Fortunately, the Help staff responds quickly to membership problems, but when the same problem repeats over several months you can't help but feel that some deeper solution is required.

The music catalog contains mysterious holes; a recent search for Sting, for example, delivered most of that artist's complete albums, but only one song from *Soul Cages*. Still, the inventory encompasses enough artists and albums to keep anyone browsing for a good long time. More troublesome is the excessively long buffering period that precedes each streamed song.

At publication time, Pressplay was promoting "portable downloads," which can be burned in audio format to CD and transferred to a portable player. Members get 10 of these special downloads per month, or 120 right away by paying for a year in advance. The annual payment deal isn't worth it, and there aren't enough portable downloads to satisfy any reasonably music-hungry fan. Watch for the ceiling on portable downloads to be raised in the future; we can hope, anyway.

Pro & Con Pressplay is your best bet for authorized major-label downloads. The service is far superior to MusicNet (RealOne) in presentation, performance, and subscription terms. Even so, the copy-protected files are a deal-breaker for many people, quite understandably. Regardless of any justification concerning the economics of music, forcing users to use a tiny selection of authorized players is unacceptable in today's marketplace. Ripping the downloads into unrestricted MP3 files using software described in other chapters is feasible, but doing so violates Pressplay's user agreement and terms of service, and so can't be recommended. The upshot? There is value and enjoyment to be had in this service, but the hope is that future versions will more realistically address the demands of modern music consumption.

MusicNet (www.real.com)

The first point to realize about MusicNet is that you don't subscribe to a service by that name. MusicNet is created by an affiliation of three major record labels, a scattering of smaller labels (just one at this writing, but I'm willing to be optimistic), and RealNetworks, an online audio distribution company. The music included in MusicNet is part of the RealOne service fashioned by RealNetworks. If you want MusicNet, you subscribe to RealOne. In this chapter I refer to both brand names depending on whether I'm talking about the music portion only, or the broader service and the RealOne program that delivers that service. (See figure 4.4.)

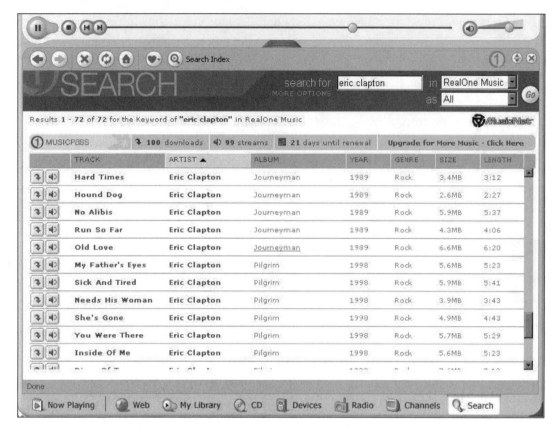

Figure 4.4. A music search result list in RealOne, distributor of the MusicNet catalog.

❓ **Info Update** MusicNet might distribute its content through other services over time; the arrangement with RealOne was the first such service arrangement, and as of this writing remains the only one. America Online is a promised distribution partner, but the world's largest online-access service refused to carry the first version of MusicNet. Time will tell with version 2. Check this book's Web site (www.digitalsongstream.com) for news affecting MusicNet.

RealOne began with the rockiest start imaginable. RealNetworks (the parent company) shocked observers by daring to inaugurate the service, and begin taking money for it, with a beta version of the program (meaning an incompleted program still in testing mode). Such beta releases are usually preliminary, unofficial, free programs that users are invited to try at their own risk. In this case, testing proceeded in the hands of paying customers, and the result was ugly. Speaking anecdotally, I have rarely in my ten-year online career seen such a ragged, buggy, generally horrendous and universally panned product launch. I can't read everything, but I didn't see a single positive review, and I contributed a few scorchers of my own. Early users complained of dysfunctional service on many levels, inoperative streams and downloads, inability to install the program, multiple crashes, and other interactive atrocities—not to mention the initial, unattractive subscription terms.

At publication time, after using RealOne for almost a year, the experience has dramatically improved, but is still beleaguered by unchanging drawbacks, which include:

- **Stingy subscription terms.** RealOne's basic $10 monthly plan (at the time of this writing) allows one hundred streams and one hundred copy-protected downloads. The downloads expire at the end of each month, and must be renewed to continue hearing them, and the renewals count as *fresh* downloads against the new month's allowance. No burns; no transfers to portable devices. Compare this basic package to Pressplay's unlimited streams and downloads (for $15 per month) that remain viable during the entire subscription run, plus limited burning. MusicNet offers the worst subscription terms in the business.
- **Pushy video advertising.** The built-in video player makes it easy to display intrusive ads that closely resemble TV commercials. This noxious practice takes up bandwidth, stresses computer resources, and interferes with whatever audio you might be listening to from non-RealOne sources.
- **Slow performance.** RealOne is heavy with graphics, slow to load its service pages, and sluggish when buffering streams.

Pro & Con Believe it or not, there is an upside to the RealOne story. MusicNet is a small part of the subscription picture, which includes streaming video content from ABC News, CNN, Major League Baseball, the NBA, the Weather Channel, the Wall Street Journal Interactive Edition, iFilm, Old Time Radio, and many other sources. The highest of three subscription levels is required to secure the full selection, and at publication time that subscription cost almost $20 per month. Only you can decide whether a monthly fee that might be nearly what you pay for cable TV is worth dishing out for this smorgasbord of information, entertainment, and music.

And the Winner Is . . .

My highest recommendation goes to EMusic as the most worthwhile online sub-scription service, with a strong honorable mention going to Rhapsody. EMusic wins its gold star despite a lack of many A-list, headlining music acts in its download catalog; in fact, if Britney and Backstreet Boys are your cup of tea, you won't get much joy from this mostly indie service. EMusic earns its wings by delivering unsecured MP3 files in tremendous numbers, great server performance (fast down-loads), and a deep, fascinating genre catalog.

Rhapsody dishes up a state-of-the-art environment for customized streaming, and is addictively fun to operate. But the twin inescapable facts of any streaming-only service are that you never really own anything, and you can never get the music away from the computer—until the next generation of portable wireless devices are avail-able, that is. (At publication time, Rhapsody introduced CD burning of its streams for an additional charge, offering one way to get the music out of the computer.)

 Pro & Con Most music lovers have their hopes pinned on version 2 of MusicNet, and aren't bothering with the initial product. The music selection is scantier than Rhapsody's, the subscription terms less generous than Pressplay's, and the bulky service software is more meddlesome than any of the others. The advice here is to skip it until version 2 hits the Net, which might have occured by the time you read this. Check this book's Web site (www.digitalsongstream.com) for updated information.

The Independent Services

Independent services can be defined as those not owned by major record labels. That leaves services owned by small record labels (known as indies) and those owned by nonlabel companies that license music from small and large record companies. As of this writing, the second type of independent music subscription is developing faster than the first, because they are free to license music from many sources. The four such services covered here are EMusic, Rhapsody, MusicNow, and Radio MX.

EMusic (www.emusic.com)

EMusic (formerly called GoodNoise) has been around longer than any other online subscription described in this book. With that longevity comes experience and excellent operability. There's nothing difficult about navigating the site or being a subscriber. EMusic is primarily a download service that allows auditioning of thirty-second excerpts. I have wished many times for longer excerpts, but with unlimited downloads the idea is to take, take, take—and sort it out later. Unlike stingier subscriptions from Pressplay, MusicNet, and MusicNow, EMusic encourages acquisition. Whatever you take, you own for good.

EMusic is a Web-based service that requires no special program to download or play back your downloads. Songs and albums are delivered in pure, unrestricted MP3 format encoded at 128k, which sounds pretty good to most ears. The catalog is what really sells any service, and EMusic specializes in music that resides somewhat off the beaten track. Of course, that qualification depends on where your personal track lies. Mainstream hits are generally not found. But if you love folk, world, jazz, or classical music, EMusic holds vaults of content to be plumbed. All other genres (including spoken comedy) are covered too.

A few big names punctuate the EMusic inventory: Eric Clapton, Tom Waits, Green Day, Creedence Clearwater Revival. A mid-2002 arrangement with parent company Vivendi Universal put the backlists of many stars into the mix (conduct a label search for "UMG" to find Universal albums). Dozens of legendary jazz artists inhabit the catalog: Coltrane, Monk, Byrd, Armstrong. A musty feel pervades; EMusic specializes in licensing backlisted music. At the same time, in specific niches, the service is dynamically up to speed; the entire Shanachie catalog is available, for example, and when the star Irish band Solas released its fifth album in 2002, it appeared instantly in EMusic (which already had the first four), ready for downloading.

Terms of subscription are simple: ten bucks a month; unlimited downloading. This is what music subscription should be.

Power User One of the beauties of this plan is the choice between single-song downloads and whole-album acquisitions. (Figure 4.5 illustrates a typical download page.) You do need one specific piece of (free) software to accomplish the whole-album snags, and it can be one of two programs set up to work with EMusic:

- **RealJukebox.** RealJukebox is bundled into the RealOne player (see chapters 2 and 9 for more about RealOne as a stand-alone player; information about the RealOne subscription service is included earlier in this chapter). RealJukebox grabs the album and separates the tracks, automatically assigning filenames. At this writing RealJukebox is still available by

Figure 4.5. An album download page in EMusic.

itself, but that might not be the case eventually. At any rate, go to the RealNetworks site (www.real.com) for the free program download.

- **FreeAmp.** My preference, FreeAmp is slimmer, requiring fewer computer resources, and performs the same track-separating, file-naming functions as RealJukebox. (Figure 4.6 illustrates a download in progress through FreeAmp; the RealJukebox downloader looks very much the same.) Download FreeAmp from its site (www.freeamp.org).

It is quite possible that by the time you read this, RealJukebox will no longer operate to download whole albums from EMusic. Whether RealJukebox is withdrawn or not, my recommendation is FreeAmp.

Guilt-Free Music I have spent innumerable happy hours prowling through the EMusic catalog, and have acquired immense troves of music on the cheap. Like any subscription service, the more you use EMusic the farther your dollar stretches. If you download an average of an album per day, each album costs about thirty-three cents. Furthermore, aggressive downloading helps fund the artists and labels that distribute through EMusic's revenue-sharing business model.

Info. Update At publication time, EMusic had just released the EMusic Download Manager, which can replace FreeAmp and RealJukebox for both single-song and whole-album downloads. You don't need to use the Download Manager, but I recommend it. The EMusic Download Manager is

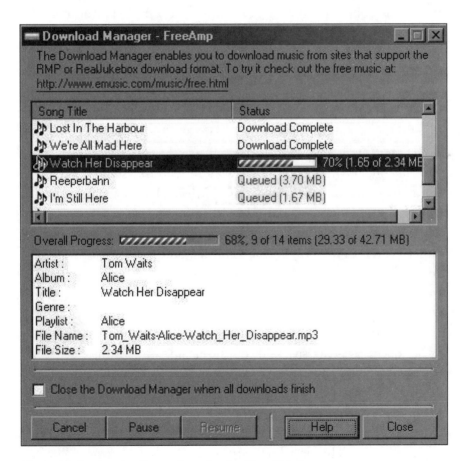

Figure 4.6. FreeAmp handles an album download from EMusic.

a simple, stable little program that looks quite a bit like FreeAmp, and does a perfect job collecting, naming, and storing your downloaded music. When you become an EMusic member, you are prompted to download and install the Download Manager when you first attempt to acquire a track or album. You may accept or decline this offer (it's perfectly free), and later adopt or discontinue your use of the Download Manager in the My Account section on the EMusic site.

Here are some tips to help you get the most from EMusic's service:

- **Take advantage of the all-in-one experience.** EMusic provides three basic functions: streaming, downloading songs, and downloading albums. Acquiring individual songs is handled by the Windows Save File feature (unless you use the EMusic Download Manager), and requires no additional software. Streaming and album-downloading each require software, and you can consolidate your EMusic experience by forcing both to occur via the same program: either RealOne or FreeAmp. You accomplish this bundling by massaging the file associations in your preferred program as already described. Album downloads are bundled into either the RM or RMP file type. Music streaming is handled by your choice of RealAudio (RAM files) or MP3 playlisting (M3U files). Assigning all these file types to the same program ensures that only one program pops up during an EMusic session. But you can avoid this hassle entirely by using the EMusic Download Manager.
- **Browse first.** Don't sign up at EMusic on my strong recommendation alone. Unlike most other subscription services, the entire EMusic catalog is open for browsing by nonmembers. Some music is dished up free of charge, so you can test the streaming and downloading performance, too.
- **Stack 'em up.** Whether you enjoy high-speed Internet or not, chances are that much of your EMusic downloading will occur at night. The service encourages massive raids on the catalog by allowing stacked downloads. Select as many albums as you like, and FreeAmp (or RealJukebox) queues them up for downloading, one by one. There is no simultaneous downloading here, as is common in Pressplay and file-sharing networks, but the queuing system works just as well considering EMusic's blazing download speed.
- **Think adventurously.** You must be tired of Britney by now. She's not

missed among EMusic fans. This service isn't about regurgitating the same corporate hits you can hear on morning-zoo radio. Prowl deeply into the catalog and pillage with vigor. You'll see many names you haven't encountered before, and will discover hours of outstanding music in every genre. Not only can your musical life be made less expensive; it can be freshened and invigorated.

- **Download first; ask questions later.** This tip is salient mostly for high-speed subscribers. Rather than puzzling out album clues from the thirty-second samples, I've found that my time is put to better use downloading likely candidates in bulk, then sorting the good from the bad later. You can always delete what you don't wish to keep—either single songs within albums or entire albums.

- **Set your filename format.** EMusic keeps a database of certain user preferences, including your preferred file-naming format. This excellent feature harks to the automatic file naming found in CD-ripping programs (see chapter 2). Figure 4.7 displays the page at which you make the setting; it's under the My Account button at the top of every

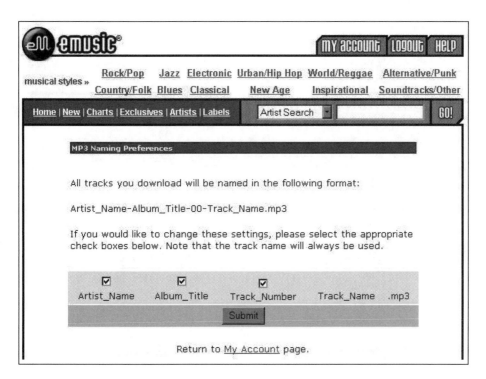

Figure 4.7. *Setting a file-naming format in EMusic—an essential task for any active subscriber.*

page. I personally dislike the use of underscores *and* hyphens, and the feature is less avoidable than when ripping. Still, it keeps your EMusic files consistent and generally readable in a chosen format. Beware, though; it all goes to hell in the classical music department, where "Artist Name" could mean composer, conductor, orchestra, or concerto soloist. The result is often overlong and confusing filenames. I have made frequent use of the Bulk Rename Utility, described in chapter 8, for cleaning up EMusic classical downloads.

- **Complete the ID3 tags.** EMusic does a good job filling in basic ID3 tags: artist name, song title, album title, and track number. None of the ID3v2 tags is filled in (see chapter 8), and neither is the genre field of the ID3v1 tags. If you like sorting music by genre in your desktop organizer (see chapter 9), you need to fill in that genre field.
- **Search by label.** Whenever possible, EMusic licenses entire label catalogs. Each album page is cross-referenced by hyperlinks to the artist and label pages. Clicking that label link can yield the most spectacular

Figure 4.8. A small portion of the Shanachie catalog in EMusic.

windfalls of great music. Figure 4.8 illustrates a typical label page, showing a fraction of the artists available in the Shanachie folk and world music catalog. Each artist might be represented by several albums. Multiply this bounty by thousands of labels, and you can see that you're getting fantastic value for the $10 monthly subscription. Also, try clicking the main "*Label*" link on most EMusic pages for an alphabetical descriptive list of participating labels; that's a great way to browse too.

Pro & Con EMusic has everything to recommend it, and almost nothing to dissuade you from trying it. As a veteran subscriber who is involved with every major service and plenty of minor ones, I can say that EMusic remains at the center of my online musical life. The absence of mainstream hit music and the distracting hype that inevitably accompanies it is a benefit, in my view. I have traveled hundreds of miles to see concerts by bands I discovered on EMusic. My classical collection is immeasurably enhanced by that department's downloads. I cannot imagine ever squeezing the last drop out of this vast and deep catalog. EMusic gets my highest recommendation as a must-have component of the digital-music lifestyle.

Rhapsody (www.listen.com)

The Rhapsody subscription service is a development of Listen, a well-established digital music directory site. At publication time, Listen had enjoyed greater success licensing major-label music than any other independent. The result is a streaming service featuring albums and artists from all of the five majors, several indie labels, and the Naxos classical label. That's not to say that all music from those five majors is accessible by any means. But a rich and growing selection is available for streaming-only listening.

Rhapsody is both a preprogrammed Netcaster and a personalized playlister that invites members to build personal stations. You might be perfectly satisfied with the fifty-two genre-divided stations provided by the service, but Rhapsody really rocks and rolls when you search for music and drag it into your own "library." The term *library* is somewhat misleading because you don't store any music in your computer. (Rhapsody does, in fact, keep some frequently accessed content on your hard drive, but it's impossible to see or access it as local files.) Each person's library is merely a

Figure 4.9. *Streaming an album in Rhapsody; use the Save icons to build playlists.*

list of cues that activates songs stored on Rhapsody's servers. As in any streaming environment, you must tolerate buffering delays and occasional interruptions and stutters. For the most part, though, the server performance is unblemished by hassles. I've listened to Rhapsody for hours while tooling around the Web, writing, and otherwise making demands on the computer, all the while noticing nary a glitch in the music flow.

Best of all, the service is presented with simplicity and style that must be the envy of competitors (see figure 4.9). You probably will never need the Help menu. Four service levels make it easy to try Rhapsody, and even the most expensive (affording access to the entire catalog) was, when paid quarterly, less than $9 a month when this book went to press. You must get the highest membership tier to hear any major-label music. The Naxos classical catalog is available by itself. A modest burning plan is available for the Naxos collection by itself.

Frustrating holes do exist throughout the catalog, because participating labels and artists have withheld certain albums, certain songs on included albums, and newer material. Still, the inventory is far more current than that of the MusicNow service. And with Listen's history of aggressive licensing and catalog improvements during Rhapsody's infancy, there is reason to hope for continual progress.

Power User Rhapsody is accessed through a dedicated program that you download and install after subscribing. Try the following tips to maximize the Rhapsody experience:

- Remember that you can listen to (and add to your library) whole albums in those cases when every song of an album is available. Look above the song list (see figure 4.9) for the listen and add buttons next to the album title.

- A superb drag-and-drop relationship exists between the My Library and Current Playlist panels. Use your mouse to drag songs and whole albums down to Current Playlist. Dragging upward to My Library is foolproof, because the software won't let you mistakenly put one artist's song into another artist's album folder.

- When installing the Rhapsody program, you must determine the size of a hard drive cache (dedicated storage area) that assists the service in keeping the streams unbroken. Your choices are 250 megabytes, 500 megabytes, or a full gigabyte. If you think this is a startlingly greedy requirement of an online service, I agree. The good news is that I've extensively tested Rhapsody's performance with the 250–meg cache, and it delivers very few problems. So if hard drive space is at a premium, don't hesitate to choose the smallest cache size.

- The built-in search engine has some brains, returning matches to artists with similar names to misspellings. Don't forget that it's there. However, I find browsing more satisfying, even if the directory pages load rather slowly. (Why isn't that enormous cache used to store *them*, for Pete's sake?) Click the Find Music button to get started.

- On every artist or album page, make note of the "Stations that play" link just under the band's name. The result is a list of preprogrammed stations that sometimes play the selected artist. Switching over to one of those stations (especially with Auto Information turned on) is a great way to discover new bands in tightly defined music styles.

- Share playlists you've developed with other subscribers. This feature is implemented elegantly. Right-click any playlist you've stored in My Library, and choose the Send to a Friend... selection. Rhapsody causes your default e-mail program to pop open an outgoing letter that includes a list of your included songs, and the actual playlist file as an attachment. When the recipient clicks on the attachment, Rhapsody opens, connects to the service, and plays the list. Naturally, the recipient must be a subscriber. Members really could use an online space for group sharing of playlists as in Pressplay, but until then this one-to-one sharing is pleasing enough.

Info.Update At publication time, Rhapsody had just introduced a new burning service for portions of its catalog—besides the classical burns of the Naxos catalog already available. In the new plan, furnished to members subscribing to the All Access level, each burned track is charged 99¢, above and beyond the monthly subscription payment. That might seem like Rhapsody is charging you a monthly fee to shop in a music store. The good news is that the burns are accomplished in standard, unencrypted audio format. In other words, you can turn around and rip your burned tracks to standard MP3 files without any copy protection, and you own those tracks forever.

Pro & Con Rhapsody is addictively fun. You might experience moments of wondering what the heck you're paying for, because at the end of the month (or year) you don't own a single piece of music. But you've probably enjoyed a great deal of listening during that time, and discovered some new favorite music. Rhapsody does have a small burning service associated only with the Naxos classical catalog, in addition to the All Access burning for 99¢ a track. For an extra monthly charge you can burn up to ten classical tracks per month, but you cannot (strangely) use this service with a Full Access subscription. The limited nature of this initiative prevents me from recommending it, but it's a promising start and might grow into something more.

   The service software is annoying in small ways: There are no EQ (equalizer) settings. The Back button doesn't always work correctly. No bookmarking is available in the Find Music directory, forcing you to retrace your steps. But these small bottlenecks don't seriously impair the productive diversion of prowling through this robust, beautifully designed, continually improving service.

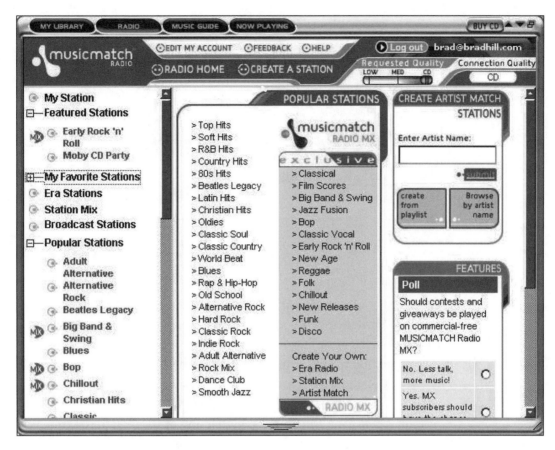

Figure 4.10. *The main Radio MX service page.*

Radio MX (www.musicmatch.com)

Radio MX is a subscription service created by and integrated into Musicmatch for use in the Musicmatch Jukebox Plus program described in chapter 9. Radio MX (see figure 4.10) is an inexpensive, high-quality, seriously interactive streaming service that encourages customization in unique ways.

As a passive listening experience, Radio MX isn't worth the money. Better to spend your time at any of innumerable more innovative programming destinations as described in chapter 7. However, you get more than your money's worth from Radio MX by making full use of its interactive features. In particular, three customizing tools make this service a lot of fun:

- **Artist Match.** Enter up to five artist or band names, and Radio MX creates a station built around their musical style. The database that drives this feature is impressive, but not infallible. If your chosen artists are too

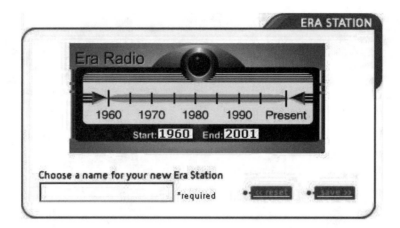

Figure 4.11. Era Radio stations invite the user to define precise time periods in pop music.

far off the mainstream track, Radio MX either won't recognize them or might confuse them with unrelated artists. Basically, though, Artist Match Stations are a fine way to discover new music.

- **Era Radio.** Delivering Internet radio matched to a decade is hardly novel, but Radio MX goes much further by letting you specify exact years on an Era Radio timeline (see figure 4.11).
- **Station Mixer.** You can smash together any of your custom stations into mega playlists.

All these toys let you name and save your custom-built stations, for easy access later. There is no downloading through Radio MX, and you don't end up owning any music. To make the service portable, you need Musicmatch Jukebox Plus installed on your laptop computer.

 Pro & Con Radio MX is saved by its price, which undercuts other monthly subscription plans. As a preprogrammed streaming service, Radio MX compares poorly with Rhapsody. But while Rhapsody allows customization of its streaming database by pulling individual tracks and albums into a personal library, Radio MX creates unique semiautomatic tools for generating wholly new stations with little work. If Musicmatch Jukebox Plus is your favored library management program (see chapter 9), then Radio MX is an irresistible add-on that cooly integrates your local files with fluid Internet content.

MusicNow (kesz-fm.fullaudio.com)

MusicNow is an underrecognized subscription service launched by ClearChannel, a major holding company of broadcasting companies and concert venues. Inaugurated on the Web site of KESZ-FM of Phoenix, Arizona, the service should be available from other ClearChannel station Web sites by the time you read this. It doesn't matter where you sign up, though; the service is identical.

MusicNow is a mostly download service that streams only minute-long excerpts of available tracks. Two subscription levels are offered at this writing: $7.49 per month for fifty downloads, and $14.99 per month for one hundred downloads. However you slice it, you pay fifteen cents per downloaded track, and this is where MusicNow gets interesting. You may exceed your monthly download ceiling at any time, and to any extent, for an additional per-download cost of fifteen cents. The value of this innovation should be emphasized. Taking full advantage of this largesse, users can back up the truck to MusicNow and indulge in downloading sprees without getting shut off in the middle of the fun.

If only the catalog were more interesting. Although MusicNow licenses recordings from the major labels, the inventory is heavily weighted toward older material by star artists. Even five-year-old albums mysteriously withhold some tracks.

The service is pain-free in the usability department, at least. The whole shebang is delivered in a browser interface, so you don't need to download any special programs. Just sign up (a one-week free trial is offered) and start browsing by artist, album, track, genre, and subgenre. Downloads are copy-protected and at publication time did not play in Winamp, Media Jukebox, or RealOne. Windows Media Player is the default player for the service, and downloaded tracks cannot be integrated into your collection if you like using some other jukebox program (which is more than likely, because Windows Media Player is arguably the worst jukebox program for library management).

Power User Here's a travel-friendly feature that makes MusicNow an extremely portable service. Because MusicNow is displayed in a standard browser, you can log into the service from any connected computer. Once there, the Synchronize feature scans your local machine for the presence of MusicNow tracks, compares what it finds with its remote record of your entire download history, and invites you to bring the local machine up to speed with a single click. If you've got a little time to wait, MusicNow will bulk download all your previously downloaded tracks to the new computer, or just selected tracks. Download performance is screaming-fast through a broadband connection.

Pro & Con Unfortunately, MusicNow's excellent features (unlimited fifteen-cent tracks; synchronizing) are neutralized by the copy-protected files that prohibit integration into the master collection, and by the Pressplay-style "music rental" system that disables all your downloads if you ever unsubscribe from the service. If the labels ever decide to sell us substantial, lasting online product, the fine features innovated by some of these services won't go to waste.

Classical Music Subscriptions

Classical music is set apart from other genres by its long, unique traditions and lack of crossover, to some extent, between its audience and the pop-music crowd. Consequently, the classical repertoire isn't packaged with the pop and jazz catalogs in many subscription services. Here are two dedicated classical services to remember along with the distinctive classical portions of the EMusic and Rhapsody catalogs.

Andante (www.andante.com)

Andante is both a new record label and online music service, bravely forging a hybrid path that might become more typical for music companies of the future. Along the way, Andante stumbles a bit over the unfamiliar terrain. But serious classical lovers almost *must* subscribe to this young and growing service, partly due to the lack of serious alternatives, and partly with joy at the high quality of Andante's unusual music catalog and outstanding information resources.

It's hard to know which part of the business Andante wants you to buy into. There's no question the site wants you to purchase expensive CDs. At the same time, the muscular online service is obviously being built with serious intent and high aspirations. With all departments under ongoing construction when this book was printed, Andante still offered plenty of value to warrant a solid recommendation, particularly to knowledgeable connoisseurs of vintage classical recordings from the 1930s through the 1960s. (The listening catalog also features concert recordings made as recently as six weeks before the present—a powerfully alluring feature.)

The CD store is part of the mix, but you don't need to be an online subscriber to purchase discs. The online service consists of three main content areas: feature writing, reference works, and streaming music. The single-plan, $10 monthly subscription (or $99 per year) opens the door to the entire site's content. Everything is Web-based, and no extra software is needed beyond either Windows Media (probably already on your computer) or some version of the RealPlayer software such as RealOne. Downloads of any sort never occur as part of the plan.

New subscribers probably head for the so-called Musicroom first (see figure 4.12), where the listenable music resides. Unfortunately, the goodies are obscured by dreadful directory design—which is to say *no* directory at all in any

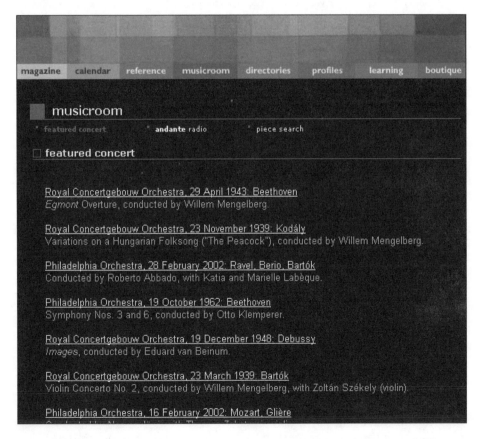

Figure 4.12. *The Andante Musicroom, where subscribers launch high-quality streams of vintage and modern concert recordings.*

sense that experienced Web surfers can use. A long list of Feature Concerts (about one hundred of them) is presented in a multipage format, and a search engine is presented for hit-and-miss music finding. The streaming catalog is exceptionally diverse, representing over seventy years of recording, and there is no practical way of using a keyword-based search engine to find anything. A comprehensive directory is desperately needed that breaks the catalog into composer, performer, ensemble, and recording-date categories. While I'm complaining, I'll mention the poor navigation that forces the user to make unnecessary clicks and view superfluous pages before hearing any music.

The Reference area is an intriguing aspect of the service, if immature in some sections and occasionally unworkable. Consisting of several dictionaries, encyclopedias, lists, and article collections all tied together, Reference highlights include:

- **Calendar.** Best for world travelers who want to catch a classical event in every port, the concert calendar is also fun for anyone to play with, and makes it easy to find out when your favorite artist is performing somewhere nearby.
- **Concise Grove Dictionary of Music.** One of the most imposing musical reference works, the Grove by itself would justify Andante's Reference section.
- **List of recordings and discographies.** Two distinct, searchable databases, but neither is user-friendly or particularly useful. The discography engine is too label-centric, prohibiting you from ever viewing an artist's complete list of recordings on *all* labels.
- **Timeline.** The graphic version, powered by Java, often didn't work during this book's test period. The text version pops up in integrated searches of the whole Reference area, and makes for fascinating historical prowling.
- **Concert notes.** All kinds of miscellaneous information about specific pieces is found here, including—most valuably—complete opera libretti in the original language with side-by-side English translations (see figure 4.13).
- **Andante Academy.** This portion aspires to be a collection of musicological essays with embedded music links. At publication time it wasn't much of anything.
- **New York Review of Books.** You might wonder what the heck this feature is doing in a music site. Every article about music published in

Tosca (1900)
Act I
Composer: Puccini, Giacomo
Author: Illica, Luigi and Giacosa, Giuseppe

ATTO PRIMO	ACT I
La Chiesa di Sant'Andrea alla Valle.	*Scene: The Church of Sant'Andrea alla Valle.*
A destra la Capella Attavanti. A sinistra un impaleato: su di esso un gran quadro coperto da tela. Attrezzi varî da pittore. Un paniere.	*R.—The Attavanti Chapel. L.—Scaffolding, däis, easel supporting a large picture covered by a cloth. Accessories of the painting craft. A basket.*
	(Enter Angelotti L., in prison garb, harassed, disheveled, panic-stricken, well-nigh breathless with fear and hurry. He casts a hasty glance around him)
ANGELOTTI: *(vestito da prigioniero, lacero, sfatto, tremante dalla paura, entra ansante, quasi correndo, dalla porta laterale. Dà una rapida occhiata intorno)* Ah!...Finalmente!...Nel terror mio stolto vedea ceffi di birro in ogni volto. *(torna a guardare attentamente intorno a sè con più calma a riconoscere il luogo.—Dà un sospiro di sollievo vedendo la colonna colla pila dell'acqua santa e la Madonna)* La pila...la colonna... "A piè della Madonna" mi serisse mia sorella... *(vi si avvicina, cerca ai piedi della Madonna*	**ANGELOTTI:** Ah! I have stalled them...dread imagination Made me quake with uncalled-for perturbation. *(shuddering, he again looks around him, curiously and somewhat more calmly, heaving a sigh of relief as he recognizes a pillar-shrine containing an image of the Virgin and surmounting a receptacle for Holy Water)* The pilar...and the column. My sister wrote to tell me "At the foot of the Madonna"... *(he approaches the column and searches*

Figure 4.13. Andante displays libretti in the original language with English translations.

this culture periodical since 1963 is stored here, accessible by keyword searching. Subscribers could use cross-reference links of authors, but quibbles aside, this collection is one of the most fun parts of the site.

Power User The audio quality of Andante's streams is perfectly adequate, but in the robustness department they are not state-of-the-Web. That means that you get more interruptions and stutters than should be expected in a paid service. I report this reluctantly but unavoidably, as it is a real problem with concert streams that can last for two hours. Andante needs to bolster its delivery of these streams for the service to become truly irresistible. In the meantime you can minimize disruption to the musical flow by choosing Windows Media over RealAudio for your default streaming format.

Power User Don't neglect the Search Entire Site option that almost always appears above the keyword-entry form on the leftmost portion of the page. For the most part, the Reference section invites you to either restrict your search to the specific reference work you're currently using, or widen the search to the whole site. Such broadening yields fantastic results, and leads to giddy dips in swirling informational pools. Try a site-wide search on the keywords *Carnegie Hall*, and enjoy the resulting reviews, interviews from *Andante* magazine, archived news, essays, Grove entries, and much more.

The Andante Boutique is where CDs are sold. The small but interesting catalog is, according to plan, just the start of an ambitious compilation goal that will release "close to one thousand CDs over the course of the next decade." Andante is concentrating on vintage recordings of great orchestras and grand, past-generation conductors and soloists. You can listen to streaming samples, but not whole pieces. One problem here is with the CD catalog numbers, which resemble twentieth-century dates: CD number 1986, for example, presents recordings of Bach made between 1929 and 1933. This unnecessary numbering scheme seems a poor choice for a record label specializing in dated twentieth-century recordings.

 Pro & Con Andante is a subscription service not quite ready for prime time. Even so, it's a lot more ready than MP3.com's Classical Channel (described below), or anything else for that matter. Its poor navigation and buggy technology might improve with time, and the satisfaction quotient is set pretty high even with the service's problems. The site's catalog evolves fairly quickly, with continual additions to the Musicroom, which retains subscriber interest. Some downloads would be appreciated. As it stands now, Andante is the main game in town for lovers of classical music, who should subscribe with enthusiasm and hope that good becomes better.

MP3.com Classical Channel (www.mp3.com)

The Classical Channel at MP3.com can be the source of much pleasure and good listening, but the frank truth must be spoken: the service is a mess. Suffering from what appears to be utter neglect, the catalog is mislabeled, filenames are derelict, and ID3 tags are egregiously incomplete. The result is that, in some cases, you don't even know the composer of a selection and there is no way to find out. Multiple movements of the same piece sometimes have

Classical Music in Rhapsody and EMusic

Classical music is not always separated from other genres. The classics are pleasingly integrated into both Rhapsody and EMusic.

Rhapsody incorporates the entire catalog of the Naxos label, an ambitious and accomplished classical record company. In fact, you can subscribe to the Naxos portion of the service by itself, without any pop or jazz music, for under $5 a month (at publication time), paid quarterly. A recent count put the Naxos catalog at 1,897 albums. The classical repertoire is thoroughly covered by artists you might not have encountered before; in other words, the catalog is broader than it is deep, with an emphasis on coverage over quality. None of the recordings is bad; some surprise with excellence. The hope is that Rhapsody will press its advantage by adding other labels to its classical department.

EMusic takes its multilabel approach straight into its classical catalog, which is served up on equal footing with the other genres. Hidden gems await you, including dozens of converted piano rolls representing rare performances from a century ago. Where else can you go online to get recordings of Debussy and Stravinsky playing their own piano music? And all for $10 a month for unlimited downloading and permanent ownership? The downside to EMusic's classical department, as with the other genres, is spotty coverage. The entire Bach-to-Boulez repertoire shows gigantic holes, and the joy of finding obscure labels and secluded delights must be balanced against often failing to locate something specific.

The upshot? I don't want to live without either one. I take Rhapsody's Naxos for unmatched repertoire coverage, and EMusic for its quirky treasures and lasting downloads.

identical filenames that must be rewritten *before* downloading, lest you merely overwrite the previous downloaded movement with the current download. Exploring this service is like hacking through a wild patch of jungle.

Why then do I include the Classical Channel, and even recommend it to some extent? Because, heaven help me, I find it so much fun. There's good music here, from unusual recording artists. It's all available cheaply, both as full streams and unrestricted MP3 downloads. I'm willing (occasionally) to put in the repair work needed to glean value from this beastly tangle, and I recognize that classical music lovers have few places to turn.

MP3.com (which is covered as an indie warehouse in chapter 6) offers many home-grown "channels," some of which are free, and almost all of which are created by musicians using the site for self-promotion. The Classical Channel is an in-house effort created by MP3.com, the corporation, and is operated as a bulk subscription service. Shortly before this book's publication, you could purchase a year's access for $30. A total of 541 albums are ripped into 128k MP3 files, ready for unlimited streaming and downloading. The catalog is wide-ranging but spotty. The entire inventory can be sorted alphabetically by composition title, performer name, or composer, but labeling is wildly inconsistent, making it difficult to troll the lists

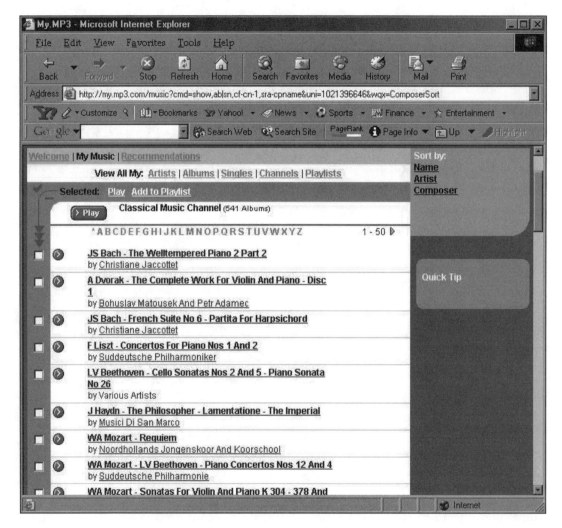

Figure 4.14. MP3.com's Classical Channel delivers good music, but lists it badly.

(see figure 4.14). Composers are sometimes designated by last name, but just as often by first initial: Vivaldi or A. Vivaldi, for example, throwing that composer both toward the top and bottom of the alphabetized catalog. Beyond the bad labeling, inexplicable deviations from order and the lack of keyword entry make targeted searching a wistful, unrealized dream.

On the upside, the Classical Channel outperforms its competitors in two important modes. First, you can download the entire catalog if you like, and keep it forever—a striking improvement over both Rhapsody and Andante. Second, the catalog is far more varied than Andante's (though less than a third the size of Rhapsody's complete Naxos catalog).

You must establish a My MP3.com account (it's free) in order to subscribe to the Classical Channel. Go to my.mp3.com to get started. See chapter 6 for more information about the complete My MP3.com experience.

Power User When using the Classical Channel, remember this most important tip: always rename files in the Windows Save As panel before you download them. Figure 4.15 illustrates the danger of not renaming first.

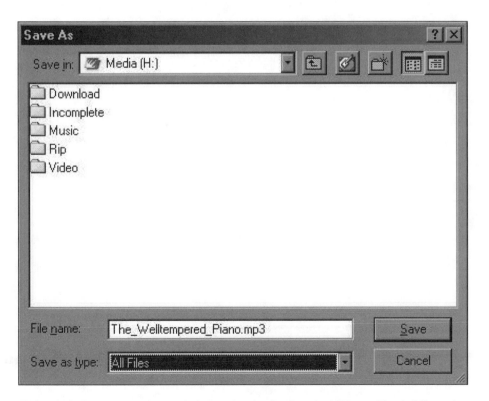

Figure 4.15. Be sure to rename tracks before downloading from the MP3.com Classical Channel.

Notice the filename, "The_Welltempered_Piano.mp3," which is identical to every other filename of this album, *The Well-Tempered Piano*. If you don't create unique filenames as you download, Windows will attempt to overwrite the original file with each subsequent download. And since the ID3 tag fields are entirely empty in this example, there is absolutely nothing to distinguish one track from another. The alternative to all this work is to use the Classical Channel simply as a streaming service, and never download.

5

The Gray Area of Music Trading

I'll start the chapter by immediately contradicting its title. There is nothing "gray" about sharing copyrighted music files online: the practice is illegal, pure and simple. But the networks in which files are traded all operate legally as of this book's publication. Several have been sued, but almost all file-sharing litigation has been interrupted by one delay or another, and no final American courtroom decision has been rendered against any file-sharing company as of mid-2002. One European court in the Netherlands ruled in favor of Dutch file-sharing company KaZaA, decreeing its right to continue operating.

So the gray area of music trading is made up of legal networks, on the one hand, being used rampantly to infringe copyright, on the other hand. Furthermore, the "rightness" of file-sharing as a cultural force is debatable, and fierce arguments are waged concerning the supposed damage wreaked upon CD sales by trading music. While the strict legality of sharing files is not in question, the means and the results of doing so are murky aspects of an ongoing evolution of the music marketplace.

This chapter defines song-swapping and offers some background of the major participants in the phenomenon, but does not document the operational details of file-sharing networks and their access programs. These pages take you through some history, explore the social phenomenon of illicit music-trading, and promote a responsible attitude toward the unarguable allure of unauthorized networks. See chapter 11 for finer details of copyright.

Before and after Napster

The emergence and stunning popularity of Napster marked the start of digital music in the popular imagination. But while Napster was important, its rise and fall represents just a mile marker on the highway of downloadable music. Digital music really began with the introduction of the CD in 1982. Online song-sharing was under way on a small scale before MP3 gained traction in 1997, and began steaming along for certain when AMP (1997) and Winamp (1998) made it easy to play back downloaded MP3 songs.

Early file-sharing venues included Web sites, private FTP (file transfer protocol) servers, Usenet newsgroups, e-mail, and IRC (Internet relay chat) rooms. These virtual environments still set the scene today for robust song-swapping. FTP downloading remains vigorous through the AudioGalaxy network, although that aspect of the service is far from effortless. (Just as this manuscript entered production, AudioGalaxy ceased operations, at least temporarily and perhaps permanently, to comply with a lawsuit settlement.) Usenet and IRC are as vibrant with song-swapping activity as ever. Instant messaging (IM'ing) represents another means of one-to-one music sharing, one that will probably gain prominence in the future.

You might say, then, that Napster was the first P2P (peer-to-peer) music-sharing environment, allowing users to scavenge music directly from each other's hard drives. But again that would be a mistake, because IRC represents an earlier version of P2P, albeit one much thornier and tougher to learn than Napster's simple interface.

And that is exactly where Napster's claim to history really lies: in the ease of its interface. Just as early versions of Windows plastered a friendly GUI (graphical user interface) over the already established DOS operating system for personal computers, so Napster provided a simple point-and-click ambience through which users accessed an underlying P2P infrastructure that already existed. The result was similar: a sudden stunning rate of adoption, thanks to ease of use.

As with the timing of Windows, the necessities of P2P file-sharing came together at roughly the same time (1998 to 2000), combustibly. They were:

- Napster's point-and-click climate;
- the popularity of residential high-speed Internet connections;
- decreasing memory prices, leading to huge computer hard drives;
- the proliferation of programs that rip music CDs into the MP3 format; and
- the increasing popularity of CD burners for archiving MP3 collections and creating music CDs from MP3 data files.

Other, related industries quickly got into the act as well, including manufacturers of portable devices for carrying music outside the computer (see chapter 10). But there's no question that Napster was the lynchpin of the entire phenomenon. The program's network furnished the source of the music—abundantly, easily, freely—and helped create the millions of large MP3 collections necessary to fuel the surrounding hardware and software businesses.

Just as Napster didn't start file-sharing, but consolidated it, neither did Napster's demise end file-sharing; it dispersed it. Even during Napster's heyday, from mid-2000 to mid-2001, alternatives were brewing, motivated by Napster's legal vulnerability and some built-in drawbacks. One drawback limited trading to MP3 files, forcing people to use an add-on program called Wrapster, which camouflaged other formats (such as pictures, videos, text, software, games, and non-MP3 music) and made them look like MP3s. That was a confusing situation for everyone involved. Improvements to the basic interface also became necessary as users got acquainted with power-sharing.

But it was looming litigation that created a window of opportunity for programmers wishing to take Shawn Fanning's innovation to the next level. As the RIAA (Recording Industry Association of America) began to hammer against Napster in court, the service's approximately 60 million users downloaded frantically while testing other waters at the same time. By the time Napster ceased operations in mid-2001, four major alternative networks were either up and running or poised to go online:

- **Gnutella.** An open-source (available for development and exploitation by anybody) effort that is accessed by many separate freeware programs.
- **FastTrack.** A proprietary (owned by a company that develops and exploits it) effort that was accessed until early 2002 by three programs:

Why Was Napster So Popular?

The question might seem foolish. Free music is obviously attractive, and naturally moves quickly. Ever since Napster's rise, panicky record labels and their lobbying groups have preached darkly to the media: free music is dangerous, and consumers, given free reign, are criminals at heart. When that message is headlined often enough in the media, it's easy to believe that when it comes to free access, the "free" is more important than the "access."

But it's clear from countless user interviews that the "access" part is just as important as the "free" part—perhaps more important. A study written by industry expert Phil Leigh in January 2002 claimed, "Surveys have demonstrated that the two most important reasons that users employed Napster were (1) they could find just about any composition they wanted and (2) they could access it immediately without having to take a trip to a retailer or waiting for a mail delivery order. Surprisingly, the free price ranked as only the third most attractive feature."

The unprecedented glory of Napster was the astounding depth and range of its selection. Its inventory was determined by the contents of its users' hard drives, resulting in a wondrous selection of hard-to-find music. I've heard innumerable stories of P2P triumphs in which long-lost music was found. Napster was adopted not only because the music was *free*, but because the music was *there*, unconstrained by distribution, marketing, and format bottlenecks that seemed suddenly arcane and artificial.

We live in an increasingly digitized, liquid, on-demand media world. Napster was the first loud wake-up call to the corporate controllers of music properties. The message wasn't that music needs to be free. The message was that music needs to be available, unencumbered by marketing ploys, untethered from the disc, and packaged in formats that correspond to the digital lifestyle. That message continues to be driven home by Napster's many descendants.

Morpheus, KaZaA, and Grokster. In March 2002, Morpheus left FastTrack and became a Gnutella program.

- **AudioGalaxy.** A proprietary Web-based music directory connected to a satellite program for managing downloads.
- **OpenNap.** Even though the Napster client was taken out of operation, the network it used still exists and is serviced by dozens of clients and Java interfaces. WinMX is the most popular.

Other, nonheadlining services launched at about the same time, including Aimster (which changed its name to Madster under pressure from America Online whose AIM instant-messaging product was Aimster's inspiration), IMesh (the most popular alternative network), Jungle Monkey (a project of the University of Michigan's computer science department), eDonkey (whose members specialize in trading TV shows and other video files), and FreeNet (created by Ian Clarke, one of file-sharing's great visionaries).

Driving a spike into Napster scattered its membership, but failed to slow the momentum of file-sharing in society at large. To the contrary, P2P downloading became more popular, and music traffic over alternative networks increased. At the time of the 2002 Grammy Awards, the RIAA estimated (perhaps accurately, although such guesses are shots in the dark) that 3.6 billion songs were downloaded via P2P connections each month.

A Brief History of Gnutella

Gnutella loyalists claim that this network represents the future, an entirely new type of distributed computing, the reversion of the Internet to its file-sharing roots, and the eventual adjustment of society's view of intellectual property and copyright. They might be correct. Certainly, the Gnutella project has come a long way in a short time, evolving from a fledgling network hobbled by moderate traffic while lurking in Napster's shadow to a robust global infrastructure of decentralized sharing accessed by several slick programs.

Gnutella is not a program or company: it is an open-source development project with the goal of potentially linking every Internet user in a shared, but strangely unidentifiable, network. Far more decentralized than Napster was, and FastTrack is, Gnutella has been compared to a bucket brigade, passing search requests along a path that might never be replicated, and is never reinforced by a fixed host or a permanent circuitry connection. If the network could be mapped, it would be as a constantly shifting topology. Beyond these analogies, any description of how Gnutella works would be too technical for this book (and possibly its author). Suffice to say that Gnutella sharing has a sort of built-in intelligence that fosters effective searching and transfers. Accordingly, though searching takes longer than in FastTrack, transfer speeds (in my experience) tend to be faster.

The specs for the first version of Gnutella's network were created by Justin Frankel, the fellow who, arguably more than Napster inventor Shawn

Fanning, is responsible for the revolution of online music. With Tom Pepper, Frankel birthed Gnutella in a couple of weeks during March 2000. Frankel had already made history by developing Winamp, the first consumer-friendly (you might say consumer-seducing) MP3 desktop player. He and his company, Nullsoft, had been acquired by America Online.

In fact, that acquisition created something of a conflict. When Gnutella was ready for release to the open-source community (a large, informal collection of programmers who cooperatively develop public-domain software without remuneration), Frankel put up a Web page and posted the software code for open distribution. Within hours, AOL—corporate face burning over its newest, hippest acquisition releasing a subversive file-sharing network to the world—took down the page and yanked the code offline. Too late, though; it doesn't take long for digital content to distribute online, and developers immediately pounced on Gnutella and set to work.

Gnutella started as an alternative to Napster, and has emerged in the post-Napster space as a benchmark technology that might endure beyond all the private peer-to-peer networks and contribute far more profound changes to the digital lifestyle. For now, though, for most users, it's simply a file-sharing network that competes with FastTrack, AudioGalaxy (if AudioGalaxy resumes operation), and OpenNap.

A Brief History of FastTrack

Leading the P2P pack after Napster's suspension, Morpheus became the poster program of the neo-Napster universe, overshadowing other alternatives as the up-and-coming file-sharing realm. Featuring a private network that can be searched very quickly, Morpheus quickly gained enough of Napster's fragmented audience to assume the high-profile spot as the default watering hole for people interested in sharing music (and other media).

Morpheus climbed to prominence as one of three programs accessing the FastTrack peer-to-peer network, the other two being KaZaA and Grokster. In March 2002, Morpheus and its partners suffered a falling-out that shifted the balance of power in the file-sharing industry. At that time Morpheus leased its access to the FastTrack network from KaZaA, FastTrack's inventor. According to KaZaA, Morpheus failed to pay a required licensing fee. According to Morpheus, KaZaA upgraded a crucial piece of code without telling Morpheus. In the midst of this corporate soap opera, the only thing Morpheus's users could feel was their pain at not being able to log into the network. In the end, Morpheus cut its losses, severed its ties with KaZaA and FastTrack, and tried to abbreviate the migration of frustrated users away from its program. Morpheus hastily became a Gnutella client and relaunched as the Morpheus Preview Edition—still widely known, simply, as Morpheus.

In order to get up to speed with Gnutella quickly, Morpheus licensed heavily from another Gnutella program, Gnucleus. As a result, Morpheus looks just like Gnucleus with the following cosmetic differences:

- Morpheus uses one integrated window instead of multiple windows.
- Morpheus presents an opening splash page filled with company promotions, ads, and links to destinations within the Morpheus Web site.
- Morpheus launches a volley of pop-up ads onto your screen, whereas Gnucleus is ad-free.

Alert Morpheus belies its affiliation with Gnutella and that network's many other programs by referring to its ability to "exchange information with other Morpheus users around the world." While true, the implication that Morpheus is the network, not merely an on-ramp to the network, is misleading. It's important to understand that you can observe and participate in Gnutella with roughly equal effectiveness through any of its programs—as far as Gnutella is concerned, they are identical.

Guilt-Free Music There is one feature that does distinguish Morpheus from every other program, and that's the MusicCity network of cooperating indie artists. Through this venture, musicians who have released their own CDs can use MusicCity's security software to release their music into the P2P network with some level of security on the files. This security limits the downloader's ability to copy and redistribute the song, to whatever extent the musician wishes. The result could be the first peer-to-peer network controlled by artists who are using its distribution power to increase CD sales.

Info.Update As of this book's publication, the new MusicCity operation was inching off the ground and still soliciting participation by musicians. It was not clear whether the secured songs would be fed into Gnutella, or a dedicated P2P network, and whether users needed a separate program besides the flagship Morpheus client. Version 2.0 of Morpheus was also promised soon, and might be available by the time you read this. Two sites keep you up to speed with every development:

- the Digital Songstream (www.digitalsongstream.com); and

- MusicCity (www.musiccity.com).

Also, Morpheus itself delivers updates on the opening splash page.

Privacy and File-Sharing

File-sharing is not for those obsessed with computer privacy. The essential principle involves reaching into another person's hard drive, and opening your own hard drive to the gropes of others in the network. As such, file-sharing differs importantly from the client-server interaction that people got used to with the World Wide Web. With client-server networking, your computer is *served* content (Web pages, for example) from a hub computer that is simultaneously serving many other clients (personal computers visiting the site at the same time). The client requests information from the server, so the server is the more powerful partner in the relationship.

With file-sharing, the partners in the transaction are equals. Your computer can act as both a client and a server, requesting files from somebody while serving files to somebody else. Everybody involved is, you might say, a peer of everyone else. In fact, that's just what the participants are called— peers—and that's why file-sharing is known as peer-to-peer, or P2P.

You might wonder, in the midst of the democratic milieu of peer-to-peer music-sharing, whether it's a safe environment for your computer. Haven't we all learned (sometimes the hard way) to protect our hard drives from direct contact with strangers? Indeed, both in theory and in fact, viruses are a risk of online file-sharing.

The first known virus to propagate through a P2P network spread through Gnutella in February 2001. An executable file camouflaged as a music file, it created more alarm than actual damage, and it proved the theory that viruses can be transmitted in this fashion. Since then, the virus threat has been more theoretical than factual. I have never personally heard any virus stories from other downloaders.

Still, if you prefer to keep the very possibility of viruses at arm's length, file-sharing might not be for you. Remember, though, that all downloading is essentially the same and the antivirus protection you currently use watches your P2P downloads as well as client-server downloads. The extra risk of file-sharing comes from the multiplicity of sources (millions of individuals offering downloads) and the lack of any controlling server to filter the files.

Sharing and Sharing Alike

Although song-swapping implies a one-for-one method of trading, most of the time no such barter obligation exists. You don't necessarily earn a download by making a corresponding upload. Usage studies indicate that a small percentage of participants provide most of the uploads, while more users engage the network primarily to download. There is, though, an unofficial sharing ethic that pervades some corners of the file-swapping realm, sometimes expressed by admonitions written into the ID3 tags of available files (see chapter 8 for information about ID3 tags). These brief manifestos (for example, "SHARE OR BE CUT OFF!") might carry a threatening tone, but most ardent P2P jockeys don't really monitor very closely the uploads reaching into their machines. In any event, the worst that can happen, if a download is indeed cut off, is that it will resume with another source.

That said, there is logic to the prickly attitude of the fervent users. At the most passionate level, they believe that file-sharing heralds a new world order of liberated content and neighborly cultural empowerment, and that the whole system can blossom only with a critical mass of participants working both ends of the equation—giving and taking. In that light, those who only download are viewed as vagrants who burden the system.

Still, many people keep their sharing folders relatively empty, preferring to download mainly, and for a couple of reasons. First, the legal onus is on uploading copyrighted material, not downloading it, so a certain sense of technical absolution results from not feeding the system. This reasoning fails to consider the relentlessly circular nature of file-sharing that is fed on both ends, but that is a philosophical and psychological point. More important, uploading requires bandwidth just as downloading does, and those with slow telephone modems have a hard enough time getting music down without clotting the line with outgoing songs.

Anonymity when Sharing

Whether online or offline, there are two types of invisibility in this world: apparent invisibility and true invisibility. Apparent invisibility occurs naturally in very large numbers, such as in a crowded city or in a popular file-sharing network. There, anonymity is bestowed by sheer massive assemblage that renders almost everyone pretty much faceless. True invisibility is difficult to accomplish in the physical world, although it's technically possible to erase a person's identity records. In an online community traceless anonymity is likewise feasible and likewise rare.

Generally, when engaging in file-sharing, you are less anonymous than you might wish to think. Although apparently invisible, it should be clear from the detailed registrations some programs require that your offline identity would be traceable from your online persona, if push came to shove. This fact is a worthy consideration for any high-volume music uploader, as the recording industry increasingly (if still tentatively) shifts its litigious sights from the network to its users. It's possible that by the time you read this a highly publicized lawsuit against an individual will be launched in an attempt to discourage use of file-sharing networks.

The noisy breakdown of Morpheus in early 2002, which motivated that company's shift from the FastTrack network to Gnutella, was caused partly by authentication problems through which the program failed to recognize users as they attempted to log in. That fact alone should alert FastTrack users that they are hardly anonymous: if they were, the program wouldn't care who they were during log-in. Gnutella puts greater emphasis on anonymity—there is no registration process in some cases so usernames are not displayed—but it is fairly easy to determine the FTP (file transfer protocol) or IP (Internet protocol) address of an uploaded file, and from there it's a short step to determining the individual user. Freenet is an open-source sharing and publishing network that claims to be completely anonymous, but its transparency has not been challenged or tested.

Regardless of the particular network, media companies have contemplated, and will continue to contemplate, forging legal-remedy paths that could lead directly to your computer and your true, bad self. One tactic has been to lean on ISPs (Internet service providers) to curtail file-sharing activities among their customers. This initiative hasn't gotten off the ground, partly for political reasons (for example, AOL Time Warner, the parent company of one big record label, is also the world's biggest ISP) and partly because some legal precedent has been established absolving ISPs from liability when their users behave badly. Another industry strategy is to assess your MP3 collection through drive-scanning and reporting software bundled into desktop players. RealNetworks, inventor of RealAudio technology, got into considerable public-relations trouble when it released such software to unsuspecting consumers and was forced to immediately scale back its secretive ambition to examine the contents of your hard drive.

The point is that you are rarely as invisible as it might seem, and most file-sharing doesn't transpire with any substantial anonymity.

The Shared Folder

Even the most immodest online citizen might be daunted at the thought of exposing his or her entire hard drive to rummaging strangers. Fortunately, song-swapping doesn't work that way. All file-sharing programs allow you to identify a folder as the single portion of your hard drive exposed to the network. This dedicated folder, usually called "Download" or "Shared," is often set by the sharing program during installation, but you can always change the default to a different folder.

The "Download" folder is both where downloads are automatically stored and, in effect, the "Upload" folder, because it is (unless the default settings are changed) the folder that other users have access to. Active traders leave either the original downloads or copies of them in the "Download" or "Shared" folder, to spread the music around. But there is nothing to stop them from removing downloads as they are received.

Searching versus Browsing

When you shop for CDs in a music store, you might or might not be looking for a certain album. Physical stores encourage browsing with bright display racks and listening stations. Even online CD stores present a modified ambiance for virtual ambling in the product aisles.

File-sharing offers an experience that could hardly be more different than store browsing. All of the post-Napster programs furnish a keyword-search interface that demands you have a fairly explicit idea of what you want to find. You don't need to know exact filenames or song titles, although it's helpful to have correct artist names. The basic process involves typing a keyword and waiting for results.

The FastTrack programs, KaZaA and Grokster, allow browsing within the "Shared" folder of any user who appears in a results list, and this is an extremely important feature. If you find someone who seems to share your taste—say, for example, by owning every recorded song by your favorite band—you can pick among that person's other files with the hope that she or he has discovered great music you don't know about yet.

FastTrack notwithstanding, the point to remember is that file-sharing is ineffective for general music browsing. Browsing is better accomplished in the paid subscription services (see chapters 3 and 4), or in a record store where you can audition CDs before buying them, or at an online retailer like CD Baby that furnishes song samples of a decent length.

Songs versus Albums

Since the advent of LPs (long-playing, 33–rpm vinyl records), the music marketplace has been accustomed to thinking of the ten- or twelve-song album as the essential recorded music product. Of course, the singles industry has thrived during certain periods. I remember the eagerness with which I bought 45–rpm singles (doubles, really, counting the B side) and the plastic inserts that kept the discs centered on the turntable spindle. But most recorded songs throughout the album-oriented decades have been available only on the albums. The recording industry has founded much of its success on bundling hits into these more expensive compilations.

Digital music, and in particular online song-sharing, shakes this presupposition to the ground with tectonic force and devastating effect—devastating to the labels, that is, but liberating to the consumers. Whether the album's grave has been dug remains to be seen, but it is certain that in the file-sharing zone the song, not the album, rules. It is possible to search for music by album title (more effectively in some programs than others), but search results are generally delivered as song lists. The association between a song and its album is fundamentally broken, and completely unapparent unless the uploader has the ID3 tags in order (see chapters 2 and 8). It takes some work to assemble an album from a Gnutella or FastTrack results list, and there is no way to tell, within the programs of those networks, whether you have found and captured every song on any album.

Thinking of music as songs instead of albums might be an advantage. But being forced to think that way by inadequate file-sharing systems points only to the inherent sloppiness of these networks, and to the window of opportunity given the labels to build a better downloading search-and-retrieve service.

Getting What You Pay For

Free music is problematic enough on the face of it, with copyright infringements, legal gray areas, and the learning curves of mastering something new. People find it worthwhile because of the unparalleled selection and instant availability, but other problems drive home the "get what you pay for" reality of the situation. The downside of sharing music on free networks can be summarized by these hard truths:

- Download speeds are slow.
- File quality is inconsistent.
- Search results are erratic.

The following sections describe in detail these three drawbacks.

Noninstant Gratification

Slowness is the curse of file-sharing, and it cannot be solved with any consistency by a high-speed connection at home or work. One advantage of the client-server arrangement of licensed music subscriptions (unlike peer-to-peer sharing) is that the server regulates download speed, keeping the pipes clean to everyone's advantage. Also, there are usually fewer "hops" (data-routing points that exist between two ends of a connection) between a client and a server than between two peers in a file-sharing network, lessening the distance and potential bottlenecks that can slow down a transfer.

In a P2P network, the top download speed is always defined by the slowest link in the transfer chain. That bottleneck might be a switching point, or it might be the 28k modem in the computer of the person whose files are being taken. Most programs allow users to view the probable transfer speed of any file, and also to filter slower connections out of your search results list. Even so, most people's experience is that the speed estimates should be taken with a big grain of salt; like mileage estimates on new-car stickers, they are for comparative purposes only. Think of the file-sharing network as a living, breathing, multitentacled kaleidoscope of ever shifting connection tendrils. One file from one user can come screaming into the receiving computer up to a point, then inexplicably slow to a crawl. Generally, there is much more crawling than screaming, as transfers find the lowest common denominator among many connection variables.

Alert It is a tech industry truism that downloadable music is the single online feature most responsible for driving broadband penetration. Translated, that means that people invest in cable modems and DSL lines to download music. Nothing wrong with that, but be aware that, in the province of free file-sharing, a high-speed Internet connection doesn't make as much difference as you might expect. Because of the network uncertainties already described, high-speed lines perform very much like telephone modems. Speedy downloads that flaunt a cable modem's capabilities *sometimes* occur, but rarely and unpredictably. The benefit of broadband is more evident in the server-based subscription services, which can blast music into your computer with mind-twisting speed.

Living at the Uploader's Mercy

It is not only the uploader's slow modem that can pollute the file-sharing experience. When you download a song through a free network, you are receiving entertainment content prepared by an amateur whose file-creation and organizational preferences might not be remotely compatible with yours. Bad and surprising results can ensue, mostly in these three areas:

- file-naming;
- file-tagging; and
- sound fidelity.

The most egregious file-naming sin is to completely lose track of the song being named, and mislabel it entirely. The result is that you might spend a half hour in a grueling low-bandwidth download of an obscure song that took weeks to find, only to discover that some bonehead packed Britney Spears's latest confection into that filename by mistake (or with capricious intention). Short of receiving the wrong song, you are at the mercy of uneven and bizarre file-naming practices that include misspellings, excessively long filenames, the archaic and unnecessary use of underscores instead of spaces, weird abbreviations, and other aberrations that require alteration before the music can be added to your tidy collection.

Bad filenames are troublesome enough, but generally less of a hassle than poorly maintained ID3 tags for MP3 files, which are often a terrible mess. This issue isn't urgent if you generally access your collection through Windows Explorer, or some other file manager that displays filenames. But if you organize your music through a desktop player like Media Jukebox, utter confusion reigns if the ID3 tags aren't accurate. Song names appear as album titles; artist names appear in the song position.

ID3v2 tags, which are more elaborate than ID3v1 tags and provide more fields for what might be called creative tagging, furnish a special challenge. These extra fields are often used by file-sharing broadcasters to deliver sharing manifestos, keywords, Web site promotions, and other junk. To be fair, in certain cases the excessive tagging is useful; sometimes these extra fields provide album information or a short history of the file. Uploaders use that space to give details of homemade concert recordings shared as MP3s, for example. Whether useful or not, the tags often need to be changed before the file is maximally useful in your collection.

Then there is the issue of file quality, from the high-fidelity perspective. The default standard for encrypting MP3s is 128k, which is a measure of how many digital snapshots of the music are taken per second. MP3s created at that bit rate (chapter 2 has more about bit rates) sound pretty good to most ears. However, there's no question among most discerning listeners equipped with very good speakers that higher bit rates sound better, and deliver copies more faithful to the original recordings. And as storage memory (hard drives and blank CDs) has become relatively cheap, there is a growing willingness to devote space to larger files encoded at 160k and 192k, or even higher.

But the general desire for high-quality files is unevenly distributed, and you never know what you'll find in a P2P network. You might spend months searching for a live MP3 of a certain Grateful Dead concert, finally to find it, only to discover that the uploader has encoded the file at a measly 92k. On the other side of the coin, you might *not* wish to devote storage space to big files that sound pretty much the same to you as 128k files. In that scenario, you might become increasingly frustrated by the audiophile trend in file-sharing.

Pro & Con The file-sharing inadequacies point to the advantages of paid music subscriptions. Despite their many drawbacks, subscriptions deliver consistently named files at a middle-of-the-road bit rate, without excessive and extraneous ID3 tagging.

The Shrinking File-Sharing Inventory

When measured by program use and download traffic, free music downloading is more popular now than it was during Napster's heyday. But the file-sharing experience has deteriorated in two important ways:

- There are more ads.
- The selection is worse.

The advertisement problem is severe, and caused by the commercialization of file-sharing by companies trying to turn the Napster idea into a revenue-generating business. Much the same phenomenon occurred with the World Wide Web, which was quickly glutted with ads after a brief initial period of noncommercialism. Napster was an ad-free environment of pure music searching. Its progeny deliver a range of screen clutter from no ads to a strangling attack of pop-ups. Some Gnutella programs derive a light-advertising or no-advertising attitude from their open-source heritage. FastTrack programs, though, take no prisoners. Morpheus, the most popular program immediately after Napster's shut-down, continued its hostile ad barrage even after switching from FastTrack to Gnutella.

Pro & Con It might seem ungrateful to complain about advertising while using free software to download free music, but that's not the point. New intrusive online advertising formats are rendering much of the commercial Web space unusable, and file-sharing is in the same danger of driving away its users. At this point a rough tradeoff exists between fast searching performance and an ad-free climate. The FastTrack network is bottled lightning compared to Gnutella, but users pay for this fine performance with a screen-shaking barrage of pop-up ads in both KaZaA and Grokster. And Gnutella is a clean ride only through certain programs, while others display modest ads or reminders to upgrade to an ad-free paid version.

But forget about the ads. More problematic is the dwindling music selection of the post-Napster universe. There is no way to quantify this, but many file-sharing enthusiasts, devoted and casual alike, notice that fringe music is harder to find than during Napster's glory days. At its peak, Napster truly seemed bottomless. Now, with the file-sharing community splintered into competing networks, there doesn't seem to be the critical mass at any single location that benefits everyone with vast accumulated musical taste and libraries. Mainstream music is still bountiful, but file-sharing's best asset is delivering music that's unavailable in other venues, or individual rare singles that, in the physical world, are tied to unsavory CD compilations. As that asset deteriorates, the rewards of file-sharing are reduced.

Is File-Sharing Worth It?
Questions of social responsibility and conscience aside (those issues are discussed in the next section and in chapter 11), there are many situations in

Adware, Spyware, and Third-Party Scandals

In the ethics of online customer relations, there is a distinction between ads that support a free program and invisible, manipulative add-on programs that take control of your computer to some extent. Some file-sharing programs, born of a spirit of free sharing, have crossed over to the dark side by violating privacy and user control. In so doing, some of them created well-publicized scandals.

The company whose product suffered the worst slam to its reputation is Sharman Networks, owner of KaZaA, the popular FastTrack program. In the spring of 2002 it was discovered that a new version of KaZaA bundled a small program from another company that, unknown to the user, detoured the computer's Web browser at certain times and in certain ways that earned affiliate income for that other company. This occurred in the midst of growing user impatience with KaZaA's ad-glutted environment. The result was a migration of customers away from KaZaA and out of FastTrack—or, alternatively, they were driven to KaZaA Lite, a renegade KaZaA clone with all the third-party junk stripped out.

That incident and others before it have put users on the defensive against all kinds of adware (bundled programs that deliver a steady stream of ads) and spyware (software hooks that assess the contents of your hard drive and report back to the host company). Secretive software installments represent another in a long list of reasons to forego the scurrilous file-sharing programs entirely. If you do install a file-sharing client, it's best to opt out (by reversing the default choices) of any bundling of third-party software that is offered. The program authors don't like this advice because revenue generated from adware pays for the program, which is delivered to you free of charge. But without considerable research it is difficult to identify innocent versus invasive bundling.

which any experienced P2P enthusiast can't help but wonder whether the hassles are worth the time.

Pop-rap star Eminem's 2002 album release, *The Eminem Show*, provided a perfect laboratory in which to measure the rewards and frustrations of obtaining new music by means of unauthorized downloading. *The Eminem Show* was launched amid the most frenzied industry hype seen in two years. The album's release date was advanced more than once after digital leaks spilled the tracks onto P2P networks. Retail stores jumped the gun on the final release date to satisfy crushing demand, creating more file-sharing

It's Not Just about the Music

Napster was specifically a music-sharing application. It put not only music-swapping but also file-sharing on the map. Although Napster couldn't understand any type of file besides MP3s, its descendants are true file-sharing platforms with no file-type limitations.

As a result, all kinds of digital material are being shared through modern P2P networks. Music is the most evolved media universe in play, thanks to the vast dispersed library of MP3 files held by individuals. Increasingly, though, users turn to KaZaA, Morpheus, Gnutella, and the other sharing programs for digitized movies, TV shows, music videos, pictures, games, MIDI files, and application software. Each of these media types enjoys the free distribution, and suffers at the hands of bootlegging, according to formulas, regulations, and trends unique to their fields.

leaks before everybody could get their hands on the disc. Some source (probably associated with the record company) uploaded repeating ten-second loops of each track, disguised as full tracks and intended to thwart downloaders, to the file-sharing networks. The trading community approached the situation as a blood sport, determined to push the album through the unauthorized realm as vigorously as possible.

In this paranoid and illicit environment, it became unusually easy to identify the entire album and download it. Uploaders were more careful than usual to tag and name the tracks accurately, making whole-album identification clearer than normal. Even so, downloading *The Eminem Show* was hardly a piece of cake. At one experimental moment when the agitation was at its height, the FastTrack and Gnutella networks combined displayed over three thousand matches to the keywords *eminem* and *the eminem show* using three file-sharing programs. On FastTrack, it was impossible to find all twenty album tracks. On Gnutella, most of whose programs don't read ID3 tags and thus don't display album names in a separate column, the twenty tracks *could* be found, from several different sources. Those files no doubt varied in encoding quality and tagging accuracy.

So, obtaining the whole album was easier than usual, but still problematic, which points to P2P's inadequacy as an album-oriented delivery mechanism. Rarely have uploaders, as a group, showed so much determination in illicitly pushing an album around the Internet as a whole unit. Even with that group effort, no fan with any kind of life and a decent amount of disposable cash would brave the hassles rather than just buying the unaltered product at a store, once available.

Socially Responsible File-Sharing

Should file-sharing play any part in the digital music lifestyle? Each individual must seek a personal balance in an unsteady marketplace saturated with newly liberated music. To whatever extent P2P networks find a place in the household music computer, this book recommends a type of socially responsible sharing that seeks to do no damage. All unauthorized file-sharing is illegal, but not necessarily damaging to the copyright holder. The "Don't download!" admonition of record labels is obviously ineffectual and futile in a market dominated by tech-fluent kids. As copyright theory grows increasingly irrelevant to digital reality, there might remain some chance to shift consumer awareness away from legal concepts toward the idea of damage, and damage avoided.

The socially responsible approach is defined by three rules:

- Never download and keep music that you would purchase if file-sharing didn't exist.
- Use file-sharing as a means of auditioning music for possible purchase from authorized distributors.
- Do not expose purchased files to file-sharing networks.

Online music distribution is in a state of flux, and responsibility remains in the hands of individuals, not the online networks, the record labels, or the courts. The technology is not going away, but nobody (who thinks it through) wants the music marketplace to disintegrate. If the persistent popularity of P2P eventually jolts the recording industry into building new, online-friendly distribution channels, file-sharing will have fulfilled its most important purpose. In the meantime, being a modern music consumer doesn't mean scavenging for as many free tracks as possible. Rather, the point is to enjoy the benefits of new formats, conveniences, near universal access, and legitimately lowered prices.

6

Skirting the Fringe

Do you need unauthorized file-sharing to get *free* music? And do you need inadequate subscription services to get *good* music? Hardly, on both counts. Good, free, and guilt-free authorized music intersect at indie watering holes, where the unsigned musician and the adventurous listener meet for tuneful revelry. Creative artists who don't fit the major-label mold, or who haven't gotten lucky, hunger to be heard. Music-loving collectors who crave unrestricted music files, and who have tired of the big five's refusal to meet market demand at any price, hunger for new streaming and download opportunities. This chapter points to online destinations where both sides of this musical appetite are sated.

Indie sites are struggling to figure out how to make money in the online realm, just as the big labels are. They are forced to try less expensive and less restrictive approaches to file distribution because their content isn't as famous. Fortunately, in a nonphysical realm there is room for everyone. If the owners of Top 40 content are not making the best use of the online space, you are always one click away from other sites, business models, and musicians.

At the time of this book's publication, five years have passed since MP3 was launched into the mainstream by the release of Winamp, and five years of Internet time represents generations of product development and business reevaluation. During that time, the multinational media holding companies that control most recorded music have not moved appreciably beyond the initial panic that often accompanies new technology. By all appearances, they remain in denial of the marketplace requisites that are more firmly established with every passing day: unfragmented catalogs, unrestricted files, protection of personal-use copying, and instant access to media that the Internet offers. Price is negotiable, but transparent access and hassle-free files are not.

In crossing over to the indie universe, you might be astonished to find that the quality differential isn't as noticeable as you supposed. Your musical palate might even be refreshed by the comparative adventurousness and freedom from formulaic production values that you find at the fringe. Thousands of creative and inspired musicians hunger for an audience. They are eager to distribute their files and CDs in a more consumer-friendly fashion than do the signed stars and their business handlers. Of course, mediocrity exists in the middle class of the music industry, where struggling artists try to make ends meet. There is banality at all levels of the business. The difference is that in the indie realm, you are far more in control of your choices.

The major record labels claim to fill an important role as talent scouts and content filters for consumers who would presumably be overwhelmed by mediocrity without them. Indeed, in some cases the discovery and marketing of new talent unleashes outstanding culture into our sound space. But I challenge any reader to spend a month exploring the fringe of indie download sites described in this chapter, and the edgy Internet radio stations featured in the chapter 7, then turn on Top 40 mainstream radio for another listen. See if you don't think the major labels should reconsider their value as cultural determinants. Then spend your time, bandwidth, and money accordingly.

Let the adventure begin.

MP3.com (www.mp3.com)

One of the first and most famous of the Web-based music download sites, MP3.com survived severe legal miscalculations and remains one of the largest repositories of indie music anywhere. The site does not implement any kind of audition or filtering process; the doors to musician participation are wide open. Anybody with an original recorded piece of music may construct a page on MP3.com and offer that recording for download, streaming, or as part of a physical CD.

MP3.com's open-door approach results in a lush, tangled catalog. Navigating through the site is like hacking through a jungle. A competitive atmosphere permeates, as musicians practicing guerrilla online marketing fight it out for placement in the site's popularity charts. Frankly, mediocrity pervades. Yet MP3.com remains more than worthwhile, and I find myself visiting the site all the time for one reason or another. Even established indie artists distribute their stuff through MP3.com; why not? Most online indie catalogs offer nonexclusive agreements, so musicians tend to place themselves at several destinations in the endless quest to be heard.

Under the stewardship of Michael Robertson, MP3.com's founder and former CEO, the company once attempted to create a legitimate online listening station based on the personal CD collections owned by individuals. The site would verify that you owned a certain CD, then would allow you to listen to its tracks, streamed through any computer connected to the site. It was thought that this service, using an interactive verification system called Beam-It, would solve music portability issues and allow laptop-equipped travelers to leave their CDs at home when on the road. This service was the basis of My MP3.com, a modified version of which still operates, and gave birth to the "celestial jukebox" idea. However, the necessary creation of a universal library of digitized music ran afoul of copyright law (predictably, many observers claim in hindsight). The venture was shuttered insofar as it applied to major-label CDs, though it still operates with CDs sold through the site's artist pages. MP3.com was eventually acquired by one of the majors—Vivendi Universal—which continues to operate the site and its earthy features.

Innovative uses of technology, such as Beam-It, are hallmarks of MP3.com. The site seems to introduce a new bell or whistle every month. Furthermore, MP3.com is increasingly serving as a promotional and free-content destination for major acts. In mid-2002, Eminem, Linkin Park, Nelly, P. Diddy, Nappy Roots, Goo Goo Dolls, and Pink were a few of the headline acts streaming singles through MP3.com. (Capturable downloads of star musicians are usually not forthcoming.)

Navigating through MP3.com

While the site's home page is the official entry port to the unkempt feast within, the Genres page is a less daunting place to start (genres.mp3.com). This page serves as a minimum-hype on-ramp to the site's artists. Lack of content is never a problem at MP3.com, but distinguishing the good from

Figure 6.1. An artist page at MP3.com.

the bad is tricky. Be prepared to listen up a storm. A typical visit involves rampant surfing, starting streams, abandoning them, and moving on. The site offers musicians various self-promotion tools beyond the basic free page and warehousing of files, so you can expect unsavory music placed front and center: that prominent spot was purchased.

On many pages, and certainly on the artist pages, you have various listening and track management choices. Figure 6.1, illustrating a small portion of the artist page for Ikarus (an excellent world music artist), shows your options for two of the many tracks on the Ikarus page. Each artist has control over which track options are offered. Some choose to tempt visitors toward CD purchases by dishing up just one or two tracks, or perhaps by streaming every track but offering no downloads. Others, seeking uninhibited distribution, authorize streaming and downloading of everything, in addition to CD products. Here are your choices for fully enabled tracks:

- **"Lo Fi Play."** Use this link if you are connected to the Internet with a telephone modem. The sound quality is thin, but adequate for auditioning music.
- **"Hi Fi Play."** A near-CD option for broadband visitors. Both "Lo Fi Play" and "Hi Fi Play" open whichever program is assigned to play MP3 files (not M3U files, as is often the case with streaming links).
- **"Download."** Click this link to save an unrestricted MP3 file of the song. These files are encrypted at 128k.
- **"Transfer2Device."** A smart bit of behind-the-scenes technology sniffs out whatever portable MP3 player you have connected to the computer and downloads the track to the player. Don't forget to connect the player to the computer before using this feature.
- **"Add to My.MP3."** This link adds the track to your "Artist" and "Singles" folders in My MP3.com. (The next section describes My MP3.com in more detail.)
- **"Email Track to a Friend."** This link leads to a form in which you can send a link to the track (not the track itself) to any e-mail address. The recipient sees an image of the track's CD cover (if available), and both "Lo Fi" and "Hi Fi" links to the track's stream.

At the top and bottom of each artist's track list are three time-saving options for those who want to hear it all. With a single click, you can play all the tracks in a "Lo Fi" or "Hi Fi" stream, or add them all to My MP3.com. That last option is a good way to bookmark an artist you wish to know better, but don't have time to explore at the present. Next time you visit My MP3.com, an artist folder is in your collection, with each track listed and linked to its stream.

Using My MP3.com

After its courtroom denouement, My MP3.com reinvented itself as a personalized portal to favorite music at the site, significantly easing navigation through the undergrowth. Through My MP3.com, you can save artists, their track streams, MP3.com *channels* (streaming playlists created both by artists and by MP3.com), and your own custom playlists. The site also feeds recommendations to your page, in a no-graphic, nicely unintrusive manner. I've discovered some great music by exploring those recommendations.

Get started with My MP3.com by visiting its self-evident URL my.mp3.com. On that page, you are prompted for a username and password... and then you're in. The service is absolutely free.

Changing Filenames of MP3.com Downloads

You'd think a site that helped catalyze the entire MP3 revolution would name its download files better, but alas, it doesn't. Beware, when indulging in an MP3.com download spree, because the default filenames fail to include the artist name. The result, if you download twenty tracks without paying much attention to detail, is a file list of twenty song names with no indication of the artist. Because MP3.com doesn't deal with household-name acts, for the most part, you might never find your downloaded artists again.

The solution is to edit the filename before the download, in the Windows Save As panel (see figure 6.2). If your browser settings force through downloads without showing the Save As panel, follow these steps routinely in MP3.com and any other download site in which you want to check the filename before saving:

1. **Right-click the download link.**
2. **Click the Save Target As... selection.** The Save As panel appears.
3. **In the Save As panel, modify the filename.**

You can also use this panel to choose the download destination, which is another good reason to right-click download links as a matter of habit. If you don't, most browsers place your download in the same folder as your previous download, and if your previous download wasn't a piece of music, that folder could be anywhere.

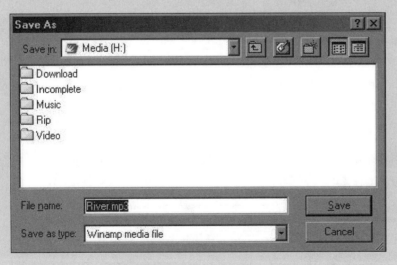

Figure 6.2. Change filenames before downloading anything from MP3.com, lest you end up with uninformative titles.

Notice that you can easily change your default fidelity setting at the top of every My MP3.com page. You must choose one or the other, and that assignment affects how your streams in My MP3.com are played; you don't have a choice with each track. Making this setting, though, doesn't affect your listening in MP3.com at large, where you still may choose the bandwidth quality with each streamed track.

Figure 6.3 shows an artist folder in My MP3.com. You may immediately begin a stream of all tracks from all saved artists, or all the tracks of any single saved artist. Use the check-boxes to select artists whose tracks you want included in the stream. Click any artist's link to see a list of the tracks you saved from that artist's page, then use the check-boxes to select which tracks you want streamed. If a track is available for downloading, you can get it from the artist folder in My MP3.com.

The beauty of My MP3.com is its personalized quality and its portabil-

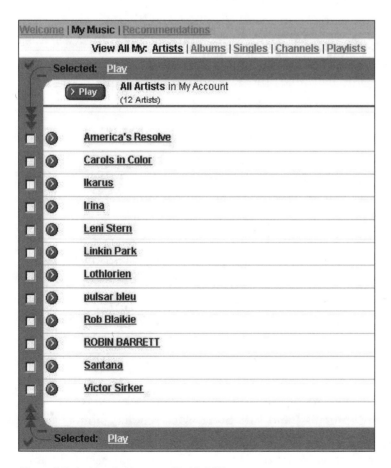

Figure 6.3. *A view of artists saved in My MP3.com.*

ity. Using the feature often develops a robust collection of hand-picked streaming music. And you can listen to it from any Internet-connected computer in the world.

Buying CDs at MP3.com

Many MP3.com artists sell CDs of their work through the site. You can link from an artist page to a CD-purchase page for that artist, or go directly to the MP3.com CD director (store.mp3.com). There you find top-selling artist CDs plus in-house compilations, by genre, of MP3 artists; this latter group comprises MP3 CDs, with 110 songs on each disc. Most MP3.com artist CDs contain audio tracks and corresponding MP3 tracks for easy transfer to your hard drive collection. Of course, if the 128k bit rate at which the supplied files are encoded isn't up to your standards, you can rip the CD to higher-fidelity files.

If 128k files are sufficient, and online access to music is more important than local storage, consider the MP3.com's netCD, which most artists make available. Priced less than a physical disc, the netCD purchase adds an album's tracks to your My MP3.com account instantly; from there they can be streamed through any computer you connect with your username and password. The same instant online access is provided with regular artist CDs purchased through MP3.com too.

Epitonic (www.epitonic.com)

Epitonic is an indie music site with fun technology, good music, and biting attitude. All the content at this site is free, and it includes excerpts, whole-song downloads, whole-song streams, and full-album streams. The underlying emphasis is on CD promotion, and Epitonic presents a diverting atmosphere in which to discover new talent. At the same time, personalization features invite you to build a listening home in the site, which then becomes a worthwhile music destination in itself, even if you're never lured into buying a CD.

There's nothing to stop you from wandering the site as an unregistered visitor, surfing the streams. A better bet, though, is to undergo the painless free registration so you can download songs and keep a personal Blackbox. The Blackbox is an on-site playlist organizer with category folders. You can choose from an extensive drop-down list of mood-evoking folder names such as "Brimming with Angst," "Underpaid and Overworked," "Temporary Schizophrenia," and "Ah, Sweet Melancholia." Similar to My MP3.com, but without its extensive feature set, Blackbox (figure 6.4) turns into a custom Internet radio station once you pile up enough selected tracks.

Name	Artist
Add selected to playlist: - New Playlist - ▾ add	
- New Playlist - ▾	
Move selected to folder: Test move	

[Select All]   [Deselect All]   [Delete Selected]

☐	Name	Artist
☐	The Room (Fila Brazillia Mix)	Harold Budd
☐	Pantomime ... (with Zeitgeist)	Harold Budd
☐	Breathless ... I (with Zeitgeist)	Harold Budd
☐	Harmonic Cross Sweep (Overtone Series of C Chord Progression)	Ellen Fullman
☐	Acoustic/Folk Genre Walkthrough	Epitonic.com
☐	Future Tropic	aFRO-mYSTIK
☐	Infinite Rhythm (Swag's Universal Re-Edit)	aFRO-mYSTIK
☐	Huffer	The Breeders
☐	Cansada	The Verbrilli Sound
☐	Drum & Bays	The Verbrilli Sound
☐	Styles Crew Flows Beats	Peanut Butter Wolf

[Select All]   [Deselect All]   [Delete Selected]

Figure 6.4. *The Epitonic Blackbox, the site's personalizing feature.*

Reminder When surfing the site and assigning streaming tracks to your Blackbox, remember that many pages contain time-saving bulk-assignment links. Look for Copy Songs to Inbox; from the Inbox you move songs to one of your Blackbox folders. Also, keep your eye out for the "Stream This Page" link, which gives you at least a few songs uninterruptedly, on most pages.

Epitonic Radio delivers a more effortless streaming experience than Blackboxes. Click the "Radio" link to find a genre page. Choose multiple genres, if you like, as well as the number of tracks altogether, that you want included in the radio playlist. You can't see the artists or tracks on this page, but you can see them all at once in a long list, while the custom "station" is playing in Windows Media Player. This handy list allows you to jump around among the tracks.

Epitonic genres lean heavily toward electronica and edgy flavors of rock and grunge. At the same time, there is an interesting classical catalog, featuring tracks from New Albion and Atlantic Classical albums. In all genres, the thrill of discovery is emphasized. Epitonic is a site for adventurous ears. (Britney lovers, stay away. You'll only get hurt.) When in the mood to dive deeply into a genre, start off with the Walk-Through for that genre—a streaming production highlighting important artists, recordings, and historical illuminations of that musical style.

House of Blues (www.hob.com)

For many years the House of Blues site has been poised at the cutting edge of online media, taking the initiative in transferring its offline brand and content to the online realm. Set up as a promotional vehicle for the many House of Blues clubs and venues around the country, HOB.com is a potent musical destination in its own right, fueled by set recordings and concert footage from the clubs. Any lover of blues (and jazz, some rock, and even some hip-hop) *must* get acquainted with this site. Two of its features are particularly noteworthy:

- **HOB Radio.** Seven genre stations are available for streaming. Pay particular attention to The Green Room, a collection of nearly a hundred programs hosted by well-known blues, soul, jazz, and pop recording artists presenting tracks that influenced their development. These programs are entertaining, unique, and must be heard.
- **Concert Archives.** The HOB vault continues to earn its superlative reputation with an asounding collection of audio (and some video) concert streams, mostly in House of Blues venues.

HOB.com dishes up all this glorious content free of charge. The site also promotes live music heavily, both at its affiliated locations and everywhere else that features blues, roots, and acoustic music.

IUMA (the Internet Underground Music Archive)

Legendary is the word for the Internet Underground Music Archive. It has been a haven for indie musicians and bands since long before the Web was mainstream. The site's tagline, "IUMA is music you should know about," seems fair enough. With little glitz to distract from the core genre directory (see figure 6.5), IUMA serves up a meat-and-potatoes diet of hard-core indie music. Experimental music is treated respectfully here, so visit in a spirit of adventure.

IUMA has been around so long that its community space is far more developed than at most sites. Visit the Bulletin Board section to browse through thousands of posts about the music, specific artists, and the site itself. These discussions offer the best guidance and editorial direction in the site, because formal reviews are not to be found. This utter lack of hype

Figure 6.5. *The genre directory at IUMA.*

and editorial coercion lends IUMA a rare purity and integrity. To an unusual degree, the music must speak for itself.

IUMA's operators segregate recently contributed tracks, so frequent visitors can find new music quickly. A handful of Featured Artists enjoy front-page promotion as well. Top-forty lists divided by genre give clues about the popularity of artists and tracks. Throughout the directory, you have a choice of listening to tracks in RealAudio or MP3 format—the latter provides whole-song downloads—and everything is free of charge. Even registration isn't required.

Garageband (www.garageband.com)

Tears were shed when Garageband fell with the dot-com implosion. Then, to great and widespread jubilation, it came back! Just in time for inclusion in this chapter, too. This unique venture seeks to create Internet-bred music stars in an organic competition fueled by reviews and votes of registered visitors. Everything is free for the nonmusician participant. Registration is semipainless, and definitely worth the slight effort.

This all-indie site of musical hopefuls makes it easy to gravitate directly to the best (or, at least, most popular) music, if that's your intent. Just click the rankings links to see current top-ten lists. Music is streamed in RealAudio format, and having RealOne installed is a great advantage. While the full song streams in the top panel, the lower browser panel is used to deliver the means of voting, the results of voting on the track currently streaming (review clips scroll across the panel like news headlines), as well as the entire site for browsing. In other words, the on-site experience switches entirely from your Web browser into RealOne, where it becomes an integrated music/information rapture. Look for those green Play buttons everywhere: each one is a full song ready to stream.

The songs are also ready to download, directly from RealOne. Click the Download MP3 button in the top panel. You might also want to click Add to Playlist; this button throws the stream link to a general list kept under your username, from which you can later sort tracks into folders.

Garageband has returned. Let the addiction begin anew.

CD Baby (www.cdbaby.com)

There is no more respected, even hallowed, site and business in the online music industry than CD Baby. As a textbook example of how to survive the disastrous indulgences of a bubble industry, CD Baby is unparalelled. The e-commerce store began as a one-person (founder Derek Sivers, who still runs the place) shop operated as a favor to musician friends. Derek rode every day's CD orders to the post office on a bicycle, and the shoestring sensibility still holds sway in the cheap-at-all-costs office. CD Baby claims to have been utterly untouched by the dot-com crash—every bit as untouched as it was by venture capitalists who made futile investment overtures. Remaining sparse and lean, CD Baby has thrived.

More important to indie musicians, CD Baby offers generous revenue splits, attracting a bang-up catalog of independent CD releases. The store accepts *only* unsigned, unagented submissions, and listens carefully to each one for proper placement in the site's directory.

For consumers, the important points are two-minute song auditions (of selected songs—the artist or band chooses which ones), good prices (again, set by the artist), and the heartwarming understanding that hard-working indie musicians are solidly benefited by each sale.

In the community of professional observers who track the present and future of digital music, CD Baby is universally lauded as a model of how the Internet can be leveraged to benefit all parties—musician, retailer, and consumer. The company has been profitable since its second month of operation, and employs eight people. At publication time, Derek Sivers had written checks to musicians totaling well over a million dollars. In a market environment whose integrity is damaged by purchased shelf placement, thirty-second online excerpts, and massive promotional payments to obtain radio airplay, the pristine credibility of CD Baby illuminates the hope of a future open, fair music industry for both artists and consumers.

7

Surfing the Internet Radio Stream

In the continual furor over downloading, ripping, and burning that seems to define digital music, streaming audio and Internet radio are sometimes overlooked. Part of the nonchalance might be attributable to the longevity of Internet audio, which predates the consumer MP3 scene by a few years. That extra time has been put to good use in two ways. First, the sound quality of streaming audio has improved sensationally. Second, the range of programming content has expanded dizzyingly, to a point of overwhelming variety and global reach.

Relative newcomers to the online experience (that is, those who joined the party sometime after the World Wide Web was instituted) might find it hard to understand what a thrill it was to experience the first meager attempts at online audio streaming. Most people got their first listen through RealAudio, a streaming format that once utterly dominated the Internet audio scene, and still is a major participant. The first version of RealAudio, erratic and thin though it was, presaged marvelous things to come—in particular, the long-awaited transformation of the Internet from an information medium to an entertainment realm.

Contemporary streaming flows with exceptional quality, rivaling the sound of a CD in some cases. Using a high-speed connection helps receive the highest-caliber streams, but telephone modems perform adequately receiving somewhat lower-fidelity Netcasts that still sound better than many car radios in traffic.

The scope of Internet programming has been astounding for years, and becomes more so with every new technical innovation (such as MP3 streaming from home computers) and with the simple passage of time. An uncountable number of traditional broadcast stations (sometimes referred to with a touch of sanctimony as "terrestrial" stations) simulcast their entire programming day online; you can listen locally through a radio or from any point on earth through a Net-connected computer. New Internet-only programming ventures eschew the airwaves entirely and pump their playlists into the virtual realm exclusively. Big music licensers create genre-defined, all-music, no-talk "stations" and distribute them through major online services like Yahoo! and America Online.

The result of this programming bonanza is a range of listening undreamed of several years ago, when passive listening was confined to traditional broadcasts and relatively unpopular cable-radio subscriptions. Now, you can arrive at your desk at work, browse through a bookmark list of Internet radio streams, and pick a station from almost anywhere in the world. Or, ease into the day with an uninterrupted selection of tightly defined genre music. Streaming audio fits right into digital music's mandate to empower users in the programming of their life soundtrack.

Info.Update Just as this chapter was being written, political forces were threatening to overturn the applecart. A government-enforced royalty and rules structure could drive out of operation most of the small and mid-sized Webcasters whose streams contribute such inexhaustible richness to Internet radio. (See the section later in this chapter entitled "The Politics and Uncertain Future of Webcasting.") The outcome is up in the air as this book goes to production. If some of the stations mentioned here cannot be found, or the general lay of the land seems changed, visit this book's Web site (www.digitalsongstream.com) for updates.

Streaming versus Downloading

A fundamental distinction exists between downloading and streaming, a distinction sometimes lost on reporters covering digital music, to the confusion of many. The two functions break down in this way:

Internet *Not*-radio

Calling music streaming "Internet radio" is one of the least imaginative appellations possible. An audio stream is not radio by any stretch. First, it is not transmitted through the air or picked up by a radio receiver. Audio streams consist of data packets, not radio waves. Also, the underlying one-to-many broadcast model is violated by the Internet's one-to-one (many times) method of distributing content. In fact, this explains why Internet radio is so expensive to operate: each listener represents a distinct stream to whom music must be launched from a server, and each of those streams takes up bandwidth that must be paid for.

- **Streaming audio** is not meant to be captured and stored on your computer. As such, it requires no discrete downloading process of acquisition, though, in truth, some hidden downloading is going on in the background. Streaming is an on-demand method of listening to digital music, and ideally performs nearly instantaneously. In all cases, streaming requires some degree of buffering before the Netcast begins to sound: the buffer stores a bit of the forthcoming audio stream in advance, protecting the stream from interruption. (Portable CD players do the same thing to protect against skips caused by jostling.)
- **Downloadable music** is meant to be captured, and is generally not audible during the download. As such, downloads are more time-consuming than streams, and less immediately gratifying. Downloads are not on-demand components of online listening (although they become so after they are downloaded). However, downloads are more permanent, and a more solid part of your local music collection than a stream is.

Streaming operates with a fair degree of effortlessness on your part. At the most transparent level, you click a link and within a second or two begin hearing music. At the other end of the spectrum, you must boot up a program, select a genre or a station, and start it off. However, your computer has to perform some work; streams launched from the Internet need to be played through one program or another. In most cases, the streaming format (RealAudio, Windows Media, MP3) is associated with a program that pops open to play the stream. So, a RealAudio stream might activate the RealOne player; a Windows Media stream might launch Windows Media Player; and an MP3 stream could spark Winamp to action. The specific format associations are up to you, and are determined within the program you wish to use.

Reminder The file associations between streaming formats and players can be changed at any time (it's done within the programs, in the Options or Preferences settings), so that one program can handle all streams in any format. Most people prefer to leave the initial settings unchanged, and don't much care which program surfaces to deliver an Internet radio station or a CD excerpt at Amazon.com. Furthermore, many streaming opportunities give the user a choice of formats (RealAudio and Windows Media are the two most commonly paired choices in commercial sites) and therefore a choice of players.

Like a Web page, an audio stream is (sometimes) represented by a URL (Internet http:// address). One cumbersome way of launching a stream is to copy the address into a desktop player that accepts streaming URLs, such as Media Jukebox, Winamp, and many others. Naturally, this method is less convenient than simply clicking a link, and involves right-clicking the link, copying the address, and pasting it into the player. Note also that it doesn't always work, because Javascript links are sometimes used to hide the location of the streaming file.

The Many Shades of Webcasting

The Internet is an alluring opportunity for terrestrial broadcasters to expand their reach, breaking out of the confinement of geography and the distance limitations of radio waves. At the same time, the dot-com boom of the 1990s attracted entrepreneurs interested in building new Internet audiences for streaming programs, offering alternative music mixes with few or no commercials. Many of those early pioneers have gone the way of other dot-com failures, leaving large operations and swarms of tiny ones.

Consolidation in Netcasting is rampant, yet balanced by a vibrant entrepreneurialism and grassroots spirit that has survived the 1990s. As in other entertainment media, the big players attempt to dominate the space with a bevy of attractive products, so that most people don't bother prowling through the shadows for hidden gems. Microsoft and RealNetworks, owners of the two dominant streaming formats and two of the most commonly used desktop players, feed a broad buffet of streaming nourishment to the Internet masses. Along the same lines, AOL, the world's largest Internet service provider and sibling of a big-five record label, delivers simple-to-use, genre-based Internet radio to its millions of subscribers.

Around the edges, small and medium-sized commercial companies deliver intelligent, adventurous programming. Individuals use Shoutcast, Live365, and other streaming enablers to Netcast their homegrown playlists. The indie Net programmers are found through exploration, just as indie CDs and downloads are. The final section of this chapter highlights some worthy candidates for an adventurous listener's bookmark list.

Webcasting streams in several distinct categories:

- **Terrestrial simulcasts.** Broadcast radio stations large and small provide links on their Web pages that initiate a stream of the station's real-time programming. For the stations, simulcasting is a way to let you listen to favorite radio personalities even when out of town, thus cementing loyal listenership. For the most part, these stations make no additional money through Web streams, and it does cost money and require expertise for them to offer this service. Not every station simulcasts, but an amazing number (all over the world) do. Americans are force-fed a terribly standardized radio diet formulated by market-dominating chains of stations, so getting your radio online is a fantastic way to break out of cultural stagnation.
- **Packaged terrestrial programs.** DJ-style programming is hard to package, but other formats can be broken down and reconstituted online. National Public Radio (NPR) has been practicing this tactic for years, offering streaming repeats of some popular network programs on demand, even as many of its member stations simulcast their entire program day.
- **Internet-only programming.** Many music streams originate online and never go outside the virtual realm. The quality of these stations runs the gamut from homogenized to exotic. Almost all of it, though, differs from terrestrial broadcasting by reducing personality. Internet-only stations dish up very little talk and fewer ads than most broadcast stations. This type of Internet radio has become startlingly ubiquitous in music sites ranging from corporate presentations like Yahoo! Music, to small record label sites that stream their artists, to online CD

stores. One-click listening is the order of the day, usually delivered through a Web interface that pops up a control panel that lets you adjust volume and station selections.

- **Dedicated desktop streamers.** Not as popular as they once were, dedicated streaming programs have been supplanted somewhat by Internet radio "tuners" built into integrated players like Windows Media Player and RealOne. Still, pioneers like Spinner are continuing to thrive, even as others like Wired Planet and Rhythm Radio are sorely missed. Spinner and other survivors require downloading a desktop program through which you make station choices and register programming preferences.
- **Subscription Netcasting.** Most Internet radio is free, supported by advertising or slowly going broke, but some companies turn their streams into revenue by charging a monthly fee. Rhapsody and Radio MX, described in chapter 4, are two prominent examples.
- **Personal Netcasting.** Using the MP3 streaming format, individuals with an MP3 collection can become Internet programmers with the help of support sites like Shoutcast and Live365. These sites provide the necessary software for Netcasting an MP3 playlist, host the streams, and provide a directory of stations. These quirky, singular stations contribute some of the most interesting and valuable programming to the Webcast scene.

 Power User Of these categories, the generic type of Internet-only programming, provided in nearly identical fashion through major online services, is the least interesting. Aimed at the mass Internet market and widely embraced for its ease of use, these online stations are both the simplest and least rewarding audio streams. Even so, run-of-the-mill genre stations offer far more variety and personal choice than terrestrial radio. With the exception of NPR, traditional broadcast radio has fallen off my radar entirely, at least indoors. (I still listen to my car radio sometimes, skipping the interchangeable music stations in favor of local talk radio.)

The Politics and Uncertain Future of Webcasting

Between 1998 and 2002, a debate ensued between Webcasters and record labels over the fair amount to charge Webcasters for the use of music owned by the labels. The argument was started when the U.S. Congress ruled that Internet radio, unlike broadcast radio, would be liable for some kind of royalty payment to recording artists and their labels. Broadcast radio pays low fees that get distributed to songwriters and music publishers, but pays nothing to performers and their record labels. A longstanding relationship between traditional radio and record labels defines broadcasting as a promotional vehicle that benefits record and CD sales; in fact, music labels have paid enormous amounts of money to radio stations (before that practice was deemed illegal) and then to independent music promotion companies (which feed music selections to radio stations) in order to get their music on the air.

Why isn't Internet radio considered in the same light, as a superlative promotional opportunity that labels have an interest in cultivating? It's a good question, addressed by a tangled knot of answers. Internet radio is very new, first of all, and it's easy to imagine that record labels might want to build a different sort of remunerative relationship with this fresh medium. Also, there is a control issue to consider. In proposing rather lofty royalty rates, the labels have been accused of trying to destroy Internet radio. But the real motivation might be a desire to control the space, not eliminate it, because only the major labels and their broadcast colleagues have the deep pockets needed to afford high royalties, and, in some cases, are positioned to make those payments from one subsidiary of a parent company to another. Squeezing out independent Webcasters wouldn't destroy Internet radio, but it could homogenize it in the same fashion as broadcast radio, preserving the hit-oriented, mass-market, top-down musical culture so tediously transmitted by big radio chains.

In mid-2001 it was clear that the ongoing negotiations between the Webcasters' trade group and the record labels might go on forever. The two sides were far apart. The U.S. Copyright Office stepped in with the CARP, or Copyright Arbitration Royalty Panel. (The acronymn perhaps unintentionally perfectly suits the relationship among the parties involved.) The CARP listened to the arguments, did some figuring of its own, and in February 2002 came down between the two sides with proposed royalty rates for Webcasters.

The headline figure in the proposed rates was $.0014 per song, per listener. That meant one-fourteenth of a penny would be paid to the labels every time a song is heard by a listener. If one thousand listeners hear a single song, $1.40 would be paid for that song. Assuming a steady listenership of one thousand, and assuming fifteen songs streamed per hour, the royalty payments would add up to $21 an hour, $504 a day, $183,960 a year. (The proposed rates were much lower for nonprofit Webcasters, and Netcasts of terrestrial broadcasts would pay only half of the $.0014 per song.) Consider the case of Live365, a consolidated directory of home-based Netcasts and small-business Internet stations. The total Live365 portfolio of stations delivered about 6 million listening hours in February 2002 (according to Arbitron as reported by CNET). At fifteen songs per hour, that delivery rate would cost Live365 $126,000 per month, and over $1.5 million per year.

In a brand-new industry just getting its bearings, trying to grasp unestablished revenue sources, numbers like these seemed to forecast nearly universal destruction. At least, that's what the Webcasting community preached to the media, even as the Recording Industry Association of America (RIAA) complained that the compromised rates were too low. (The royalties were, on top of it all, due retroactively for three years.) The real problem for small Webcasters lay in how the proposed rates were framed: as a per-song-per-listener charge, rather than a percentage of station revenue. Because royalties are a sort of tax, it doesn't make sense to charge high-profit companies the same amount as low-profit companies. The proposed flat-fee rates seemed designed to discourage the operation of small-time Netcasting. Those parties arguing in favor of the flat fee, though, pointed out how difficult it would be to verify the accounting of large multimedia houses, like Yahoo! and AOL, which have many bottom lines to which streaming revenue could be assigned to avoid paying Webcast royalties.

After CARP announced its proposed settlement, a waiting period ensued, during which the Librarian of Congress (James H. Billington) was charged with reviewing the proposal and ruling summarily on it: yea or nay. Come May 21, 2002, Billington ruled nay, and the CARP plan was rejected. A month later, Billington issued a revised royalty plan, the most important point in which was the halving of the infamous $.0014 per song, per listener rate. This is a statutory rate, which means that any Netcaster can stream any content at that rate without obtaining explicit permission; at the same time, performers and labels can arrange private licensing deals that undercut that rate. While the royalty change (from $.0014 to $.0007) might have seemed like good news to small Webcasters, it failed to reverse the per-unit plan in favor of a percentage-of-revenue system, so independent programmers continued to sulk. More than that, many of them immediately closed shop, and others were expected to follow when the first retroactive payment became due in October 2002.

The cavalry appeared on the horizon, though, in the week before that due date in October 2002. A coalition of small Webcasters negotiated a settlement with the RIAA, formulating a legislative bill called the Small Webcasters Amendment Act. The agreement finally forged a percent-of-revenue plan that replaced the per-song, per-track arrangement. The revised royalty system applied to some extent to each of three tiers of "small" Webcasting, defined by overall revenue.

The Small Webcasters Amendment Act was expected to pass both the House and Senate unanimously, and so it did in the House. When the Senate stepped up to the plate, Sen. Jesse Helms put a "hold" on the bill—every Senator's prerogative, and one which stops a bill in its tracks. Helms did this just as the Senate was winding down its legislative session in early October 2002, and the bill was scuttled. It seemed as if small Webcasters, so close to having their future resuscitated, were doomed after all.

The succession of eleventh-hour redemptions continued, though, as the RIAA and SoundExchange (the agency charged with collecting Webcast royalties) agreed to waive the first retroactive payment for small Webcasters, in the hope that the Senate would resolve the issue and pass the bill—or some altered version of it—when Congress reconvened in November 2002.

Such is the situation as this book goes into production. And if this whole saga weren't enough fun by itself, it starts all over again in 2003, because the Webcast rates, by law, last only two years, and the 2002 resolution finally came at the end of a two-year period. The real question is how a toddling industry can get its legs when the economic rules change every couple of years. When I put this question to John O. Jeffrey, an executive vice president at Live365, just after Billington's final ruling, Jeffrey predicted an eventual long-term agreement between the labels and the Webcasters. After all, the Copyright Office got involved only because private negotiations had been fruitless for two years. The process was expensive for everyone involved, so perhaps some "do-it-ourselves" motivation will kick in.

In the meantime, a Webcast shakeout is in progress, much to the unhappiness of devoted listeners. As inevitable as short-term consolidation is, though, so is the long-term prognosis: Webcasting will be huge—far more enormous in impact and programming range than it has been. Even as this book is published, we are at the beginning of the digital music revolution in all aspects. Stay tuned. Keep prowling the underbrush for hidden gems, which for the next couple of years will probably take the form of venture-capitalized midsized Net stations, and very small operations that have cut private licensing deals with alliances of musicians and indie labels.

Info.Update The state of Webcasting is one subject this book covers that is certain to be updated by the time you read this. In addition to the *Digital Songstream* Web site (www.digitalsongstream.com), two other important sites can bring you up to speed quickly:

• Radio and Internet Newsletter (www.kurthanson.com); and

• Save Internet Radio (www.saveinternetradio.org).

If activism surrounding this issue is still called for in late 2002 and throughout 2003, those two sites make it easy to write, call, or fax the appropriate lawmakers. Internet radio is worth saving. Small-scale Netcasts, freed from the limitations of geography and the strangling cultural influences of corporate trendsetting, represent a deeply enriching contribution to the enjoyment of music around the world. And if fringe Webcasting is saved, we all should feel a happy obligation to support it. Make the extra effort to go beyond MSN, AOL, Yahoo!, and other mass-market generics. Seek out the college radio simulcasts. Spend time with the grassroots MP3 streamers. Your musical life will be elevated while you cultivate an invigorating young industry, an antidote to the deep malaise of morning zoos, weary and identical playlists, and other distressing symptoms of consolidated broadcasting.

The Ins and Outs of Desktop Streaming

Streaming audio isn't hard to master; in fact, it's probably the easiest digital music skill, far simpler than downloading files, ripping, and burning. Although there are several elements working in the background to deliver any single stream, the inventors and enablers of streaming audio have worked to make the experience as transparent, intuitive, and effortless as possible. That doesn't mean they have necessarily succeeded in every case. Furthermore, that very transparency is what herds listeners together at the most unadventurous Webcasting points. For both reasons—to understand problems when they develop, and to take your listening off the beaten path—I've put together this list of points to remember:

- **You need some basic streaming software to hear any music.** The good news is that you probably have some or all of it in your computer already. It's a rare PC sold these days without Windows Media Player and RealOne (or RealPlayer) already bundled. Windows Media Player is definitely included with any recent version of Windows. Both are available free for the downloading, and almost any stream that can't get started on your machine launches an explanation with a link to the download site. For MP3 streaming I find it best to use players designed from the bottom up for MP3 playback, such as Winamp and FreeAmp. As of this book's publication, Windows Media Player and RealOne both were unable to play certain types of MP3 streaming formats (particularly PLS files) when correct URLs were loaded into the players. (See the next point for file-type information.)

- **You can assign most players to respond automatically when you request (click on) streams in certain formats.** Using the Preferences or Options panel in any player you can assign stream types by knowing these streaming file extensions: WMA, ASF (Windows Media); RAM, RM, RMJ, RMP, RM, RMX, RMM (RealAudio); MP3, M3U, PLS (MP3). Windows Media Player does not let you get so specific with file-type assignments, but the list in that program's Options panel does allow you to assign "Windows Media file" and to uncheck all types of MP3 playback, which I recommend. RealAudio is not an available format in Windows Media Player, although Windows Media files can be played in RealOne. Keep your life simple: let each player handle its native format, and assign MP3 streams to Winamp, FreeAmp, or some other MP3 program.

- **Sound quality varies tremendously from stream to stream.** This variation is not a fault of you or your computer; it depends on the fidelity with which the streaming source encodes its files. Lower bit rates (measured in kilobits per second, or kbps) take less bandwidth, making it possible for the server to accommodate more simultaneous listeners. The trade-off between sound quality and audience size is handled in a variety of ways, and the upshot for you, the casual listener, is that some stations sound a lot better than others. Many Internet radio tuners (like Windows Media Player, but not RealOne), display the bit rate of every listed station before you kick off the stream, inviting you to make your choices partly on the basis of sound fidelity. Almost every player displays the bit rate of a stream in progress, offering an after-the-fact explanation of lousy-sounding audio. Complicating your evaluation of stream quality, though, is that bit-rate standards differ among formats. Windows Media, for example, compresses more effectively than MP3, so it requires lower bit rates to sound good. As a rough guide, think of 128kbps as a near-CD standard for MP3 and RealAudio streams, and 64kbps as a roughly equivalent standard for Windows Media streams. But always let your ears be your final guides.

- **Interruptions and stalls are part of streaming's charm.** That's a stretch, but charming or not, expect somewhat flawed listening across the board. Delivering data packets is far less reliable in the current Internet environment than delivering radio waves through the air. The faster your Internet connection, the smoother your streams, especially at high bit rates. No matter how slick your home connection, occasional drop-outs are inevitable. They can sound like a mild, brief stutter, or a dramatic interruption that takes thirty seconds to recover. You can wait out such interruptions, restart the stream from the original link, or move on to another streamcast. (You were probably getting sick of that Indonesian techno-funk station, anyway.) If you experience frequent problems, try listening to stations with lower bit rates.
- **When you launch an audio stream from a Web site, one of two things happens.** A browser window might pop up with start/stop, volume, and other controls. Figure 7.1 illustrates such a pop-up controller from Radio Free Virgin. The other possibility is that RealOne, Windows Media Player, or some other software installed in your computer boots up to play the stream. (One of your players is powering the stream even through the pop-up browser window.) In either case, the original browser window in which you clicked the stream link is free and available for further browsing. The stream continues even as you move away from that page.
- **An Internet radio stream might and might not display the artist, album, and track currently playing.** Most Web-based stations that pop up a dedicated control window do list that information (and helpfully provide links to CD-purchase pages at Amazon, CDNow, or some other online retailer). When a station plays through a desktop tuner like Windows Media Player, RealOne, or Winamp, the

existence of track information depends on how the stream is coded at the source. It's a chancy proposition, but more stations are realizing the importance of identifying played tracks. It makes all the difference in my personal listening, because I use Internet radio as an unparalleled discovery medium. I don't buy CDs impulsively (and I don't recommend buying any CD on the basis of hearing one track), but I do jot down the names of bands that grab my attention, for later research.

- **Desktop streamers that you download and install are usually not full-featured players in themselves.** In most cases these programs require the presence of Windows Media Player and/or RealNow in your computer. In such cases the desktop streamer uses the playback and streaming capability of those programs without opening the programs themselves. If your computer is missing a needed program, or a certain component of a program, the desktop streamer notifies you of the requirement and provides a download link. In the best cases, that link accomplishes the download and installation of the missing component with a single click. When further clicks are required, simply follow the instructions that appear on your screen. Generally there is little to fear if the streamer is from a reputable source such as those mentioned in this chapter. Beware, though, of any installation process that claims the necessity of disabling or uninstalling any program in your computer; it bodes ill, and could result in profound headaches later.

- **Track-advance capabilities are not a given.** In this digitized, random-access, on-demand age in which we enjoy music, you'd think that any Internet radio stream would offer a track-advance feature whereby you can skip past any song that you're not enjoying to the next song in the station's playlist. Technically, advancing tracks is no problem. But licensing the right to implement that feature from the record companies is another matter. Major labels appreciate the promotional benefits of pushed, passive programming, but when technology gets too personalized, interactive, and "pulled," the labels become cautious. Even Rhapsody, a subscription service, was launched to paying customers without this feature, attributing the lack to licensing roadblocks. Still, track-advance is occasionally found, either at stations that have finagled appropriate permission from the majors, or less ambitious stations that play less finicky indie labels.

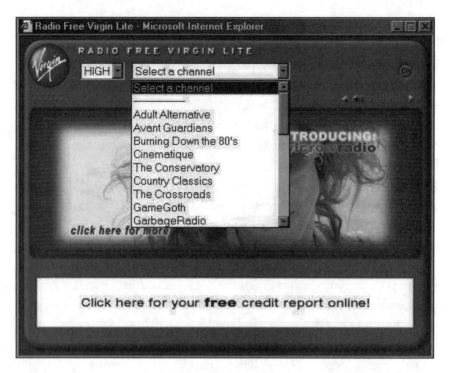

Figure 7.1. A browser pop-up controlling an Internet radio stream, in this case, Radio Free Virgin.

Using Internet Radio Tuners

Although I rant against corporate programming in both the broadcast and virtual realms, that doesn't stop me from using desktop players from the big Internet companies to find alternative programming. In fact, Windows Media Player and RealOne (owned by Microsoft and RealNetworks, inventors of two of the three major streaming formats) provide indispensable Webcast tuners. Although each company produces a Web-page portal with plenty of streaming links, I find it best to ignore those interfaces and stick to the dedicated players. The portals are heavily involved with promoting affiliated artists and with selling CDs. Inside Windows Media Player and RealOne the environment can't be called noncommercial, but the focus is more sharply on delivering a wide range of stations, and on streaming for its own sake.

Internet Radio with Windows Media Player

When version 7 of Windows Media Player (WMP) was released, it was immediately clear that Internet streaming comprised one of the program's best features, and one that has been continued in subsequent versions of the program. Incorporating a large directory of online stations that use the Windows Media format, WMP doesn't distinguish between online simulcasts of broadcast stations and Internet-only streams. It simply divides all available stations into genre categories, while also letting you search by keyword. (Keywords do not find programs; they find station call letters.) Oddly, WMP invites you to search for stations by zip code, a peculiar feature both because one of the charms of Internet radio is its freedom from geography and because the feature doesn't work very well.

Get started by clicking the Radio Tuner button on the main WMP panel. Once in the Radio Tuner, the links are self-evident. As you can see in figure 7.2, the program gives you a choice of surfing to the station's Web site or initiating the stream directly, a welcome option because most people have little interest in detouring unnecessarily to the Web site. Saving favorite stations is a good idea: just click the "Add to My Stations" link beneath any station listing.

Figure 7.2. Surfing Internet radio in Windows Media Player.

Alert WMP's Radio Tuner doesn't always present Internet stations in their best light. When a station offers a bandwidth choice—streams with differing bit rates—Windows Media Player sometimes proffers the weakest choice most visibly. An example is Radioio (noted later in this chapter), which, at its site, provides listeners with a choice of six streams of varying quality. WMP displays the worst-sounding stream on its Editor's Pick page, burying the higher-quality stream deeper in the directory. The lesson here is to visit the station's Web site if you're dissatisfied with the stream quality. There's a possibility you can get a better-sounding stream directly from the source.

Internet Radio with RealOne

As in the Radio Tuner of Windows Media Player, RealOne Radio offers a diverse directory of simulcast and Internet-only radio stations (see figure 7.3). Each station link initiates the stream without a detour to the source's Web site. The directory is organized by genre. Surprisingly, no bookmark feature exists to store favorites. But RealOne does keep track of recently

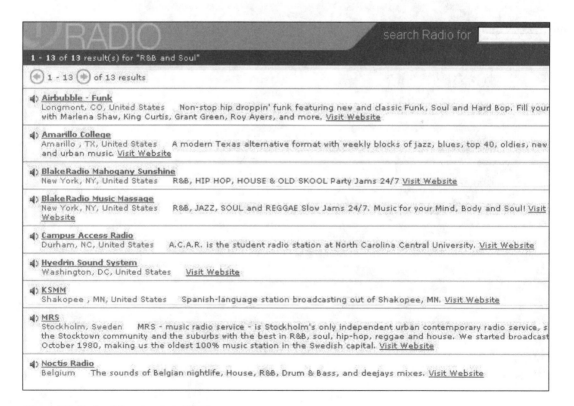

Figure 7.3. Surfing Internet radio in RealOne.

played stations, displaying their links for easy return visits to favorite streams. However, there is no way to expand or save the list, so a bit of random browsing can easily push a real favorite off the list.

RealOne provides the best way to find Internet stations using the RealAudio format, naturally. By the same token, Windows Media Player is the most convenient directory of Windows Media stations. Unfortunately, most listeners don't give a darn about the streaming format; they care about the music. Stations that use both formats (and many stations do) are likely to felicitously appear on both programs. But format fragmentation is a real problem, corresponding to catalog fragmentation among the download subscription services (see chapter 4). Independent desktop Internet radio tuners, described in this chapter, solve the problem to a large extent by listing stations in all three major streaming formats: Windows Media, RealAudio, and MP3. Let's explore three format-neutral station directories: one that operates through your Web browser, and two that run as stand-alone programs on the desktop.

vTuner (www.vtuner.com)

Desktop stream-finder vTuner can be operated directly from the company's Web site, but downloading the desktop version is handier. Even more jazzy is vTuner Plus, selling for $24.95 at publication time, which lets you save favorite stations and schedule streams for launching at particular times. The program isn't much to look at (see figure 7.4), and its cosmetic blandness is exacerbated by a nonresizable window that is locked into a too-small size to easily display its various features.

The vTuner is not a player, and it handles different streaming formats by automatically launching Windows Media Player or RealOne to handle the actual streaming chores. So using vTuner adds an element to your desktop that you don't need when using either of those streamers by itself. The advantage is vTuner's format neutrality; it finds and initiates RealAudio and Windows Media streams, both audio and video.

Oddly, the search engine at the vTuner Web site, which is supposed to mimic the searching facility of the desktop program, delivers better results than its downloadable counterpart, but both the site and the desktop searcher did better in my *Bulgaria* test than did Windows Media Player and RealOne. Searching for Internet radio streams from Bulgaria never delivers a very long list of results, so I use that search to test a search engine's ability to prowl the fringe. (I also have a quirky love for Bulgarian folk music. Don't laugh until you've tried it.) Running the Bulgaria test in four settings produced the following results:

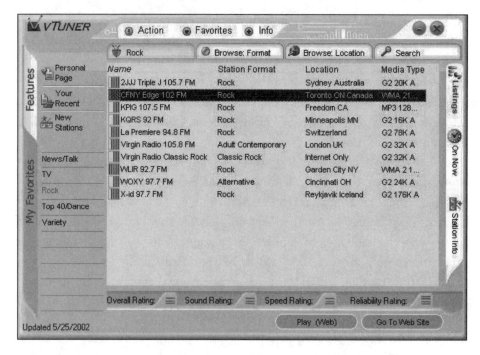

Figure 7.4. The vTuner desktop Webcast organizer finds and plays streams in all formats.

- Windows Media Player: no stations.
- RealOne: six stations.
- vTuner desktop tuner: eight stations.
- vTuner Web site: eleven stations.

At any rate, vTuner allows you to assign streams to a Favorites list, and invites searching by genre, location, and keyword. Using keywords (click the Search tab), you can locate specific shows, a great feature when you're out of town with a laptop and want to catch *A Prairie Home Companion*.

VirtualTuner.com (www.virtualtuner.com)

One advantage to a Web-based radio tuner is that you can use it from any computer. Registration at VirtualTuner is free, impersonal, and painless. Registering lets you use the bookmarking feature, set various preferences for return visits, and see more information about each station.

VirtualTuner provides more than the typical genre-based station directory. You can browse for streams by location (continent, country, or U.S. state), language, bandwidth (sound quality), source type (broadcast simulcast or Internet-only), or by streaming format. (Internet TV is covered on equal footing with Internet radio.) Use the "Advanced Search" link to specify multiple criteria. In an attempt to provide an immersive radio experience, VirtualTuner provides weather and Webcam links for every station. The site does not provide an on-site player; instead, it pops open the programs assigned in your computer to handle various streaming formats.

Sonicbox
(www.imnetworks.com/products/tuner.shtml)
Sonicbox, from iM Networks, is fast, clean, slick, pretty, and it owns a chunk of my desktop. While this tuner doesn't offer the greatest selection, the convenience factor of its swift, classy interface makes it a fun and headache-free desktop streamer. And good-looking? Sonicbox is the one streamer you most want impressionable friends to see on your screen (see figure 7.5).

Sonicbox is a back-end service provider, which means it furnishes streaming technology and soup-to-nuts Webcasting solutions to broadcasters and would-be Netcasters. Sonicbox is a tuner/directory of Internet radio streams affiliated with iM Networks. In other words, it's iM's clients that you hear through Sonicbox. The selection runs from mainstream to eclectic. Each stream begins with a little promo from Sonicbox while the station stream is buffering. Sonicbox contains a limited selection, but consistent streaming quality throughout its portfolio of stations. Unlike the gigantic tuners from Microsoft and RealNetworks that play music of many thousands of client companies, iM Networks' small size results in greater uni-

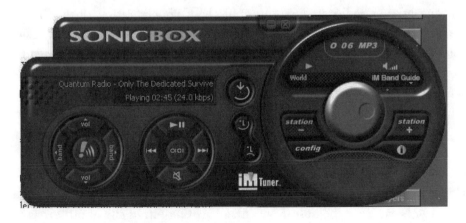

Figure 7.5. The Sonicbox Internet radio tuner.

formity of bit rate and streaming reliability. Sonicbox sounds good, doesn't take much room, is pretty to look at, and does the job with nary a hassle.

Sonicbox's interface is so simple that, at first glance, you might wonder if it has any usefulness at all. Spinning the big tuning dial with your mouse is enjoyable in a virtual-retro sort of way, but in the end is too haphazard for daily use. Look for the iM Band Guide and click it. Or, easier still, simply right-click anywhere on the program and run your mouse down to the Guide selection. Either way, the iM Band Guide genre directory pops open, with subdirectories unfolding as you run your mouse cursor down the list. Click any selection to start the stream. Any station can be saved to the so-called Z-band—basically a bookmark list of favorite streams.

Selected Internet-Only Programming

Once you dive into any of the Internet radio tuners, it becomes obvious that online streaming is an overwhelmingly fertile field. Any attempt at a comprehensive recommendation sheet would be foolish. The following sections describe a bare few of the Internet-only programmers putting out interesting and valuable work. Check this book's web site (www.digital songstream.com) for updates and evolving recommendations.

Shoutcast and Live365
(www.shoutcast.com; www.live365.com)

These two streaming sites are commonly lumped together as providers of homegrown Netcasting in the MP3 format. Both companies provide stream-enabling tools to anyone with a desire to Webcast their MP3 playlists. The result is an immense collection of small-company and one-person Internet radio stations, most of them concentrating on a single, sometimes narrowly defined genre. Shoutcast and Live365 streams furnish some of the most interesting on-demand listening in the virtual domain. However, at this writing it remains unclear whether these two big aggregators will survive the royalty regulations that are being considered by the government. Shoutcast and Live365 are poised to be hit extremely hard by any royalty decision based on a per-song flat rate rather than a percentage of revenue, because each site houses an enormous number of streams. At this point their revenues come from the sites, not from the streams, so the royalties levied on their enormous song traffic could have a devastating effect.

Still, hoping for the best, I encourage visiting either site and browsing through the directory of streams. Starting any station in Shoutcast is gen-

Figure 7.6. A portion of the Shoutcast directory of MP3 Internet stations.

erally a point-and-listen affair. In Shoutcast, click the Tune In! button next to any listing (see figure 7.6). Whichever MP3 desktop program you have associated with PLS files pops open to play the stream.

Live365 is not as simple. Click the speaker icon next to any listing, and a browser pop-up window opens to test your system for connection speed and MP3 compatibility. Then the window suggests you download and install the Live365 Player. Doing so is painless, requiring nothing from you except waiting a few seconds. But this pop-up player doesn't allow you to search for other stations, so you remain anchored to the main site. Furthermore, clicking a second station in the main site opens a second pop-up player that begins making noise in competition with the first. This cacophony is alleviated through the use of Start365, a desktop player that accesses the directory and keeps track of your preferences.

Personally, I prefer Shoutcast's more transparent system, using Winamp (see chapter 9) to play the streams and bookmarking any I want to revisit. But there's no question that Live365 owns an attractive array of stations, with an overall musical caliber that is perhaps higher than Shoutcast's. I recommend both destinations.

Spinner (www.spinner.com)

Spinner made a strong impression when it was first released, and it has become one of the milestone Internet radio outfits around. Spinner helped establish the multigenre online station, modeled on cable radio. With an aggressive licensing approach and laser-sharp genre divisions, Spinner tries to deliver exactly what you're in the mood to hear. At this writing, version 4.0 offered 190 genre stations from Abstract Beats to XtremeAltRock, from Summer Daze to Hair Metal.

Spinner's much-imitated features, such as the My Favorites list and a link to either Amazon or CDNow to buy whatever CD is currently playing, are still useful but no longer seem innovative. The program was acquired by AOL, which is hardly known for developing cutting-edge software. Spinner remains viable and fun, and the wafer-thin genre categories are impressive, but the programming within them isn't adventurous.

Spinner is a desktop streamer that must be downloaded and installed. It uses the RealAudio streaming format, so some version of RealPlayer or RealOne must be in your computer. Spinner will prompt you to download any needed components.

Radio Margaritaville (www.radiomargaritaville.com)

Jimmy Buffett is the visionary and essential music provider of Radio Margaritaville. Buffet's music is featured in hour-long blocks sprinkled throughout the programming week, mixed with DJ'd selections of compatible music and live Netcasts of concerts from around the world. The site and the Internet stations are touchstones of Buffet's Far Side of the World tour, which Webcasts its concert stops. Streams play in RealAudio format, in two bandwidth choices. The programming schedule is divulged two weeks in advance.

Beethoven.com (www.beethoven.com)

Claiming one hundred thousand listeners each month, Beethoven Netcasts one of the most popular classical music program schedules online. A vibrant Web site displays news from the classical world while you listen. The briefest of free registrations is required before getting started. Beethoven supplies the player, a pop-up browser window that offers a choice of RealAudio or Windows Media streaming.

Radio Paradise (www.radioparadise.com)

Featuring some of the most satisfying general rock and pop programming on the Web, Radio Paradise has gained renown and a loyal listenership. Streaming in MP3 format, the station can be bookmarked in Winamp, or launched from the Radio Paradise site. Listen for an hour or a day, and repeats are unlikely. Along the way, you'll enjoy a classy mix of old and new music in a cross-section of compatible genres.

Radioio (www.radioio.com)

Radioio (pronounced "radio i.o.") is an online version of a broadcast station, complete with announcers, commercials for online sites, feature program bits ("Earth & Sky"), and even weather. The forecasts somehow wrap up the global weather picture in less than a minute. This level of talkiness is unusual for an Internet station, and the saving grace is the music selection described on the site as "intelligent eclectic adultAlternative." The mix at Radioio is renowned among stream enthusiasts. With very little repetition, a typical hour of listening is represented by artists as diverse as Sting, Llama, Solas, Ryan Adams, and Joni Mitchell. The station doesn't challenge your ears, and neither does it bore them. Radioio is perfect office listening, and even markets itself ("From our cubicle to your cubicle") as such.

Eschewing downloadable players, Radioio streams directly from its Web site, through your choice of Windows Media Player or an MP3 player (each available in three bandwidth levels). Spicing up its prerecorded playlist, Radioio offers the occasional live concert Netcast in a low-bandwidth stream. When listening, be sure to click the "Now Playing Pop-up" link, which opens a small browser window listing the current selection and the previous ten songs.

Operadio (www.operadio.com)

More focused than Beethoven and utterly dedicated to sating the most demanding lover of opera, Operadio presents ten RealAudio channels of classical music. The operatic repertoire is divided into music periods, oratorios, instrumental portions of operas, and even a Broadway channel. A semipainless free registration gets you started, and the site pops open a browser player.

8

Folders, Filenames, and ID3 Tags

Not everyone has the time or inclination to program their own life sound-track. But for those who do, a new era of home music programming is upon us, thanks to file compression and programmable streaming. Small files enable large, centralized MP3 collections. Programmable streaming provided by Rhapsody, Radio MX, and other flexible Webcasters—and to a less customizable extent digital radio—enables something similar to all-request radio.

Programming playlists from an MP3 collection is the focus of this chapter. There's no point in housing a large collection without listening to it (although a lot of mindless hoarding goes on), and effective listening is supported by good organizational habits. In particular, *flexible* listening requires tidy collecting. When an MP3 collection is archived and tagged optimally, you can deploy it to fit your mood with the utmost pliancy: by artist, album, genre, randomness, or many other categories.

The level of programmability made possible by MP3 files and certain jukebox programs far exceeds the ordered playback and shuffling of CD players, and even the complex programmability of multidisc CD changers. The problem with CD-based programming is the disc itself. Compact though it is, it's a bulky relic of the uncompressed era compared to an untethered MP3 collection. The slimness and independence of an MP3 file, compared to an on-disc music track, makes all the difference. Not only can you assemble a much larger collection of music than is possible even in one-hundred-disc changers, but the organizing and reordering possibilities are more easily handled on-screen than they ever were on a CD player's front panel or remote control. Also, crucially, ID3 tags—underlying pieces of identifying information attached to an MP3 file—enable instant reorganization according to various parameters that, as you'll see in this chapter and the next, dramatically increases the usefulness and pleasure of a large digital music collection.

Power User Organizing a collection isn't nearly as fun and sexy as downloading, ripping, burning, and blasting music. And I freely admit that if you become as obsessively natty about your files as I am, maintaining your MP3s requires some drudge work. I don't think a day goes by that I don't clean up filenames, rewrite ID3 tags, create new playlists, or toy with my library settings in Media Jukebox (an MP3 management program covered later in this chapter). But I'm listening to my collection while performing these chores, so it's not unrewarded toil. And the pleasure of drilling effortlessly into a large collection from any number of angles is worth the work. Just keep imagining how you'll impress everybody at your next party.

Organizing a Musical Hard Drive

Most MP3 music, whether downloaded or ripped, starts out on your hard drive. And for those people who don't emphasize music portability, the computer hard drive is their collection's primary permanent home, and the launching pad for most in-home listening. But no matter how you carry your music and in what environments you hear it, orderly storage pays off when it comes to finding what you want, and it becomes more important as your collection grows.

In both the Windows and Macintosh environments, the folder-creation system makes it easy to apply an organizational structure to your music collection. In Windows, when planning for a varied collection, the first thing to do is get out of the "My Music" folder, located beneath "My Documents" (by default, on the C drive). Windows might sometimes try to place downloads there, but the most disorganized approach is to let Windows make placement decisions for you, which invariably ends up throwing all your songs into a single undifferentiated folder. Jukebox programs can sort out

Clarifying Filenames and ID3 Tags

By focusing on organization of a music collection, this chapter is really about clearly and functionally identifying your downloaded and ripped tracks. There exist two equally important identifying features of every MP3 track: the filename and the ID3 tags. Both are under your control, and can be customized to your collecting style.

The filename is an identifier that appears in Windows Explorer and any other program that presents the unfiltered contents of your hard drive. Every filename ends with a file extension, which, in the case of MP3 files, is *mp3*. (The file extension might not appear in Windows Explorer when certain settings are chosen. To carry out some suggestions in this chapter, the List or Details setting must be selected under the View menu of Explorer. I use List, not Details. Also in the View menu, choose Folder Options... and select the Classic Style option.) The filename of any MP3 track might and might not contain the artist name, song name, album title, or other intelligent identifiers. Sensible filenames are necessary to locate music through Windows Explorer.

The ID3 tags are attached to the MP3 file, but don't appear in the filename. These tags are divided by information fields, into which can be typed the artist name, album title, song title, track number on the originating album, year of release, genre, and (in some cases) other information. Two levels of ID3 tagging exist: ID3v1 and ID3v2. The latter version contains additional information fields, removes the thirty–character length limitation of version-1 tags, and allows for non-text insertions such as pictures. Most jukebox programs invite you to alter the ID3 tags, which is fortunate because they are so often a mess even when the tracks are obtained from authorized sources. Intelligent ID3 tags are necessary to locate music and rearrange playlists through jukebox programs.

that kind of chaos, but only if your ID3 tags are impeccable. So, because you must place every song you download and rip *somewhere*, you might as well give some thought to your folder structure from the start.

The foremost decision facing you is how specific you wish to get with your hard drive folders. At the most inexact end of the spectrum, you would dump everything into a single folder called "Music." That leads to trouble as your collection grows. At the most fastidious end of the organizational spectrum, you could create a dedicated folder for every artist and band in your collection, and even folders for individual albums. In fact, some sorting and ripping programs attempt to do exactly that when placing your files. The problem here is folder clutter, forcing you to dig into a complex haystack of folders with excessive mouse-clicks to find an album or a band.

 Reminder Keep in mind these two central principles:

- Effective file naming can do the work of detailed folders when accessing your collection from Windows Explorer.

- Effective ID3 tagging can do the work of detailed folders when accessing your collection from a jukebox program.

It seems best to create a moderately detailed folder structure on your hard drive, while letting your preferred jukebox program handle rearrangements according to ID3 tags. You might choose to create folders according to music genres, or any other specialties that you enjoy collecting. Figure 8.1 illustrates the folder setup of a 10–gigabyte music library. The collection exists on a hard drive partition called "Media" (H:), and includes a "Download" folder and a "Rip" folder, as well as the big "Music" folder with many nested folders within it. This arrangement is a good example of a folder structure of middling complexity that holds a substantial music library (about 160 hours).

The illustration raises a few questions. How does one create a folder? What is the advantage of a single "Download" folder, and how do you arrange for all downloads to land within it? Why the "Rip" folder? Why is there one album folder ("Great Pianists Sampler") in what is otherwise a genre-based organization? The following sections take up each of these questions, and lead to helpful acquisition and storage habits.

Creating Folders

For all practical purposes, Windows places no limits on the number of folders you may create on your hard drive, or the number of levels you may create beneath a folder. Those levels are called the folder hierarchy or nested folders. Creating a folder is simple:

1. **Click on the folder or hard drive icon under which you wish to create a nested folder.**
2. **Click the File menu and select New.**

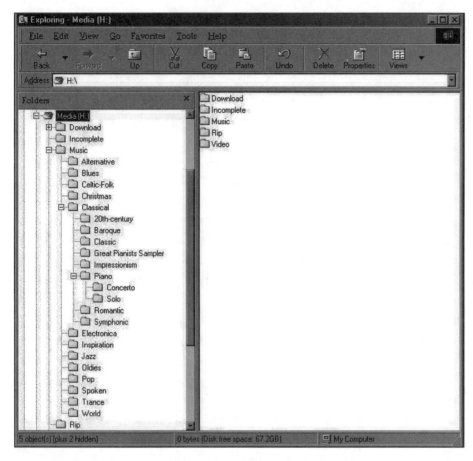

Figure 8.1. *A moderately complex folder structure for a music collection.*

3. In the next drop-down menu, click Folder.
4. Type the name of your new folder.
5. Press the Enter key.

Your folder now exists and is ready for content. Windows provides a generous limit to the length of folder names, but for your own sanity keep the names short; otherwise you'll be continually resizing the Explorer panels to see your complete folder names. Save the longer identifiers for filenames within folders.

Consolidating Your Downloads

If you use several programs for downloading, sorting, and playing your music collection, it becomes evident that a behind-the-scenes struggle is waged for ownership of the location at which your files are stored. Many programs wish you would let them decide where to place songs on your hard drive. This trait is especially noticeable in file-sharing programs and music subscription services, which invariably attempt to create a "Download" folder nested in the folder that holds the program. That is to say, Morpheus has its own "Download" folder, BearShare has its own, so does Pressplay, and so on. The result of this fractured approach is that if you download from several sources (which, of course, the programs don't want you to do) your music gets scattered all over the place. That means extra work for you gathering it together and redistributing it to your own folder system.

The solution is to create a master "Download" folder, somewhere close (in Windows Explorer's view) to your master "Music" folder tree, and direct all downloads to that folder. The redirection requires that you enter the Preferences or Options panel of each download program you use (see chapter 4) and change the default location of the "Download" folder. It's not hard to do, but you must remember to do it. Forgetfulness leaves you scratching your head, wondering where the heck your downloads went, then scouring your hard drive to find them.

Besides the obvious convenience of not having your downloads scattered, finding them all in one place helps you accomplish some inevitable chores before shifting them to their permanent folder homes. It's not important to investigate their ID3 tags at this point, but it is important to clean up their filenames (as described later in this chapter).

 Power User It's a good idea to keep a dedicated "Rip" folder for temporarily storing MP3s created from CDs. Keeping music permanently in the "Rip" folder is possible also, if you want to segregate CD-sourced MP3s. It's not a useful plan, though, if you rip a lot of discs. My preferred method is to consider all files, whether ripped or downloaded, essentially equal and subject to the same organizing rules.

Storing Hopeless Files

You might notice in figure 8.1 that the directory tree includes one folder corresponding to an album, *Great Pianists Sampler*. That folder is an example of filenaming so awry that remedial work isn't worth it. In this case, the source is a double CD of very short classical piano pieces, each performed by a different pianist. The file-identification on the CD is so haphazard that no rip-

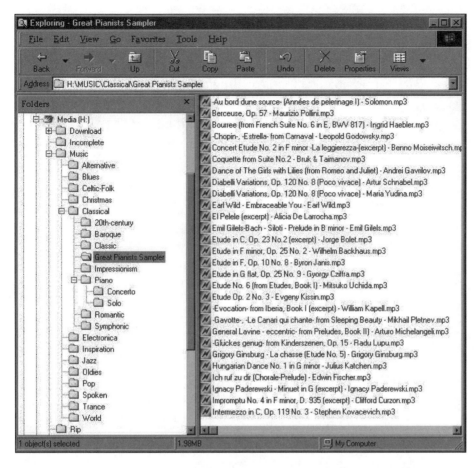

Figure 8.2. *Some filenames defy easy adjustment, even when ripped from the same CD.*

ping program's auto-titling feature could make sense of it. In some cases the pianist's name comes first, in others it's the composer or the piece title. Sometimes the pianist's first name is included, sometimes not. Various punctuation marks enclose composition titles in some cases; not in others. The composer is missing from several. Figure 8.2 illustrates what a muddle exists in that folder. Rather than attempt to make all sixty-eight files adhere to a consistent file-naming scheme and integrate them into the "Piano" folder, the easier solution was to dump the whole collection into a dedicated folder.

Another common (and regrettable) reason for breaking the organizational scheme is to accommodate files that cannot be played by your preferred program. In particular, some of the music subscription plans deliver copy-protected downloads that can be played only in the service's program, or some other approved player. For example, MusicNet and Pressplay, described in chapter 4, use copy-protected Windows Media files that are played either in the service programs or the Windows Media Player. I dislike mixing those downloads into folders filled with unrestricted files, because it confuses matters when creating playlists in a jukebox program. If you forget which files can or cannot be played in that jukebox program, your playlists won't work as expected. So, thanks to the record labels' attachment to copy-protection, restricted files from the authorized services are generally unfit for integration into your larger personal music collection.

Name That File

Chapter 2 describes the automatic file-naming features bundled into ripping programs, which solve the file-naming chore with elegance and consistency. That's fine for music ripped from commercial CDs, for which the program can supply complete and accurate artist, album, and track information. There are many situations in which rewriting filenames is necessary to keep a tidy music collection. Here are some of the filename problems you're sure to encounter if you acquire music from multiple online sources.

Lengthy filenames are sometimes assigned by overzealous subscription services. Though you want your files to be labeled with crucial information such as artist name and song title (and possibly album name and track number), the basic rule of thumb is that short is good. When burning MP3 files to CD, your filenames are in most cases restricted to sixty-four characters (including dashes, underscores, and spaces).

Even lengthier filenames are common for classical music tracks, no matter what the source. Classical music recordings simply have more information pieces. In a concerto, for instance, there are composer, conductor, orchestra, soloist, composition name, key, opus number, and movement number. If all these chunks are included, the result can look something like this:

Rachmaninov_Piano_Concerto_3_op30_Vladimir_Ashkenazy_
ChicagoSymphonyOrchestra_Fritz_Reiner_mvt1.mp3.

That filename contains ninety-nine characters, and is no exaggeration of what I typically find in download services that provide classical tracks. Not only would the filename get truncated in a CD burn, but it would make a window-stretching eyesore in a Windows Explorer view of its folder.

Outright inaccuracy is also a problem, no matter the source, and forget about files from unauthorized file-sharing networks. The names are a mess.

Renaming is the only solution, chore though it be. You can revise file-names manually, one file at a time within Windows Explorer, or use a utility dedicated to bulk renaming. I'll get to each method in its turn. First, here's a list of essential renaming tips:

- **Eliminate repetitions.** Classical filenames are full of them, inexplicably, as if there weren't enough information to stuff in without duplicating it.
- **Eliminate first names.** This one is tricky, but I've made it a general principle in all musical genres, and I follow the rule more than half the time. In the above example, I know who Ashkenazy and Reiner are, and I don't need Vladimir and Fritz taking thirteen valuable characters. Likewise, I know who Clapton is without the four-character Eric. The tricky part happens when you don't know the artist well, and need that first name to identify him or her. I also have trouble when I mentally refer to the artist with both names, as with Alison Krauss, whom I never think of as "Krauss." Band names, of course, are not subject to this rule at all; Limp Bizkit probably shouldn't be reduced to Bizkit.
- **Separate information chunks with one dash and no spaces.** My preferred separator is a single hyphen surrounded by spaces, like this:

Kit Watkins-Mirage.mp3.

But when push comes to shove, and characters are at a premium, get rid of the spaces and leave the hyphen. (Underscores separate effectively, too, and make a more visually definitive break with no spaces than hyphens do.) You can also use spaces with no underscores or hyphens in all versions of Windows starting with Windows 95.
- **In classical music, cut the opus numbers and movement names.** Leave in the movement number, though; it's needed to keep the files in order when viewing them through Windows Explorer. (The ID3 tags keep them in order when viewing through a good jukebox program.)
- **Place the track number before the song title, and always use double digits.** If you place the track numbers *after* the song titles of an album, the numbers will not work to list the tracks in album order. Furthermore, using 01, 02, 03, and so on, prevents the single-digit songs from being listed after 10, 11, 12, and the other double digits.
- **Put the artist name first.** Generally a good idea, but of course it's up to you. If you have an entire folder dedicated to an artist or band, obviously you don't need to include the artist in the filename.

These rules of thumb hold whether you're renaming one file or a batch. Naturally, when performing the sort of bulk renaming described later, you must concentrate on an unchanging part of the filenames—that is, not the song titles.

Changing Filenames in Windows Explorer

Windows allows you to change one filename at a time. Skip this section if changing filenames in Windows is old news. If you've never done it, fear not; it's easy. Follow these steps:

1. **Right-click the individual filename you wish to change.** A selection menu pops open.
2. **Click Rename.** The selection menu disappears and the filename remains highlighted within a rectangular text box (see figure 8.1).
3. **Alter the filename.** At this point you may press Delete to remove the entire original name, or click the mouse cursor anywhere within it to Backspace of a portion or type a new portion.
4. **Press Enter.** The new filename is attached to the file. You may repeat the process whenever you want.

 Reminder No matter what else you change, leave the file extension (which for an MP3 file is *mp3*) in place at the end of the filename. Without it, most MP3 players won't recognize the file as playable.

You can use the Windows copy-and-paste function with filenames, and it comes in handy. If you're changing many filenames in a similar way, but the original names are too disparate for the Bulk File Renamer described in the next section, try this trick:

1. **Right-click the individual filename you wish to change.**
2. **Click Rename.**
3. **Alter the filename.**
4. **Highlight the new filename by clicking and dragging the mouse across its entire length.**
5. **Press Control + C.** This copies the new filename into the Windows clipboard.
6. **Right-click another one of the filenames needing a change.**
7. **Click Rename.**

8. **Press Control + V.** This pastes the improved filename into the second file's space.
9. **Press Enter.**

Once you've repeated steps 6 through 9 above for each of the files needing renaming, you can go into each one individually to make whatever alteration is unique to that file, such as song title or track number. Believe it or not, this procedure saves work.

Changing Filenames in Bulk

There exists a simple Windows utility that every serious digital music collector should be using, and it's free. Called the Bulk Rename Utility, it is a clear, intuitive, and fairly powerful program for making identical changes to groups of filenames. I don't know how much time this little piece of freeware has saved me, but I wouldn't want to be a music collector without it. Created by an English chap named Jim Willsher, the program can be downloaded from this location:

http://www.jimwillsher.co.uk/Site/Software/BRU_Intro.html.

As you can see in figure 8.3, the program allows you to add or remove extensions, change the case, make bulk replacements, add prefixes and suffixes, and insert numerals to the start or end of the filenames. Some typing is generally required when making replacements, but it's well worth the effort. Keep in mind, though, that the Bulk Rename Utility works best when dealing with groups of files that already have identical portions. In that case you can alter the identical portions, or insert something before or after the portion. Because this is the purpose to which I most often put the program, when making adjustments to all the files of an album, I'm including a step list below:

1. **Use the left-hand window pane to select the folder holding the filename group needing change.**
2. **In the right-hand window pane, use the mouse and Shift key to select a group of similar files.** Click on the topmost file, press the Shift key, and click the bottom file. Those two files and all files in between become highlighted.
3. **In the Replacements section of the bottom panel, position the mouse cursor in the Replace text box, and type the filename portion that needs changing.**

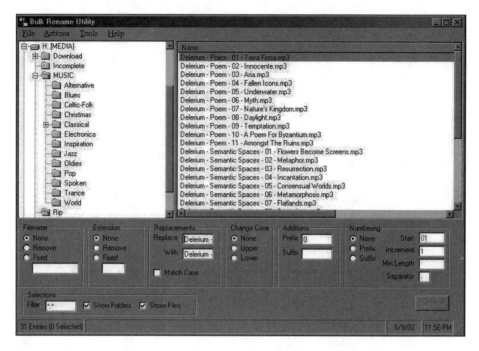

Figure 8.3. *The useful Bulk Rename Utility.*

4. **Position the mouse cursor in the With text box and type the new filename portion.**

5. **Click the Rename button.** You see the files change in the right-hand window pane, and if Windows Explorer is open on your screen you see the filenames change there, too.

I use the Bulk Rename Utility primarily to change filenames in whole-album downloads I get from EMusic and other online sources, both to remove unwanted information and shorten the filename. It's also great for adding track numbers, composers, or some other information.

 Reminder Note that Musicmatch (covered in chapter 9) also has a wonderful bulk filename editor built into the program, specially tailored to music files. The files must be "added" (a short process of importing file information to the program) before the filenames can be bulk-changed—an easy procedure that could be worthwhile just for that feature. The Bulk Rename Utility works directly with files as they appear in Windows Explorer.

9

Desktop Players and Organizers

This chapter investigates the most publicized and popular desktop music organizers, commonly called desktop jukeboxes, exploring the largest, most powerful, and most complex MP3 programs available. These integrated programs incorporate ripping, burning, library management, music playback, recording, and sophisticated playlisting. The library management and playlisting features are of particular focus in these pages; ripping and burning are covered in chapter 2.

Managing a Music Collection with Media Jukebox

Media Jukebox receives my highest recommendation for an MP3 management program. Upgradable freeware that delivers powerful extra features in its commercial version (Media Jukebox Plus cost $24.95 at publication time), this program combines format flexibility with unmatched library tools to manage, sort, and play a sprawling collection—or multiple collections belonging to different members of a household.

As the name implies, Media Jukebox handles more than just music, and is meant to be a one-stop solution to all your desktop multimedia needs. This book's focus is on the musical features, but, for the record, you can use the program for DVD playback and playing video files, in addition to play-

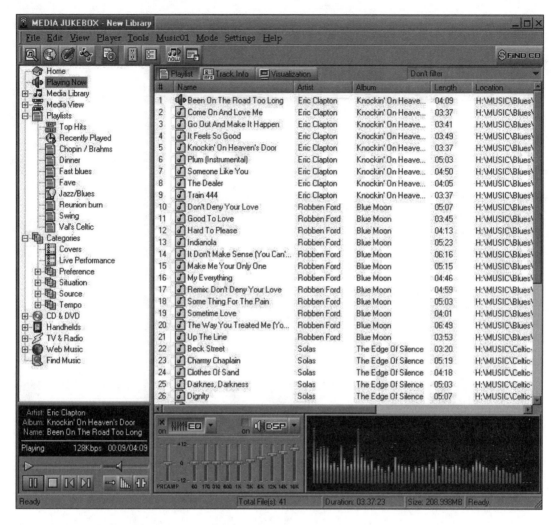

Figure 9.1. *The main playback window of Media Jukebox.*

ing CDs, ripping, burning, tuning in Webcasts, and managing all of your compressed tracks.

Media Jukebox's pliancy is its main selling point. The program doesn't care what your preferred file type is, though its virtuoso handling of ID3 tags makes it perfect for MP3 management. Likewise, it doesn't enforce a certain type of organizational structure as many other jukeboxes do. You can set up your library to mimic your hard drive folder structure, or to cut across that structure by sorting according to artist, album, genre, or playlist. Best of all, you can hedge your bets by creating multiple library views that incorporate the same collection in different ways, or distinct collections in the same way.

Choosing software is a personal matter. In this case, Media Jukebox's advantages stand so far above its competitors that I can't quite imagine leading a fulfilling digital music lifestyle without it. (I also respect Musicmatch Jukebox, which is described later in this chapter.) At the very least, I urge all readers to try the free version, spending enough time with it to get comfortable with the depth of its features, then decide whether to upgrade. Not a day goes by that I don't use Media Jukebox.

Media Jukebox Basics

No question about it, this program is a monster. While not nearly as deep and complex as an advanced database program, or a highly evolved consumer application like Microsoft Word, Media Jukebox bristles with features that make it daunting at first. Once downloaded, the best approach is to explore simple tasks and work your way into more powerful management of your collection. Media Jukebox is best suited to large collections and demanding playlist requirements. Unaspiring collectors with just a few oft-played tracks will find this program's power wasted.

Media Jukebox employs a single window with multiple panes (see figure 9.1). All music listening in Media Jukebox transpires in the Playing Now pane. Start by clicking Playing Now, then dragging files into Media Jukebox from Windows Explorer, or by using the File menu to choose the Open Media File... selection. When at least one track shows in Playing Now, either double-click it or click the Play button to hear it. Simple enough. Notice how the track is displayed in Playing Now: the name, artist, album, and other column information is taken from the track's ID3 tags (more on how to edit them later).

Importing Files to Media Jukebox

If you wish to burn a track to CD, create playlists, or perform many other manipulations, you need to "import" your files into Media Jukebox. Have no fear of taking this step: importing does not move the files on your hard drive or change them in any way. Importing is a standard operation in jukebox programs. The process simply packs all the file information into Media Jukebox's memory for later use. That information includes three basic facts about each file:

- the filename;
- the file location on your hard drive; and
- the file's ID3 tags.

Once all that information for your collection is loaded, Media Jukebox is ready to arrange your collection in various ways according to your preference. Importing is quick; a 10–gigabyte collection takes about two minutes. Media Jukebox helpfully hastens the process by drilling into nested folders automatically, rather than making you tediously select each inner folder manually.

It's difficult to make a mistake when importing to Media Jukebox, and impossible to make an irreversible one, so dive fearlessly into the following steps:

1. **Pull down the Tools menu and click on the Import Media... selection.**
2. **In the Import Media Files panel, check the boxes next to file types you wish to import.** The "mp3" box must be checked to capture your MP3 information, and don't forget to check "wma" for any Windows Media files in your collection. Use Windows Explorer to look over your collection for file types. Chances are, the icons next to the files are different for differing file types (but not necessarily—the icons depend on file-type assignments made in all your playback software).
3. **Select the folder from which you want files imported.** If your collection is gathered in a folder structure nested inside a main folder, select the main folder to capture everything. Click the small button next to the Search In... field to browse your hard drive.
4. **Uncheck the Import Using Directory Structure selection.** Just a suggestion; you can obviously leave it checked. I find it pointless to replicate my folder structures in Media Jukebox. Unchecking this option forces the program to display your music library according to a more flexible genre/artist/album scheme.
5. **Click the Start Search button.** Media Jukebox tears through your folders and copies file information (not the actual tracks: just their names, locations, and ID3 tags) into its database.

 Reminder You may repeat the Import process at any time, scooping up previously unimported files added to the collection. In that case, Media Jukebox seamlessly adds the new file information without disturbing the data already gathered. If you move around previously imported files from folder to folder, the program changes its location information without altering its other file identifiers, and *does not* create duplicate entries for your moved tracks. In other words, the Import feature is a smart, three-step process of keeping Media Jukebox up to speed with your collection.

Figure 9.2. *Part of the Media View organization tree in Media Jukebox.*

Power User After importing your library (as long as you don't use the Import Using Directory Structure choice), Media Jukebox presents a broken-down display of your collection in the Media View organization tree (see figure 9.2). You have three display choices in that tree: Album, Artist/Album, and Genre/Artist/Album. All the information in these lists is taken from the ID3 tags attached to your tracks, emphasizing the importance of maintaining the accuracy of your tags. Right-click on any artist, album, or genre, then select Add to Playing Now, to hear the contents of that category. The Media View tree, when illuminated by effective tagging, is a powerful way to see your collection in a new light.

Creating a Media Jukebox Library

All this importing creates what Media Jukebox calls a "Library." The library you create by first starting to import is impersonally named "Default." You can change its name and even create multiple libraries. If you are the only user of this computer, and you always want access to the entire collection housed in that computer, then there's no reason to create a second library. However, multiple libraries represent a powerful feature in at least two situations:

- When the computer is used by more than one person, who each maintains a separate music collection.
- When a collection is so vast that it benefits from sorting into separate libraries before undergoing finer artist/album sorting within Media Jukebox.

Renaming the default library and creating a new library both start the same way, but the latter takes the process a bit further:

1. Pull down the File menu and click the Library Manager... selection.
2. In the Media Libraries panel, click the Add button.
3. In the Library Properties panel (figure 9.3), enter the new library's name.
4. **Enter the storage location of the new library.** You can store library data anywhere on your hard drive. I prefer keeping it within the Media Jukebox folder cluster where I installed the program. The "Default" library is stored in the "Data" folder, and that's where I put new libraries.
5. **Use the Clone From drop-down menu to select the "Default" library.** This choice copies the "Default" library to the newly named library, creating a duplicate as a way of renaming. If you wish to create an entirely new library, leave this space blank.

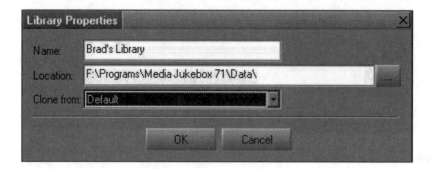

Figure 9.3. *Naming a new library in Media Jukebox.*

6. Click the OK button.
7. In the Media Libraries panel, highlight your new library and click the Load button.
8. To create a new library, import files using the instructions in the previous section.

Switching from one library to another is a simple matter of opening the Library Manager, selecting a library from your created list, and clicking Load.

Media Jukebox Options

As in many programs, Media Jukebox's power and ease-of-use lie in the Options panel, which has twelve groups of settings. Eleven of these groups pertain to music or general display options. Open the Options panel in the Settings menu, or simply use the Control-O keyboard combination. Click the left-hand

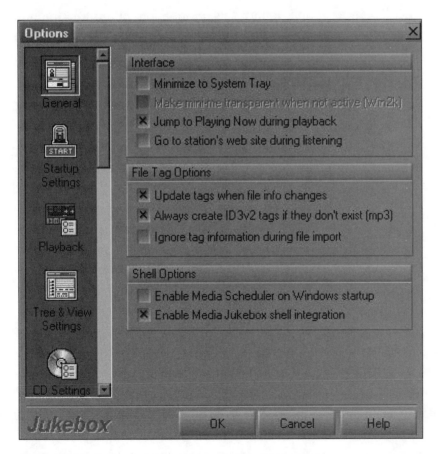

Figure 9.4. The Options panel in which you configure Media Jukebox.

group icon to see the options for that group (see figure 9.4). This section contains a rundown of essential preference choices and my recommended settings.

 Power User I cannot possibly cover all selections in the Options panel, so I have described the ones most important to track playback, program display, and library organization. If you dive deeper into the Options panel, refer to Media Jukebox Help for explanations of exotic settings. With the Options panel *closed*, press the F1 key of your keyboard. Type in the Options category in which the questionable setting is located, then double-click on that category when it appears in the contents list.

General. The most important option here is Update Tags when File Info Changes. Make sure that this option is checked for seamless ID3 tag editing. I also keep the next option checked, Always Create ID3v2 Tags if They Don't Exist (mp3), as it handily replicates ID3v1 information in the ID3v2 slots. The next option, Ignore Tag Information during File Import, should be used only selectively, when importing files whose tags are in such disarray that it's easier to build them by scratch than revise them. I have never used this option, though, and I suggest it remain unchecked always. Importing ID3 tags along with the files is crucial to general sorting and, in particular, creating SmartLists.

Startup Settings. I keep everything on this panel unchecked. Showing the splash screen on boot-up is unimportant. Use Open Media Jukebox in Mini-me Mode only if you typically listen to the same playlist over and over, and screen space is at a premium. Mini-me is Media Jukebox's half-minimized display format that hides the library and sorting functions. You might want to enable the Startup Volume slider if changing the volume on your computer is difficult. I leave the Startup Page setting, which determines which portion of the program is displayed when Media Jukebox is first opened, on Playing Now. Checking Expand Subfolders inevitably results in contracting them again manually, because they take up too much room with a collection of any size at all—so I suggest leaving it unchecked.

Playback. This group of settings contains important choices that affect your day-to-day listening satisfaction in Media Jukebox.

- In the Playback Mode portion you can control how much space (if any) exists between tracks in a playlist and how the program responds when you jump from one point in a track to another. I usually leave both on Standard. Beware the Gapless setting in the Seeking drop-down menu! It creates a two-second lag before jumping to the new point in the track. During those seconds the track continues playing, but the net effect is quite frustrating and slow. The only setting that makes a quick jump is Standard. The three Smooth settings are fun to play with, each creating a cross-fade of a different speed. They are likewise entertaining in the Between Tracks setting. You can easily try them all out by choosing one, clicking the OK button, and playing some tracks. Return to the Options panel to try another.

- Under Performance, the slider position determines how your computer prioritizes Media Jukebox's demands on the processor. Playing music by itself does not stress the computer much. But when you're perform-ing six other tasks at the same time, the music might stutter as the computer juggles demands. Moving the slider toward More Skip Resistant puts Media Jukebox higher on your computer's priority list.

- The settings in the Output portion might seem exotic. The defaults work fine for most people. In the Bitdepth menu, the default 16–bit setting reduces the processing quality of music playback from the internal standard deployed by Windows. Doing so makes little appre-ciable difference to most ears, and keeps the music flowing smoothly. Increasing the bitdepth acts upon the performance of Media Jukebox's built-in equalizer and DSP (digital signal processing) effects, and might be worth experimenting with on a powerful computer. The Do Not Play Extended Portions of Silence setting is useful, as it knocks out those seconds of silence that can follow the end of a song, putting a big gap between tracks. I routinely check that setting.

Time and View Settings. This option group influences how Media Jukebox displays the two most important panes of its window: the left-hand sorting pane and the large track-listing pane.

- First, select which sorting categories you want from the Organization Tree Fields menu. My advice is to select all of them, because they eas-ily fit in the long vertical pane.
- Then, to the right, select which columns you wish to display track information from the Content View Fields list. These choices get their information from the ID3 tags associated with each track. In addition to Name, Artist, Album, be sure to check the important

Location and Track # selections, both of which help keep your tracks in album order.

- At the bottom of the panel you can empower the program to automatically sort tracks in Playing Now when you first pull them in, according to several criteria listed in the drop-down menu. (Don't forget to check the Enable box.) I prefer to sort by Location first, then resort to my heart's content later.
- In the middle of the panel, the Appearance settings let you determine whether pop-up "tooltips" appear when you run your mouse cursor over tracks and the sorting categories in the Organization Tree. Also, you can display grid lines to separate tracks (see figure 9.5), which is useful in large playlists and when many columns are set to display.
- Use the bottom-panel buttons to set the program's font, and which buttons appear in the toolbar.

📄 Playlist	📑 Track Info	🖥 Visualization		Don't filter
#	Name	Artist	Album	Length
1	♪ Been On The Road Too Long	Eric Clapton	Knockin' On Heave...	04:09
2	♪ Come On And Love Me	Eric Clapton	Knockin' On Heave...	03:37
3	♪ Go Out And Make It Happen	Eric Clapton	Knockin' On Heave...	03:41
4	♪ It Feels So Good	Eric Clapton	Knockin' On Heave...	03:49
5	♪ Knockin' On Heaven's Door	Eric Clapton	Knockin' On Heave...	03:37
6	♪ Plum (Instrumental)	Eric Clapton	Knockin' On Heave...	05:03
7	♪ Someone Like You	Eric Clapton	Knockin' On Heave...	04:50
8	♪ The Dealer	Eric Clapton	Knockin' On Heave...	04:05
9	♪ Train 444	Eric Clapton	Knockin' On Heave...	03:37
10	♪ Don't Deny Your Love	Robben Ford	Blue Moon	05:07
11	♪ Good To Love	Robben Ford	Blue Moon	03:45
12	♪ Hard To Please	Robben Ford	Blue Moon	04:13
13	♪ Indianola	Robben Ford	Blue Moon	05:23
14	♪ It Don't Make Sense (You Can'...	Robben Ford	Blue Moon	06:16
15	♪ Make Me Your Only One	Robben Ford	Blue Moon	05:15
16	♪ My Everything	Robben Ford	Blue Moon	04:46
17	♪ Remix: Don't Deny Your Love	Robben Ford	Blue Moon	04:59
18	♪ Some Thing For The Pain	Robben Ford	Blue Moon	05:03
19	♪ Sometime Love	Robben Ford	Blue Moon	04:01
20	🎵 The Way You Treated Me (Yo...	Robben Ford	Blue Moon	06:49

Figure 9.5. *Using grid lines clarifies (or clutters) Media Jukebox's display.*

CD Settings. The settings in this group can remain in their default state without causing trouble in most cases. One check-box you might want to activate is the Enable CDDB CD Lookup Service selection. CDDB is an online track information database (see chapter 2) that provides track and album names for CDs played through desktop software. Allowing Media Jukebox to retrieve CDDB information on its own initiative facilitates playing and ripping CDs.

Recorder Settings. Settings for CD ripping are in the Encoding group. The Recorder Settings group refers to Media Jukebox's built-in real-time recorder, one of its classiest features. The recorder (activated from the Tools menu) lets you grab anything playing on your computer and turn it into an MP3 file. (It uses the format and bit-rate settings selected in the Encoding group.) Leave the Recording Source menu set to Mixer for recording Internet streams, but notice that you can change it to Microphone or Line In for recording your voice, or the tracks of a vinyl LP. Select the convenient Wait for Sound before Starting Recording for effortless and accurate start times to your recordings. Below that option, select Enable Automatic Track Splitting to command Media Jukebox to separate tracks into distinct files—but be careful of tracks with a silent part in the middle, because the program thinks any silence is a break between tracks. You can experiment with the gap levels beneath this setting to overcome such accidents, but for the most part the default settings are fine.

Sorting Your Collection in Media Jukebox

Media Jukebox shines when it comes to arranging tracks into playlists. These lists can be temporarily sorted on the fly, or permanently sorted and saved.

Sorting tracks on the fly is accomplished similarly to many programs and Web sites that present lists of one kind or another. In the Playing Now window, information about your tracks is arranged in columns, according to your choices in the Time & View portion of Options (see the previous section). Clicking on any column header orders the entire list either alphabetically by that column information, or numerically. If you keep, as I do, at least five crucial columns—Name, Artist, Album, Location, and Track #— you can order a group of tracks in many interesting ways.

You can reorganize track order while tracks are playing. When sorting on the fly, remember three important points:

- To keep tracks in correct album order, click the Track # column header first, then click the Album column. If you merely click Album, the tracks might remain out of order. If you merely click Track #, by itself, Media Jukebox plays every track #1 loaded into Playing Now, then every track #2, and so on. But if you click Track # and then Album, the program plays loaded albums sequentially, in correct track order.

- You can shuffle tracks randomly by using the Control-R keyboard combination.
- No matter how you reorganize track order on the fly, you must "update" the playback order before the changes are locked into place. Simply right-click Playing Now, then click Update Playback Order. Notice that the left-hand # column (not Track #) becomes sequential, where it wasn't before the "update."

Creating and saving playlists is encouraged in a few ways:

- Right-click Playlists, then click Add Playlist, to create a new playlist folder that can hold the tracks you want in that list.
- In Playing Now, you can drag any track into any Playlist folder. (The track must be imported in Media Jukebox to be in a playlist. Unimported tracks can be played, but not added to lists.) Alternatively, right-click any track in Playing Now (whether or not it's currently playing) and click the Add to Playlist... selection, then select which playlist from the drop-down menu that appears.
- You can build and order a playlist in Playing Now, then save the whole thing at once. Right-click Playing Now, then click the Add to Playlist... selection. A pop-up panel appears with a drop-down menu from which you select one of your created playlist folders. Be sure to click the Keep Track Order check-box if you've decided on a final order. (Of course, you can change the playlist order at any time.)
- You *cannot* drag tracks from Windows Explorer directly into a playlist folder. You must drag them into Playing Now, and move them to a playlist from there.

 Reminder To play a saved playlist, right-click the playlist folder and select Add to Playing Now. This literally adds the list to whatever tracks are already in Playing Now. If you wish to hear nothing but the selected playlist, right-click Playing Now first, and click Clear Playing Now.

Alert When you double-click any track, anywhere in Media Jukebox, whether in a playlist folder or in any portion of the extensive Media View tree, that track is placed in Playing Now and starts playing. The problem is (and this characteristic is vexing until you get used to it), doing so clears all the tracks that were in Playing Now before you double-clicked a single track. You can always right-click that track and select Add to Playing Now instead of the potentially frustrating double-click. Be sure to remember this when you're building a playlist in Playing Now, and auditioning tracks listed in other parts of the program. One careless double-click of a track could wipe out an hour of work.

Reminder Remember to frequently save your playlist-in-progress! There is no dedicated Save function when working on a playlist in Playing Now. You must right-click Playing Now, then select the Add to Playlist... selection. Media Jukebox compares your current list with your last save, and makes the necessary adjustments.

SmartLists take ID3–based organization to the max by feeding newly imported tracks into the list as they meet the list's criteria. Those criteria are defined by you, and include artist names, album names, genre, track dates, and Media Jukebox categories. (See the "Setting Categories in Media Jukebox" sidebar.) SmartLists present the steepest learning curve among Media Jukebox's many powerful management features. However, learning how to create these dynamic lists is well worth the effort.

The following steps walk you through setting up a SmartList:

1. Right-click Playlists in the organization pane.
2. Click Add SmartList.
3. In the SmartList Properties panel, click the Add New Rule button.
4. In the New Rule panel, double-click any list item. The Genres to Play category is a good place to start.
5. In the next panel (see figure 9.6), use the check-boxes to make one or more selections.
6. Click the OK button.
7. Repeat steps 3 through 6 to add new SmartList rules.

Figure 9.6. *Selecting genres for a Media Jukebox SmartList.*

If tracks appear in your SmartList that don't seem to match your Genres to Play selections, it means that the ID3 Genre tag for those tracks needs revision, a process covered in the next section.

Using and Setting ID3 Tags in Media Jukebox

The ID3 tags attached to MP3 files, as described in chapter 8, play a huge role in Media Jukebox's potent library features. Almost all the sorting that occurs within the program, which determines what order your tracks are played in, depends on these ID3 tags. Without ID3 information, most of Media Jukebox's displays would be senseless, lacking even a track or artist name, and the program would be no more helpful in sorting your collection than Windows Explorer is. Consequently, learning how to edit your ID3 tags is vital to enjoying Media Jukebox.

 Reminder Media Jukebox is hardly the only program that allows editing of ID3 tags. In fact, most desktop MP3 players let you get your hands dirty in the ID3 realm. There's nothing to stop you from making ID3 changes in another program, and enjoying the improved tagging in Media Jukebox. Just remember to reimport the changed files to Media Jukebox, so it can incorporate the new tags in all your lists (especially the SmartLists). Importing (described earlier in this chapter) is the essential process that keeps Media Jukebox up to speed with your collection. Importing never does any damage, whether the program finds any new data or not. I import parts of my libraries at least once a day.

You can edit ID3 tags for individual tracks and, in a display of convenience, for multiple tracks simultaneously. Both tasks are important, so in this section I spell out each procedure. First, follow these steps to change the ID3 information of a single track:

1. **Right-click any track showing in Media Jukebox.**
2. **Click the Properties… selection.**
3. **In the Media File Properties panel, click any information item you wish to change.** At this point, you're looking at the ID3 tags attached to the track. (See figure 9.7.)

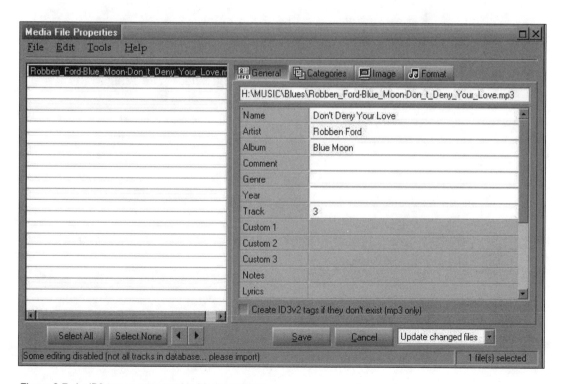

Figure 9.7. *An ID3 tag as presented in Media Jukebox.*

4. **Type your change in the selected information field.** Notice that when you click the Genre field, a drop-down menu of suggested genres appears. Genre selections are not standardized among jukebox programs, and Media Jukebox offers a large selection. You may also ignore the list and type in your own invented genre category. Make as many changes to as many information fields as you like.

5. **Check the Create ID3v2 Tags If They Don't Exist (mp3 Only) box.** There's simply no reason not to, even if you don't use the extra ID3v2 categories. Please note, though, that leaving that box unchecked does not inhibit Media Jukebox's ability to sort your collection effectively, using basic ID3v1 tags.

6. **Click the Save button.**

Setting Categories in Media Jukebox

Media Jukebox, in its organizational mania, offers additional track classifications beyond ID3 tags. These identifiers are called Categories, and their purpose is to help create playlists and SmartLists tailored to mood, listening situations, music tempos, and other important divisions that aren't represented in ID3 tags (see figure 9.8). Expand the Categories portion of the organization tree to see that Media Jukebox starts you off with several suggested folders. You are free to add others; simply right-click on Categories or any subhead, then select Add Category.

Adding tracks to categories can be done singly or in bulk. Right-click any track (or any highlighted group of selected tracks), then click the Add to Category... selection. The Media File Properties panel opens (the same window in which you edit ID3 tags under the General tab) with all your default and custom-created Categories listed. You can select one or multiple Categories for any file or group of files.

Assigning tracks to Categories might seem like just another Media Jukebox chore, part of a labored digital music fanaticism that gets in the way of enjoying the music. Indeed, you can get plenty of mileage from Media Jukebox without ever touching Categories. But I find the effort worthwhile, especially when throwing together mood-oriented playlists quickly, just before hosting company, for example. Used with SmartLists, Categories bring a steadily evolving dynamism to your listening. As you keep assigning newly imported tracks to the Categories assigned to SmartLists, the track content of those SmartLists keeps changing. With a large enough collection, Categories add an element of freshness—surprise, even—to the household soundtrack.

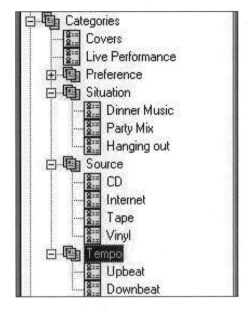

Figure 9.8. Categories are special Media Jukebox tags used in SmartLists.

When you edit ID3 tags through Media Jukebox, the program makes the changes in the files themselves, residing on your hard drive, not merely in the program's library database of file information. So, you can open an altered track in another MP3 player and see the changes you made in Media Jukebox. (You might need to import the changed track into the second player in order to see the changed ID3 tags.)

Power User Many users are unaware of Media Jukebox's powerful ability to render bulk changes to the ID3 tags of multiple files. This outstanding feature invites you to correct tagging mistakes that afflict every track of a ripped or downloaded album. You can also use bulk tagging to add information often missing from the ID3 fields, such as album date in the Year field. Extending your reach beyond a single album, you might wish to add or correct a genre in many tracks across many albums.

Alert Caution is advised when making bulk ID3 changes, because they are inappropriate to certain information fields—Name and Track in particular, because the song name and track number are necessarily different for each track. A bulk change in either field requires many tedious single-track corrections.

Follow these steps to take advantage of bulk ID3 tagging:

1. **In any track list, click a single track.**
2. **Holding the Shift key, click any other single track.** Notice that both tracks, and every track displayed between them, are highlighted. Your first and second selections should bracket and include all the tracks whose ID3 tags you wish to bulk-edit.
3. **Right-click anywhere in the highlighted block of tracks, and click the Properties... selection.**
4. **In the Media Files Properties panel, click the information category you wish to edit.** Again, be careful not to edit the Name or Track fields. Each should display "<varies>" as a warning not to assign unchanging information to the multiple tracks (see figure 9.9).
5. **Type your edit in the selected information field.**
6. **In the lower-right drop-down menu, select Update All Files.** Keep in mind that you can edit one or several (not necessarily all) of the

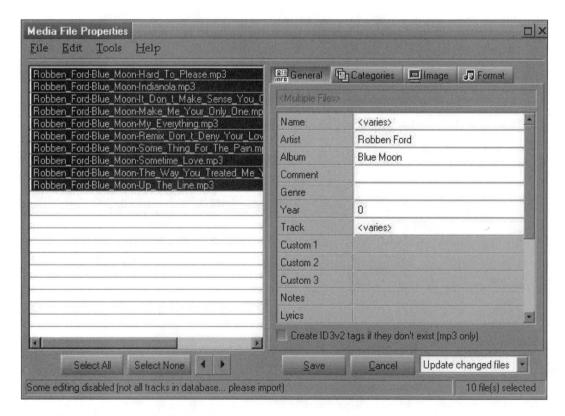

Figure 9.9. *Making bulk edits to ID3 tags in Media Jukebox.*

selected files, by reselecting them in the left-hand portion of the panel, where filenames are displayed. Use the Shift key in the same way as described in step 2. Alternatively, use the Control key to select multiple files not displayed consecutively. When you have reselected some (not all) of the window's files, use the Update Changed Files choice in the drop-down menu.

7. **Click the Save button.**

You have changed multiple ID3 tags in a single swoop. This feature is terrific for correcting annoying misspellings (all too common even with music ripped from CDs and downloaded from authorized sources) and making bulk additions of new ID3 information.

Using the Venerable Winamp

As the first consumer MP3 player, Winamp attained legendary status the moment it was first released, and each new version sits in millions of computers playing files and streaming MP3 Internet radio stations. Though Winamp is no match for Media Jukebox in library features or the management of a large music collection, it is moving in that direction with a new Media Library component in Winamp3. Even if you never use Winamp for the heavy lifting of serious library management, musical life is inconceivable without it.

One of Winamp's great charms is the immense collection of "skins" available for the program. Nullsoft, Winamp's parent company (which in turn is owned by America Online), catalyzed the skinning fad by opening Winamp's design specifications to graphic artists, with the result that futuristic, cool-looking program interfaces became almost as important as the ability to play MP3 music from the desktop. Now, thousands of designs are available free for the downloading, each of which transforms Winamp into a different, sleek beast: the black-and-white illustrations on these pages cannot do them justice.

Cosmetics aside, Winamp is one of the most convenient programs for the digital music zealot. Built from the ground up to play back MP3 files (it also handles Windows Media, MIDI, WAV, OGG, and a multitude of esoteric formats), Winamp sounds great and implements many keyboard controls that lend a casual ease to its operation. Winamp is also a popular target for plug-in developers, who write add-on programs enhancing Winamp's usefulness.

Although Winamp hit the big time and arguably is part of the establishment now, its parent company upheld its characteristic hands-off acquisition approach, allowing Nullsoft to continue its development track, and Winamp has so far retained its underground sensibility. Its Web site, barely spruced up from the early days, still seems written by college kids. (From the installation panel of a trial version came this warning: "This is beta software. Play with it as much as you like, but don't blame us if it melts your computer into a pile of scrap metal or steals your girlfriend.") More important, the program is absolutely free, it doesn't take much room on your hard drive, never bundles third-party programs, and never displays any advertising. Winamp is one of the cleanest installations around, which accounts to some degree for its popularity, and certainly for the purity of its reputation for trustworthiness.

Winamp's version 3 (Winamp3) takes the renegade doctrine to a new level by opening the program's code to outside developers and inviting them to write new functionality into the program. This new standard of decentric flexibility extends to the skins as well, so expect a new rash of designs in 2003 that present more original features than previous skins, which have been colorfully diverse but functionally equivalent.

As this book goes to press, Winamp3 is recently released, and is, frankly, something of a flop among many Winamp loyalists. Information in the following section is based on version 2.80, a massively popular version that people continue to use despite the availability of Winamp3. I expect a large installed base of version 2.80 to still be in use when this book hits the shelves. For a complete review of Winamp3, visit the Digital Songstream Web site (www.digitalsongstream.com).

Basic Winamp Operation

Winamp is preeminently an MP3 playback program. Versions 2.x and 3.x load and play files in the same basic manner. In each case it helps to display two of the programs modules, which appear as "docked" windows. (Docked windows seem to be glued together. You can pull them apart by dragging the bottom module away from the module above it. In Winamp3, press the Shift key and drag any module to separate it from its docked partners.) Those two important modules are:

• the Main Window (see figure 9.10); and
• the Playlist Editor.

Figure 9.10. The main control panel of Winamp.

The Main Window displays the stop/start controls, the Shuffle option, the volume slider, and the Repeat option. The Playlist Editor displays all the files you open into Winamp.

Alert   Note that in the Playlist Editor, Winamp displays tracks in the artist/title format, with no configurable columns for sorting the list by other criteria. This is a drawback in version 2.8, somewhat alleviated in Winamp3 by the Media Library. Even so, in the latter version, you cannot use the Playlist Editor to sort by the ID3 tag of your choice. This lack of integration represents one major reason to continue using Media Jukebox for playlisting.

Speaking of playlists, Winamp does create them, using the M3U format, and saves the lists to your hard drive. This method differs from Media Jukebox's style of creating playlist folders within the program, allowing you to dynamically sort them like any other list without reaching to your hard drive. Click the List button near the bottom-right corner (in most skins) and select Load List (look for the floppy disc icon in some skins). Then name and save the list as it appears in the Playlist Editor. You can change the order of tracks at any time in the Playlist Editor by simply dragging a track up or down with your mouse. To load a saved list, click the Load button and select Load List (look for the folder icon in some skins).

Winamp exhibits no menus in the traditional sense. The program is too cool for drop-down menus. You find everything you need in version 2.8 by right-clicking in various places and selecting from the pop-up lists. Right-click the Main Window for playback options, to open new modules, and to change skins. In Winamp3, open the Thinger module (yes, that's what it's

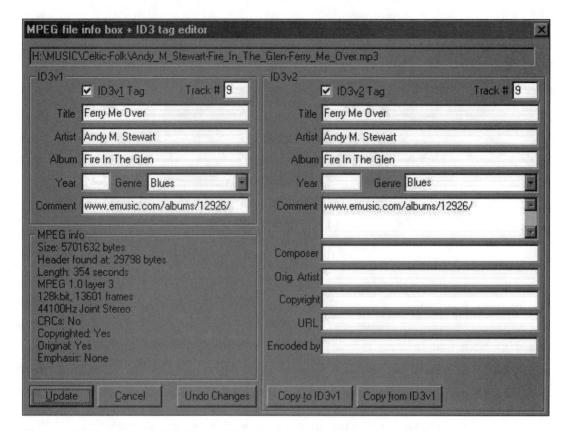

Figure 9.11. Editing ID3v1 and ID3v2 tags in Winamp.

called) and select modules from the icon display: run your mouse cursor over the icons to read what they represent.

ID3 Tags in Winamp
Although Winamp has not historically emphasized ID3 sorting, the program handles ID3 tag editing with exceptional clarity. Right-click any track in the Playlist Editor, then click File Info to see the track's current ID3 tags. (You can also click any track then use the Alt-3 keyboard combination.) Figure 9.11 illustrates the ID3 tag editor. There, you can highlight and change the information in any field, and use the buttons to copy ID3v1 tags to the ID3v2 fields, and vice versa.

 Reminder Winamp does not support bulk ID3 editing of several files at once. This feature might appear in Winamp3. If not, Media Jukebox remains a good place to correct multiple files in one swift operation.

Winamp Bookmarks

You can bookmark anything that plays in Winamp, creating a list of music you wish to access conveniently. When managing a large track collection, it doesn't make sense to bookmark individual songs extensively; it's better to use the playlist feature. However, bookmarking is a fantastic feature for organizing MP3 streams originating in Shoutcast or Live365.

An important first step is to make sure Winamp is assigned to handle MP3 streams when they are initiated on a Web site. This means that Winamp pops open in response to the stream link, and plays the MP3 station. (See chapter 7 for more discussion of Internet radio and MP3 streams.) Media file types are assigned in the Preferences panel; just follow these steps:

1. **With Winamp open, press the Control + P keyboard combination.**
2. **In the Winamp Preferences panel (called the Configuration panel in Winamp3), click File Types.**
3. **In the File Type Setup list (called the Filetypes list in Winamp3), click the *m3u* and *pls* file types.** See figure 9.12 for an illustration of the Filetypes list in Winamp3.
4. **Close the Winamp Preferences or Configuration window.** There is no OK button in either version.

You're now prepared to initiate any MP3 stream with confidence that Winamp will boot up to play it. In Winamp3, you can browse Shoutcast MP3 stations in the Shoutcast Server List module, which is easier than going to the Shoutcast site. By whatever means, once you're listening to an MP3 stream you can see it listed in the Playlist Editor as if it were a single track. In fact, you can mix streams and tracks in the Playlist Editor:

- To bookmark a station, right-click the stream and select Bookmark Item(s).
- To see your bookmark list, and select items from it, right-click the Main Window (*not*, surprisingly, the Playlist Editor) and select Bookmarks.
- You can edit your Bookmark list by right-clicking the Main Window and selecting Bookmarks, then clicking the Edit Bookmarks... selection (or Control + Alt + I). Doing so brings up the Winamp Preferences panel in Bookmarks mode (see figure 9.13). Drag any

Figure 9.12. Assigning file types in Winamp3.

item with the mouse to change its position on the list, and use the
Edit button to open any item for editing.

A well-developed Bookmark list of MP3 stations provides one of the
great joys of Winamp. MP3 streams generally buffer and start playing very
quickly, so surfing your list is almost as swift as twiddling through a real
radio dial—and the music is better.

Winamp Keyboard Controls

Working with Winamp is a fluid experience largely because of the tremendous
range of keyboard controls built into the program. You don't need to reach for
the mouse or pull down a menu to accomplish the minutiae of advancing to

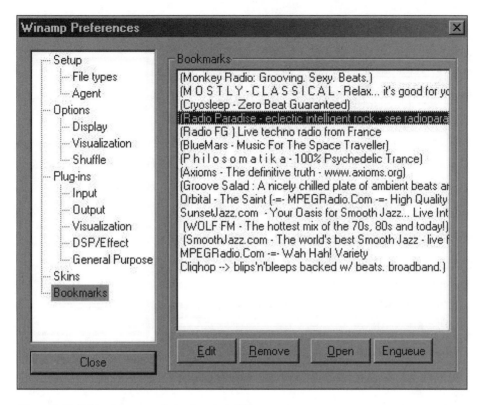

Figure 9.13. *Editing Internet radio bookmarks in Winamp.*

the next rack, starting or stopping playback, and opening the Winamp Preferences panel. Here's a list of essential Winamp keyboard commands worth learning. Winamp must be the active window on your screen for these to work. I am using uppercase letters, but you don't need to on the keyboard.

- **Play:** X
- **Stop:** V
- **Stop with fadeout:** Shift + V
- **Pause:** C
- **Next track:** B
- **Previous track:** Z
- **Skin selection:** Alt + S
- **Open Winamp Preferences window:** Control + P
- **Jump forward/back five seconds in current track:** right/left arrow keys
- **Volume up/down:** up/down arrow keys (or your keyboard's volume knob if there is one)

- **Edit ID3 tags for selected track:** Alt + 3
- **Open file(s):** L
- **Repeat all tracks on/off:** R
- **Shuffle tracks on/off:** S
- **Sort playlist by filename (not artist/title):** Control + Shift + 2

A complete list of keyboard shortcuts is in the About Winamp panel. Right-click the Main Window, then click the Nullsoft Winamp... selection.

Managing Your Collection with Musicmatch

Musicmatch is the final member of the file playback triumverate. As heavy-weight competitor to Media Jukebox, Musicmatch puts out a strong case with its library management, CD burning, and—in particular—its eagerness to deliver streaming content in addition to playing your personal collection. Although I give Media Jukebox my highest recommendation, I can't argue with the many people who swear by Musicmatch as the best single, integrated desktop answer to music management. Musicmatch is an extraordinary, ambitious program with some superlative features. I own it and use it often.

Musicmatch is a double product:

- **Musicmatch program.** The basic jukebox program is available in two versions, per industry tradition: a free "light" version, and a commercial Plus version. Almost all the features described in these pages are incorporated in the Plus version *only*. The freebie gives you basic listing and playback function. I have seen the Plus version priced between $15 and $25 at the Musicmatch Web site (*www.musicmatch.com*).
- **Radio MX service.** Radio MX is Musicmatch's subscription streaming service, described in some detail in chapter 4. A default "light" version of Musicmatch Radio is deployed for any nonsubscribers using the Musicmatch program. Subscribers get better sound quality, freedom from ads, and various interactive features. Nonsubscribers who own Musicmatch Plus do receive the Create Radio Station from Playlist crossover feature.

The Musicmatch experience is enlivened by full participation—that is, by owning Musicmatch Plus and subscribing to Radio MX. The two sides of Musicmatch support each other, and the result is truly addictive. As usual with these mega-programs, you get more mileage with a large collection. Musicmatch doesn't help you build that collection—there's no downloading—but it certainly helps manage it and discover new music related to what you already own.

Musicmatch Basics

To help new Musicmatch users get their bearings, here is some basic information about how the program works:

- The program uses a multiple-window design, unlike the integrated-window display of Media Jukebox. This layout is a strike against the program in my opinion, but it's strictly a matter of taste. Figure 9.14 illustrates the window in which playback controls are located. Figure 9.15 shows the Playlist window in File mode; that window is also used to list tracks played through Musicmatch Radio, and CD tracks when Musicmatch is used as a CD player.
- All windows are resizable except the Player window.
- As in Media Jukebox, you must *import* files into the program in order to sort and playlist them. This process is called "Adding" files, and is accomplished intelligently. Click the Add button in the Music Library window (see figure 9.16) to begin the process. In the Add Tracks to Music Library panel, you can select files from your hard drive individually or by folder. Be sure to select the Also Add Tracks from Subfolders box if you want the program to sweep through all nested folders and add the files in them (see figure 9.17).

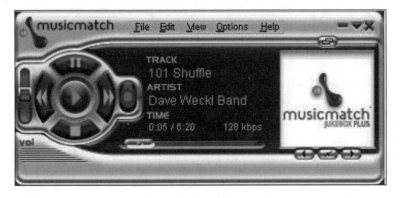

Figure 9.14. The Musicmatch Player window—the basic control panel for music playback.

Figure 9.15. *The Playlist window in Musicmatch.*

- To avoid roving your mouse between the Player and Playlist windows, double-click any track in the Playlist window to play it, even while another is playing.
- Move any track, or group of tracks, from the Music Library to the Playlist windows by right-clicking the track or group, then selecting Add Track(s) to Playlist. Select multiple tracks by selecting an entire category group, or by using the Control key (to select noncontiguous tracks) or the Shift key (to select contiguous tracks) while clicking individual selections.
- The Music Library window can be ordered by Artist, Album, Genre, or Time. Furthermore, you can move your preferred category to the left-hand column subject to collapsing into folders, by clicking the Change View icon near the top left of the Music Library window, and selecting a category from the drop-down list. Simply clicking the column headers reorders the list too, but putting your preferred category on the left makes certain Playlist selections easier. For example, try changing the library view to Genre. Now that all your genre categories are separate folders holding tracks, you can move an entire genre to

Figure 9.16. The Music Library window is where Musicmatch organizes your collection.

the Playlist window by right-clicking it, and selecting Add Track(s) to Playlist.

- In the Playlist window, use the Open button to add new tracks, as an alternative to clicking them over from the Music Library window. The Open Music window lets you select tracks by artist, album, genre, or by filename directly from your hard drive folders.

By the way, if the multiple floating windows drive you to distraction, you can clip them together in one of two ways. First, drag the *top* of any window to the *bottom* of the Playlist window. They glue together, and can be dragged apart at any time by pulling the bottom window away. If this seems too complicated, simply click the View menu in the Player window, and select Auto Arrange Components. They all clip together neatly, and can be pulled apart from the bottom of the arrangement.

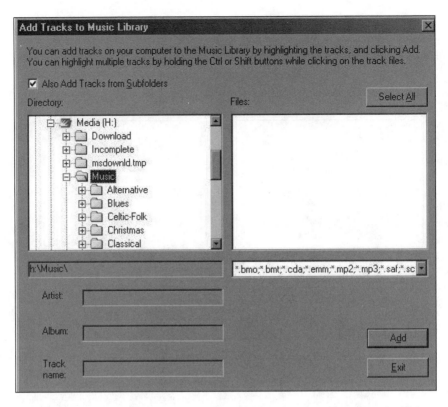

Figure 9.17. Musicmatch allows you to add entire folders of tracks to the program's database.

Tagging and Renaming Files in Musicmatch

Musicmatch has developed a superlative set of ID3 tag management features. You can, of course, edit and rewrite tags individually. Beyond that basic functionality, the Super Tagging feature enables powerful, dynamic assistance in bulk-editing and data research. I have never encountered a mightier, more effective, or more intuitive set of tools for bringing sloppy tags to order throughout a large collection. In my opinion, Musicmatch Plus is worth the price if for no other reason than to clean up ID3 tags. Granted, I'm an ID3 psychopath. Still, no matter which jukebox you prefer using for daily playback and playlisting, Musicmatch is the best choice for cleaning up your MP3 files.

Tagging begins in the Music Library window, where your collection is broken down by ID3 category (see chapter 8 for basic information about ID3 tags). Highlight any track, category, or group of tracks, then click the Tag button. The Edit Track Tag(s) panel appears (see figure 9.18) displaying the current tags. Now the fun begins:

- You can use the right-hand portion of the panel to write or revise basic ID3v1 tags: Artist, Album, Genre, Track Number. The Year field and some others are located in the More tab. While you're there you might want to select Tempo, Mood, and Situation tags, as they will help later with playlisting.

- If you select more than one file in the left-hand portion of the panel, the ID3 fields become grayed out, but click the check-box next to any field you wish to bulk-edit. (The graying-out prevents you from making careless changes that wouldn't be as damaging to a single track.) Clicking the check-box makes that field active and ready to accept a change that affects *all* the selected files. Notice that the Track Title and Track Number fields lack check-boxes, as those pieces of information can never be standardized across multiple tracks.

Two other methods of bulk-editing ID3 tags are offered. The online-enabled Lookup Tags feature compares your files to an online database of recorded music, and displays possible matches with complete ID3 tags. You

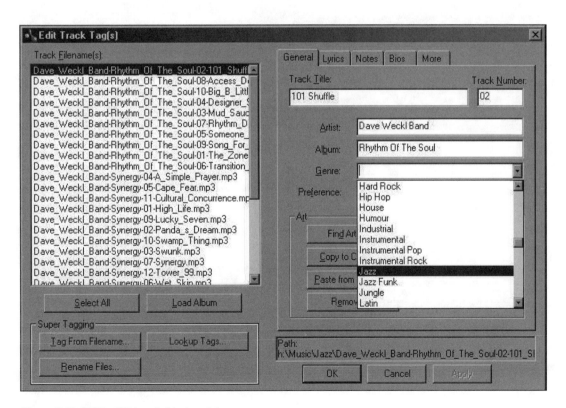

Figure 9.18. Editing ID3 tags in Musicmatch.

only have to choose the best match for each selected track, and your tags are filled in automatically, saving much time and tedium. You must be connected to the Internet for Lookup Tags to work:

1. **In the Music Library window, select a group of files.** The group can be all the tracks of a single album or disparate, unrelated tracks.
2. **Click the Tag button.**
3. **In the Edit Track Tag(s) panel, click the Select All button.**
4. **Still in the Edit Track Tag(s) panel, click the Lookup Tags… button.** The program requires a few seconds to retrieve results.
5. **In the Tag Lookup Results panel, click the correct tagging scheme for each selected file.** Figure 9.19 illustrates this panel. By and large, the blue-highlighted Selected Tag Information chosen by the program is

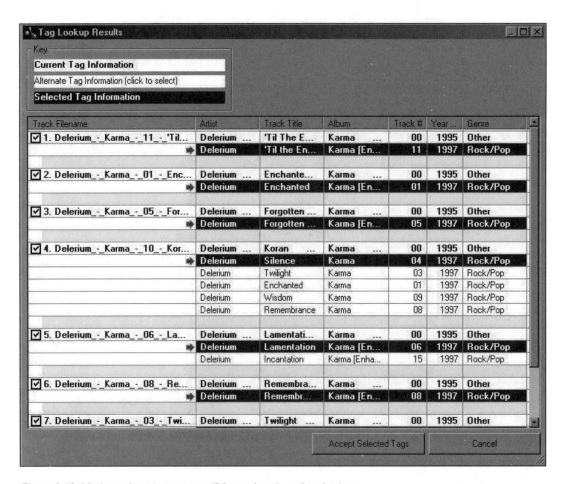

Figure 9.19. Musicmatch retrieves correct ID3 tags from its online database.

correct, although some tracks deliver several alternates. Each track also shows the current tags, so you can compare the information you're trading in with the new tags.

6. **Click the Accept Selected Tags button.**
7. **Back in the Edit Track Tag(s) panel, click the OK button.**

You have inserted new, correct, complete ID3v1 tags for all your selected tracks, without necessarily knowing the basic track information. For downloading fiends who amass quickly from many sources that don't necessarily bother with good tagging (bands and labels distributing through their own Web sites are notorious for nasty tagging and filenaming), this feature is a blessing.

The final bulk-editing feature, Tag from Filename, works best with a selection of clean filenames, each of which contains the four basic information pieces (artist, album, track number, track title) in any order, separated by some punctuation mark. With coherent filenames in place, Musicmatch can use them to generate basic ID3 tags for the entire lot. Here's how to proceed:

1. **In the Music Library window, select a group of files.**
2. **Click the Tag button.**
3. **In the Edit Track Tag(s) panel, click the Select All button.**
4. **Still in the Edit Track Tag(s) panel, click the Tag from Filename… button.**
5. **In the Tag from Filename panel, use the drop-down menus to assign ID3 categories to filename parts** (see figure 9.20). Remember, each drop-down menu corresponds to a portion of the filenames displayed in the Track Filename column. The word *field* above each drop-down menu does not refer to an ID3 field, but a filename field defined by whatever punctuation separator is used. As you make choices in the menus, the ID3 tag information changes interactively.
6. **Click the OK button.**
7. **Back in the Edit Track Tag(s) panel, click the OK button.**

If your ID3 tags are accurate, Musicmatch can use them to make your filenames consistent, in bulk. The program examines your tags, lets you determine the order in which the information pieces will appear in the filenames, and makes the necessary changes. Follow these steps to scrub an album's track filenames:

1. **In the Music Library window, select a group of files.** This process is easiest if you choose the tracks of a single album.
2. **Click the Tag button.**
3. **In the Edit Track Tag(s) panel, click the Select All button.**
4. **Still in the Edit Track Tag(s) panel, click the Rename Files… button.**
5. **In the Create Filename from Tags panel, use the drop-down menus to assign the order of information pieces** (see figure 9.21). In my collection, Artist (1), Album (2), Track # (3), Track Title (4) works best. The important point is to put Track Number *before* the Track Title. As you make selections in the drop-down menus, the prospective filenames in the New Filename column change.
6. **Click the OK button.**
7. **Back in the Edit Track Tag(s) panel, click the OK button.**

Taking the time to correct ID3 tags might seem overly complex and toilsome. These chores are far removed from the joys of listening to digital music. I recommend trial and practice to acquire a feel for just how useful

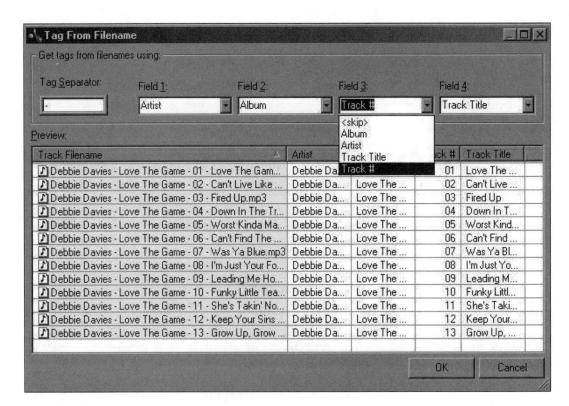

Figure 9.20. *Creating ID3 tags from filenames in Musicmatch.*

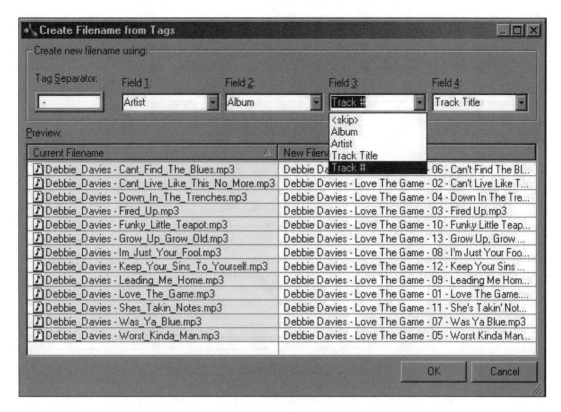

Figure 9.21. Creating filenames from ID3 tags in Musicmatch.

these tools are. If you complete tagging your whole collection in this manner, the result is a sparkling database of music that can be sorted and playlisted with maximum flexibility in any jukebox program. And that's when the fun really begins.

Creating a Radio Station in Musicmatch

Linking the Musicmatch Radio service to the Musicmatch Plus program enables the company to perform some virtuosic interactive enabling. Perhaps the most fun feature in Musicmatch Plus is the radio station creation feature. Musicmatch looks at whatever is in your Playlist window (even just one track) and custom-builds a radio station related to those tracks. Radio MX subscribers get better sound quality, but the feature works for all Musicmatch Plus owners.

Invoking this innovative feature could hardly be simpler. When at least one track is listed in the Playlist window, right-click anywhere in the window and select Create Radio Station from Playlist. The program takes a few seconds (longer if you've got a big list of tracks) to look up all the tracks, then pops open the Radio window to display the results and flips the Playlist window to Radio mode. The newly created "station" begins playing after a few more seconds. You cannot pause the music stream, but you can advance to the next track if you don't like any piece. (There's no going back to previous tracks, though.) This feature is altogether too much fun, and is a tremendous way to find new artists, and new albums by artists you already like.

Power User As your custom-built station continues to play, the tracks remain listed in the Playlist window (now in Radio mode). You can double back on the station-making process at any time by right-clicking the list and *again* selecting Create Radio Station from Playlist.

Alert Fun as this innovation certainly is, the system has glitches and a certain degree of stupidity. Some nonmainstream artists are not (yet?) recognized by the Musicmatch database, and if they are the only artists in your Playlist, the station cannot be created. Furthermore, Musicmatch is easily confused, particularly by classical tracks. In a recent experiment, I asked the program to create a station around a single Martha Argerich track; she is a legendary classical piano virtuoso famous for blazing interpretations of Chopin and Rachmaninov. Musicmatch created a station and began playing Rosemary Clooney singing "Brazil." Apparently the database picked up on Argerich's Brazilian nationality; the next station track was Tito Puente. Not a single classical selection was forthcoming.

Musicmatch Playlists and AutoDJ

Simple playlisting in Musicmatch works more similarly to Winamp's model than to the multiple-folder design of Media Jukebox. In the Playlist window, click the Save button to name and store any currently displayed list of tracks— simple as that. You can change the track order of any playlist in two ways:

- Drag any track to a different position in the list.
- Use the Shuffle button to randomize the track order.

The AutoDJ feature corresponds roughly to SmartLists in Media Jukebox. AutoDJ is a dynamic method of delivering certain types of music

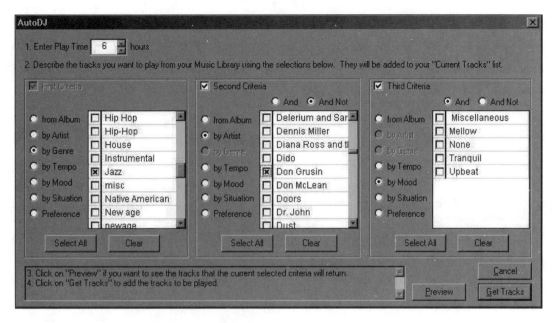

Figure 9.22. Creating an AutoDJ playlist in Musicmatch.

into your sound space. Your collection must be effectively tagged to make AutoDJ work; the ID3 Genre tag is essential, and the Tempo, Mood, and Situation tags that Musicmatch provides also help. When your collection is properly tagged, follow these steps:

1. **With Musicmatch Plus active, press the Control + D keyboard combination.** The AutoDJ panel appears (see figure 9.22).
2. **Click the radio button next to the primary criterion by which you want to sort this AutoDJ list.** For example, you might select Genre here.
3. **Use the check-boxes to select categories in your chosen criterion.** For example, you might select Jazz and Celtic here.
4. **Repeat steps 2 and 3 for the Second Criteria and Third Criteria, if desired.** Filling out second and third criteria narrows down your AutoDJ list to specific characteristics. The more you narrow down, the larger the collection you need to supply a decent amount of music. Note that you can *eliminate* criteria from the list by clicking the And Not radio button above the Second Criteria and Third Criteria.
5. **Select a time duration in the Enter Play Time menu.**
6. **Click the Preview button for a list of selected tracks.**

7. **Click the Get Tracks button to enter the completed list in the Playlist window.**

Reminder Don't forget to save the AutoDJ list as a Playlist if you wish to use it repeatedly without filling out the arduous AutoDJ panel again. Use the Save button in the Playlist window.

Pro & Con AutoDJ is not ever evolving in the same manner as SmartLists in Media Jukebox are. Media Jukebox lets you save the SmartList criteria, which continue to develop the list as you import new files to the library and continue tagging the files already imported. Musicmatch saves the resulting AutoDJ list, but not the criteria, so the list is etched in stone even if you add new files to the library that would match the AutoDJ criteria.

Pro & Con Which is better, Media Jukebox or Musicmatch? The answer depends on your priorities. Musicmatch is superb at bulk-editing ID3 tags and filenames, thus whipping a large collection into coherence. Media Jukebox is arguably a stronger playlister, but even that perception varies according to taste. Your preference for integrated display or free-floating windows makes a difference. Media Jukebox's collapsible organizing folders keeps the program looking neat. Musicmatch is in a higher league when it comes to integrating Internet information and streams with your music collection, but costs more in the long run if you join the program with Radio MX. My experience with Musicmatch is slightly buggier than with Media Jukebox, but it's possible that MJ's bugs merely bug me less than Musicmatch's bugs. One solution for eager adopters is to get both programs and develop your preference through hands-on experience. You can also use the trial periods offered by each company.

Managing a Collection with RealOne

RealOne mixes repellent desktop mannerisms with strong and innovative features, making it both offensive and irresistible. The subscription service associated with the program is definitely to be avoided (in version 1, at least), but the program itself, as a music management jukebox, has value that might compensate for its drawbacks. In the large picture of daily collecting and playlisting, the quest for a self-effacing, quiet, neutral software assistant is foiled by RealOne's resource-hungry performance, intrusive video ads, hateful file-type grabs, and exasperating message pop-ups even when the program is turned off. Outside of the disastrous, ethics-free KaZaA file-sharing interface, no digital music enabler is as pushy, baneful, and self-centered as RealOne. If power features come second to general desktop demeanor, this book does not recommend managing your collection through RealOne.

But those power features, where they exist, are charming. The program does not compete with Media Jukebox when it comes to intelligent display, or to Musicmatch in the integration of local files and Internet streams. Neither is RealOne as elegant, simple, and well behaved as Winamp when it comes to MP3 management. On top of all this, the program is slow and seems to take forever importing a large collection.

So where the heck are those power features? Primarily in two areas: bulk file renaming and the AutoPlaylist.

Bulk File Renaming in RealOne

Like other jukeboxes, RealOne lets you define how filenames are created when ripping CDs. The big difference lies in RealOne's willingness to apply your settings to all existing files (or some of them) on your hard drive. This powerful feature relies on accurate ID3 tags, so be sure those tags are in neat order when applying this feature to a group of files. (In my opinion RealOne is not the place to edit ID3 tags, because the program performs slowly and renames conventional terms in its own language. Edit your tags, in, ideally, Musicmatch, or Media Jukebox or even Winamp—then import your collection to RealOne to try this feature.)

Follow these steps to use the bulk renaming feature:

1. **Click the Tools menu.**
2. **Click the Preferences… selection.**
3. **Double-click My Library.**
4. **Click Advanced My Library.**
5. **Click the Change Filenames… button.**
6. **In the Change File Naming Convention panel, use the drop-down menus to order the information fields in your filenames.** Chapter 2

discusses this step in greater detail. Remember to put Track Number *before* Track Name.

7. **Click the OK button.**
8. **Click the Apply to Existing Media... button.**
9. **In the Apply Convention to Existing Media panel, click the Browse... button.**
10. **Use the Browse for Folder window to select files to be renamed.** You may select entire folders, but remember that subfolders will be included in the renaming process.
11. **Click the OK button.**
12. **Back in the Apply Convention to Existing Media panel, click the OK button.** Your files are quickly renamed.

Alert Be careful with the bulk renaming feature. If the ID3 tags associated with the renamed files are out of whack, your new filenames will be too. Then you're faced with performing track-by-track or album-by-album repair work in Musicmatch or Media Jukebox.

RealOne's AutoPlaylist

Media Jukebox has SmartLists, Musicmatch has AutoDJ, and RealOne has the extraordinary AutoPlaylist. Using a range of ID3 tags and other categories to define which files are added to the list and which are excluded, AutoPlaylist is arguably more flexible than either of its big-name competitors, even if some of the available categories are more exotic than practical. Here's how to create an AutoPlaylist:

1. **In RealOne, click My Library.**
2. **In your Audio Library, right-click any track or selected group of tracks.**
3. **Click New AutoPlaylist.**
4. **In the New AutoPlaylist panel (see figure 9.23), name the list.**
5. **In Basic Mode, click any genre in the left-hand pane, then check artists to include from the right-hand panel.** You can shift from Basic mode to Advanced mode by clicking the Advanced radio button beneath the AutoPlaylist's name.

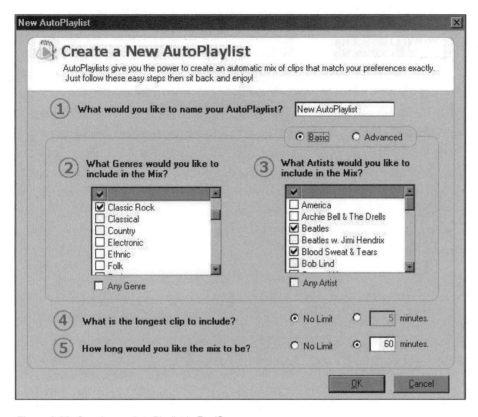

Figure 9.23. *Creating an AutoPlaylist in RealOne.*

6. At the panel's bottom, use the radio buttons to determine allowable track lengths.
7. Click the OK button.

The Advanced mode provides a long list of criteria to include or exclude from your list. The most useful of these might be the Last Played option, which accepts or rejects tracks that have been played through RealOne employing a user-determined period of time. So, if you want to keep the AutoPlaylist fresh, exclude all tracks played in the last month, or even the last few days. Conversely, you can include only tracks that have been played during that time. Or, more powerfully still, mix up the feature by selecting (for example) tracks that have been played during the last month, but not in the last seven days. When combined with typical genre and artist selections, the Last Played feature creates supple and surprising playlists.

Alert Be careful: RealOne is excessively grabby, and some installations display this alarming edict: "RealOne Player will become the default media player for common media types that are currently assigned to another player on your system." If the program does appropriate your music file associations (it continues trying after installation, even going so far as to harangue you when the program is closed), go to the Preferences panel (under the Tools menu) and select Media Types. Scroll through the list and uncheck any file types you wish to dissociate from RealOne. Now you must go into the programs you *do* want associated with those file types, and reestablish the connection. While you're in a bad mood, why not write an e-mail of complaint to RealNetworks?

10

Out of the Computer
and into Your Life

When music formats get smaller, they fit into more places inside and out of
the home. The CD, with a diameter seven inches smaller than the LP, and
the diminutive cassette tape, catalyzed music portability. MP3 and other
digital music files, freed from their reliance on a disk of any size, have no
physicality at all and are therefore infinitely portable. Of course, you still
need some kind of physical device to listen to virtual music files, but that
device can be as small as a wristwatch or a slightly fattened credit card.

Popular though tiny portable players are with the active set—joggers
and gym hounds—the athletic lifestyle isn't the only venue for music on the
go. Car players that handle MP3 files are in growing demand. And while
traditional stereo components that handle compressed files and incorporate
certain computing functions are not flying off the store shelves, demand is
maturing in that area too. Even though inexpensive, powerful computer
speakers make listening by monitor glow a sonically satisfying experience,
most people with real-world lives like to take their music away from the
desktop every so often.

This chapter delineates categories of noncomputerish new-music
devices without making specific purchase recommendations, and without
offering detailed price guides. The nature of book publishing prohibits
offering information that changes quickly. (Consult the www.digital

songstream.com Web site for current information.) This chapter does provide a shopping companion of sorts by illuminating the specifications of portable devices and clarifying which features are important.

Noncomputer MP3 Players

For the most part, taking MP3s out of the computer means transferring them to a portable player either via CD or through a USB connection between the player and the computer. In addition to devices that fall in those categories are shelftop players of various kinds and central media servers that might become more prevalent. There (currently) are five major types of noncomputer MP3 player:

- **Portable MP3 players.** These opportune and popular gadgets were the first answer to nascent consumer demand for portable song file playback. The first such player so alarmed the music establishment that a consortium of record labels sued its manufacturing company—and lost. From that point there was no stopping the stampede of new products. Consumer response hasn't been quite as tempestuous as expected, though, perhaps because these players, handy as they are, are hobbled by certain limitations, discussed later in this chapter.
- **Portable MP3 jukeboxes.** Similar to portable MP3 players, these small jukeboxes have much greater storage capacity. Whereas the players use built-in memory chips and memory-expansion cards, the more capacious jukeboxes carry internal hard drives. The similarity to computers ends there, though; the jukeboxes do not do anything except play music, and they don't go online (as of this writing).
- **MP3 CD portables.** Because music CDs are just platters with music files on them, why shouldn't portable CD players be smart enough to play compressed music files? No reason at all, as manufacturers gradually realized. MP3 CD players (whether portable or not) can play commonplace audio CDs and data CDs burned with MP3 files (and sometimes other compressed formats such as OGG and WMA).
- **MP3–enabled hi-fi components.** There's no reason that traditional stereo systems, which often are connected to the household's best speakers, should be left out of digital music. From shelftop MP3 CD players to stand-alone ripping/burning machines with internal hard drives, various products help create and manage a large file collection within the context of a hi-fi system.

- **Next-generation media servers.** Basically would-be replacements of the computer, these products are in developmental childhood as this book goes to production. Representing one side of a supremacy battle between computers and convergent devices that act like computers in sheep's clothing, household servers might offer some user-friendliness that the computer lacks, but might not overcome the enormous established base of computer users.

The next sections survey the specifications, selling points, and warning signs when shopping for a portable music device.

Choosing a Portable Music Device

Owning the right portable MP3 player is mostly a matter of understanding varying specifications and matching them to your needs. Your two big questions here are:

- How much music do you want to have at your fingertips when away from the computer?
- What other functions, besides simple MP3 playback, do you want the device to perform?

These two points support each other: the more music you carry around with you, the more power the carrying device is likely to have. And—not to forget an important point—the more expensive it's likely to be.

Memory and Music Storage

Three essential types of portable music memory exist:

- **RAM and cards.** RAM (random access memory) and card memory are quite discrete types, but are usually linked in portable MP3 players. These pocket contrivances embody a certain amount of RAM memory, which is just like the RAM in your computer. Typical RAM capacities are 32 megabytes (about a half hour of music), 64 megabytes (an hour), and 128 megabytes (two hours). If the device is large enough to accommodate one, it usually contains a slot for a memory card. The capacity of the removable memory card (which is smaller than a credit card) is added to the RAM memory to attain the device's total music capacity. Memory cards, like batteries, are usually not included with the player.

- **Hard drives.** Hard drives furnish much more storage room than even the most ambitious RAM-card combination. At publication time, no portable devices carried the hefty 40–gig and 80–gig drives typically found in desktop computers, but the ceiling on portable storage will certainly be raised as time goes on.
- **CDs.** In a sense, CDs are infinitely expandable even though each disc has a strict memory limit of 700 to 800 megabytes (depending on the disc), because you can always carry around more discs. Clearly, juggling an armful of CDs is a poor solution when jogging, but not bad when driving a car.

A small player with RAM/card memory is best when your on-the-road needs don't extend over much time. Gym workouts, jogs, and dog-walks are all perfect activities for the smallest players. Active listening that accompanies movement also benefits from the solid-state nature of these devices, which contain no moving parts whatsoever; the music never skips. Be sure, though, that your lifestyle supports frequent replenishment sessions at the computer, lest you grow insufferably weary of the short playlists these devices afford.

MP3 jukeboxes with internal hard drives provide, honestly, better value for the dollar, which might explain why the RAM players haven't inflamed consumer passion. In some cases, twice the money gets you over 180 times the storage space (6 gigabytes for $195 versus 32 megabytes for $99 when comparing two specific models at publication time). A side benefit of these cost-effective jukeboxes lies in their format-neutrality. You can store any type of file in them, and they serve as portable, backup hard drives as well as music players.

MP3 CD players require more work than other portable devices because you must burn CDs before the players have any usefulness. Busy archivers like these devices, though, because they offer profound flexibility and less planning than RAM/card units. MP3 CD players can't compete with hard drive jukeboxes in that department, but they are less expensive, and blank CDs are dirt cheap. Furthermore, they play audio CDs too.

Shopping for RAM/card MP3 Players

Where once there were few choices for shoppers interested in portable MP3 players, now there are many. It's almost bewildering. When selecting a RAM/card MP3 portable device, keep in mind these points:

The Five Types of Memory Card

Wouldn't life be simpler if everything were standardized? Bill Gates thinks so. Competition breeds innovation, though, as well as confusion, and in this area the playing field is fragmented five ways. You might already use a memory card in a digital camera. When shopping for a portable MP3 player of the RAM-plus-card type, you could limit your choices to models that accept the card format you already own. That way you could swap the card between the camera and the MP3 player. On the other hand, most song files require more room than most picture files, so you might need a more capacious card dedicated to the MP3 player, in which case the card format doesn't matter.

These are the five mainstream card formats and a few of their characteristics:

- **CompactFlash.** Prevalent; memory up to 1 gigabyte; inexpensive.
- **SmartMedia.** Prevalent; memory up to 128 megabytes; inexpensive.
- **MultiMediaCard.** Not as prevalent; memory up to 128 megabytes; expensive.
- **Memory Stick.** Used mostly in Sony devices; memory up to 128 megabytes; slightly expensive.
- **Secure Digital.** Uncommon; memory up to 256 megabytes; very expensive.

- **Memory.** The built-in RAM is important, especially if you're going for short bursts of music (no more than two hours at a time) and don't plan to invest in a memory card. The gold standard is 128 megabytes, but that might go up; conversely, you can find plenty of regressive little units with 32 megabytes of RAM. If you do plan to add a memory card, get the cheapest base unit you can find that conforms to your other feature requirements, and spend your money on the card.
- **Size.** The largest portable MP3 player fits into a pocket, but even that bantam scale might be too cumbersome for your purposes. At publication time, some models had shrunk down to just about one square inch, and others, a bit larger, can be worn on the arm or wrist.
- **Display.** Low-memory devices can play only short lists of tracks, so you don't necessarily need a big display that reels off ID3 tags and filenames. Still, some devices convey more file information than others, and if you plan to carry around a whopping memory card and hundreds of songs, a somewhat detailed display comes in handy.
- **Car adapter.** These add-ons plug into whatever "head" is already in

your car—usually a radio-cassette combination. Plugging a cassette-shaped adapter into the tape player feeds the MP3 player's music through your car's stereo system. Sometimes a power cord is also included, which plugs into the car's cigarette lighter. However, the car adapter might be utterly unimportant to your listening needs.

- **Computer interface.** Most MP3 portable players use the USB inter-face, which is convenient and yields fast transfers. Software is often included, which you can either use or decline in favor of device-load-ing software included in desktop MP3 players. (The portable devices often come bundled with the same program you are familiar with on the computer.)
- **Battery power.** All portable players use batteries, but they don't all claim the same battery life. Generally, as with back rubs, the longer the batteries last, the better. Published specs might not be entirely accurate, but comparisons are as useful as car mileage comparisons.
- **FM radio and voice recorder.** These extra features have become selling points in some models.
- **Sound quality.** This is one shopping consideration that you can't check out online, and you can't always test in stores, either. Part of any player's sonic quality depends on the headphones, so the truly discrim-inating shopper carries a favorite pair into the store. For the most part, though, people buy unauditioned devices and hope for the best. If you're listening to music while jogging down a noisy street, pristine acoustic caliber might not be so important.
- **File formats.** The ability to play MP3s is a requirement, of course, and if you have WMA or OGG files in your collection, make sure the player can handle them.

If you're buying your first portable player, shopping online is the best bet. Read reviews and survey the price scene. Online cruising is the best way to get up to speed on current models in short order.

Shopping for an MP3 Jukebox with Hard Drive

When evaluating portable players with internal hard drives, the choices are fewer and the prices are higher. Many of the feature considerations are the same as with RAM/card players, except for the presence of an FM tuner and voice recorder, which don't exist on any models available at publication time. In addition to those many points, you should also check:

- **Connection speed.** USB connectivity is an absolute must when transferring large amounts of music. USB 2.0 is even better, but make sure your computer *has* a USB 2.0 port (not the older 1.1 port) or the device will not be able to exercise its best transfer speeds. The wireless and rapid Firewire standard is also a possibility, but, again, your computer must have Firewire capability.

- **Synchronization.** This feature compares the portable unit's hard drive collection with the music collection in your computer, and automatically grabs any newly added tracks from the computer.

- **Included software.** This consideration becomes important with the greater capacity of the jukeboxes. Some are equipped with a few programs that specialize in transferring, playlisting, synchronizing, and so on.

- **On-board effects.** Presumably, you'll be doing a lot of listening through the portable jukebox, sometimes in quiet settings where sound quality differences are noticeable. Some jukeboxes contain built-in equalizers and other types of signal processing to enhance the sound.

- **Anti-skipping.** Like CD players, jukeboxes all claim some level of skip protection, and you should take it all with a grain of salt. Best not to jog with a hard drive unit.

- **Recording.** This rare feature might become more common in the future. At least one model (the Nomad Jukebox 3) lets you rip directly to the portable unit's hard drive. This property should be of special interest to those with a vinyl collection, as it is easier to get a portable unit in position with a turntable than it is to position a turntable close enough to a computer for ripping.

Finally, make sure that your chosen portable MP3 jukebox looks great, because you're going to be showing it off to a lot of people.

Shopping for an MP3 CD Player

Many of the buying considerations for the portable machines don't apply to MP3 CD players, which require no built-in memory, software, or computer interface standards. Instead, concentrate on these points:

- **Folder navigation.** MP3 CD players have been slow to accommodate the needs of experienced MP3 collectors. Each burned CD may contain between one hundred and two hundred tracks, so dividing CDs into folders is a natural enough tendency. Yet, some MP3 CD players can't cope with folder divisions.

- **ID3 tags.** Find a machine that understands ID3 tags, and can display your tracks according to track title, artist, album, and track number.
- **Playlists.** This point also relates to navigation. The player should recognize playlists saved in the standard M3U format. The CD must be burned with the M3U playlist, plus each track file represented on that playlist. The player then, ideally, lets you see the M3U list in the display, select it, and hear the tracks without further finagling.
- **Formats.** If you burn WMA and OGG files, make sure you get a player that doesn't whimper at their sight.

MP3 CD players are somewhat more appropriate devices for jogging than MP3 jukeboxes are. Expect the anti-skipping protection to be slightly more effective when playing an MP3–burned disc as when playing an audio disc.

Digital Audio Receivers and Servers

Receiving less publicity than portable MP3 players, a certain type of digitally empowered consumer electronics is helping get music out of the computer and distribute it to other parts of the home. These shelftop components are meant to be hooked into the hi-fi stereo system, either alongside or in place of the CD player. At their most full-featured, these boxes contain the following parts and functions:

- an MP3 CD player that handles store-bought music CDs, home-burned audio CDs, and home-burned data CDs with MP3 files and possibly WMA and OGG formats;
- a DVD player in anticipation of commercial music releases on DVD;
- an internal hard drive for music storage;
- a ripping function for copying CDs to the hard drive;
- a CD burner;
- some kind of home networking standard that connects the box to the computer;
- a modem for connecting to the Internet; and
- internal music software and a display screen large enough to manage the unit's power features.

Pro & Con In theory, using one of these digital audio receivers (DARs) to rip, burn, and store music files is no easier than performing the same tasks in a computer. Arguably, it's harder using the small screen built into a shelftop component. The big advantage is that, once ripped, burned, and archived, the files reside within your stereo system, and don't need to be imported from the computer. So the DAR is attractive primarily to people who don't wish to turn the computer into the household's primary stereo system. At publication time, these boxes were expensive alternatives to computer-based digital music, but the best (and priciest) of them do boast audiophile specifications that computer sound cards don't match.

Models that employ home networking to remain connected to the computer at all times create a more fluid path for music to travel around the home. In this scenario it doesn't matter where you execute ripping and burning chores, as the files can easily be archived in either location (computer or DAR), or both locations. Or, the DAR can play your computer's files directly from the computer.

When shopping for shelftop DARs (which are sometimes called Digital Music Servers), consider the following points as you browse the wide range of specifications:

Receiver or Server?

Digital audio receivers and digital audio servers are close but distinct product categories. They are bunched together in these pages, but there is a clearly defined difference between the two component types.

Receivers do not attempt to archive your music collection, and generally don't contain internal hard drives. Their purpose is to *receive* music from the computer, playing it through your stereo system. This reception is accomplished through a home networking connection to the computer.

Servers are more enabled computer surrogates that maintain your collection on an internal hard drive. Their purpose is to *serve* music from their own archive. At the same time, most servers keep a home networking connection with the computer for maximum flexibility.

- **Does it burn?** Most units with hard drives can rip CDs, but not all can burn them.
- **Is there a hard drive?** Some DARs do not attempt to archive your collection. Digital audio servers usually do contain hard drives, and rip CDs to internal storage space.
- **What network standard is used?** HPNA (Home Phoneline Networking Alliance) is becoming popular, and conveniently uses preexisting telephone wiring to connect devices in different rooms. The Ethernet standard (the same system used in cable-modem high-speed Internet setups) is also implemented in some boxes. Wireless connections using tried-and-true FM is used in at least a couple of models specializing in streaming Internet radio through the computer and directly to the stereo system. The old, reliable USB is also used, but is the slowest networking alternative, which matters when transferring massive amounts of music. Some boxes employ more than one standard, giving you a choice of connections.
- **How is album-lookup accomplished?** When ripping a CD (see chapter 2), automated filename creation and tagging saves quite a bit of tedious work. On a computer, ripping programs acquire album and track information from online databases. Digital audio servers with Internet connections (or with Ethernet networking that allows you to share a cable modem) can accomplish the identical chore. Just make sure that the box is enabled to perform a Gracenote/CDDB lookup. Alternatively, some units come with a huge album information catalog bundled into the box. In that case, going online is unnecessary; the server merely checks its own information source. It's important, though, that the box have some way to periodically update the catalog.
- **Transfers to a memory card?** You might wish to load up a portable MP3 player of the RAM/card variety from your DAR. If so, make sure the server has an interface that accommodates a card reader (USB is the most common such interface), and built-in software that can perform the transfer of tracks to the card.
- **Playlisting software?** If the digital audio server is to be a computer surrogate of sorts, be sure that it offers the same flexibility that enlivens digital music on a computer—and that means the ability to sort your archived music by artist, album, track, and genre, at the very least.
- **File formats and bit rates?** MP3 is the order of the day, but if you have a penchant for OGG files or WMA, be sure the server can read

those formats from a burned CD, and can rip CDs into those formats internally. Perhaps more important, find out the unit's encoding rates. Digital audio servers sport audiophile-level signal reproduction, so there's no point in ripping CDs into substandard bit rates. Make sure the ripping engine goes up to 320k. (See chapter 2 for more about ripping and bit rates.)

Power User In theory, it's a short step from digital audio server to digital media server, the latter of which could handle video formats as well as music formats. Such a server, called Moxi, is under development at publication time, with an expected launch date that roughly corresponds to this book's publication date. Moxi is an innovation of Steve Perlman, whose previous invention was the WebTV Internet/television service. Moxi's plan is to link every media playback system in the house (computer, stereo, television, DVR) wirelessly, fluidly serving digitized music and movies. Look for Moxi and other household media servers to begin proliferating, and consider whether to expand your household media aspirations (and budget) accordingly.

Digital Music in the Car

For some, the most imperative portable music priority is getting files to play in the car. For the most part, you have three ways of making it happen:

- **Portable MP3 player with adapter.** Some devices are equipped with car adapters right out of the box, and that off-the-shelf readiness for mobile playback is a selling point for commuters. Generic car adapters are also available at consumer electronics stores; just make sure you match plug types between the adapter and the player.
- **Factory MP3 CD players in the car.** Some car manufacturers, ramping up to speed with demand for mobile MP3 playback, have built MP3 file recognition into their onboard CD players. This simple solution allows you to burn MP3 data discs (as well as audio discs, of course) and pop them into the car's CD player with no worry. Generally, though, these built-in hybrid players don't sport LCD displays of any size to playlist your listening in the car—which would be dangerous anyway if the car were moving.
- **Auto MP3 jukeboxes.** Relatively new introductions to the market-

place, these portable jukeboxes are similar in principle to handheld MP3 jukeboxes with internal hard drives, but they are designed to be installed in the car. One such device, the PhatNoise Car Audio System, uses a removable hard drive cartridge to transfer tracks from the computer to the car player, which remains installed in the car.

Wireless digital radio provides another way of filling the moving auto with music. These recently developed systems beam genre-divided music to the car from a satellite—a kind of wireless cable-radio system for the car. This type of service is sold on a subscription basis. As a programming alternative the drawback is that you don't have any control of the selections beyond choosing a music genre. Two of the developers and providers of wireless car audio systems are:

- XM Satellite Radio (www.xmradio.com); and
- Sirius Radio (www.siriusradio.com).

At publication time, XM and Sirius were each rolling out services that included about one hundred channels of music and talk, with few or no commercials. You must purchase add-on equipment that turns your car's audio head (its radio receiver and cassette deck) into a wireless-ready receiver for whichever service you choose. As with satellite television, the receiver (which is basically a kind of mobile satellite dish) requires a fairly hefty cash outlay—in the hundreds of dollars at this writing. Both services begin their pricing (again, at publication time) at about $10 a month.

11

The Conscience of Digital Music

Most people involved with digital music know that downloading music is controversial. Napster brought unrestricted song-sharing to the mainstream, and received enormous publicity for doing so. When the original version of Napster was shut down, it became clear even to casual enthusiasts that digital music was raising thorny legal issues. Incendiary conflicts involving copyright, copy-protected CDs, and copy-limiting song files were spawned of the free-music movement that Napster popularized—which was, at the core, a revolution of replication. Copying music lies at the heart of both the convenience and controversy of MP3.

However, it is far from accurate to say that copying music is illegal, although the "ripping is bad" alarmists would have you believe otherwise. Copying for personal use is traditionally protected by American copyright law, even given recent legal enhancements that have bestowed far-reaching control upon media companies. It is when "personal use" includes going online and (sometimes inadvertently) sharing music that the situation becomes less clear-cut. Even when copyright is inarguably being infringed, there exists some confusion in the average person's mind over who is breaking the law, which law is being broken, and in general where innocence, guilt, enforceability, and social responsibility lie. Add to this legal tangle the fact that many people don't care about the legality of making song copies,

How to Sound like a Lawyer at Your Next Cocktail Party

Buzzwords lend flair to any conversation. More important, they actually mean something, and understanding them can help make sense of newspaper articles, know-it-all friends, and this book. Here are several terms you should know the next time you're gearing up for a scathing rant about digital music:

- **Intellectual property.** Any mental creation that is recorded in any fashion belongs legally to its creator, and is a type of property. It might seem strange to think of an ephemeral thing—like a song, a book, a fictional character, or an idea—as being property. Intellectual property is legally regarded in much the same light as physical property like a house or car. There are also differences between material and intellectual property, but as a starting point it's correct to recognize that mental creations are as substantial, in a courtroom, as physical constructions.

- **Property.** Specific intellectual properties are often referred to simply as "properties." A song is a property; so is a CD album.

- **Content.** Diving deeper into depersonalization, intellectual property is generally known as "content," as distinct from the service that distributes the content (like a radio station), or the device that plays it (like a CD player). Companies in the business of supplying music to distribution services are called content providers or content companies.

- **Media.** Music is a type of media (it's one medium), and so are movies, TV shows, books, paintings—any creation that can be seen, heard, or felt is broadly described as "media." Companies that specialize in owning entertainment and information properties are media companies.

- **Public domain.** The public domain represents a vast body of previously copyrighted, or deliberately uncopyrighted, works. Every piece of created media loses its copyright after some time, and this chapter discusses this crucial point in some detail. A few works, such as open-source software programs, are created explicitly as public-domain items. In both cases, PD creations belong to the public at large, and any individual can freely copy or alter them. New music is almost never in the public domain.

and you've got a turbulent situation in which everybody is upset about something. The record labels are upset with the cavalier behavior of their customers, music consumers are upset that the record labels have been trying to inhibit technology, and the musicians are upset either with their labels or with their fans.

This chapter untangles much of the confusion and, I hope, helps you take a position in which your actions as a music consumer don't betray your ethics. This book is ethically neutral. Music copyright in the Internet age has become so disabled and unenforceable that every individual must strike a deal with his or her own conscience, either following the law literally, ignoring it completely, or claiming some position in the slippery middle ground. But first you have to know what copyright law actually says, and conversely, what your rights are within the law. This chapter delineates the strict legalities, then points to commonsense approaches to digital consumerism when those legalities seem to lose their meaning. Chapter 12 takes the discussion a step further by projecting present realities to future possibilities.

Socially Sanctioned Stealing

One of the most intriguing social questions of our time is this: Why do millions of law-abiding people, who would never dream of shoplifting a music CD, harbor illegally copied songs in their computers?

Part of the answer lies in simple human naivete. Most people are not experts in copyright law, and don't wish to be. The regulations that govern intellectual property use in the United States are complex and—perhaps more important—they are counterintuitive. Sharing music just doesn't *feel* immoral or illegal to many. Most people have been doing it by nondigital means for years, making compilation tapes for friends and even copying entire CDs onto tape as gifts. Sharing culture fulfills a human urge that is not addressed by legal constraints, which is why those constraints are widely ignored at the grassroots level that lies out of enforcement's reach. Furthermore, availability carries an air of legitimacy, and the sheer existence of freely downloadable music makes taking that music seem as innocent as plucking fruit from a tree.

But the trees are growing in a commercial orchard, and most people realize this to some extent, even if dimly. Naivete and the innocent urge to share don't explain everything at this stage of digital music, when its illegal aspects have gained so much notoriety. To some extent, people are downloading *despite* their awareness of basic copyright. The following all play into this phenomenon:

- **Taking something virtual doesn't seem like stealing.** Instinctively, all people operate with a bias toward the sanctity of physical property over virtual property. The existence of virtual property (a song, a newspaper article) separated from its physical conveyor (a CD, a newspaper) is still a relatively new idea to the average person. Furthermore, intellectual property by itself has no weight, heft, or visibility—the traditional property cues we rely on to distinguish ownership.

- **If the "store" is legal, the content must be legal.** Music file-sharing really took off with Napster, a freely available program provided by a legally operating U.S. business through legitimate Internet service providers. The company's legality was challenged, but not determined (as of the completion of this book), and it's difficult for some consumers to conceive of an illegal product offered through a legal company and accessed via aboveboard service providers. In fact, millions of AOL users hooked into Napster through the parent company (AOL Time Warner) of a major record label, which also owns one of the most popular MP3 playback programs (Winamp).

- **Access to hard-to-find music.** Many people dove into Napster—and continue to use its descendants—to acquire songs that are otherwise unavailable or buried in expensive compilations. In particular, older users tend to search file-sharing networks for backlist catalogs of oldies and other obscure music types. Usenet newsgroups are famously populated by folks sharing offbeat songs and albums.

- **Temptation and greed.** Never disregard the obvious. Unlimited free music delivers an intoxicating wallop of instant gratification with no price tag.

- **Sampling music that never would have been purchased anyway.** This might be called the "curiosity factor." In this sense, unauthorized downloading takes the place of radio as a method of discovering what's out there.

- **A ferocious ethic of free sharing that has underpinned the online community for at least twenty years.** The Internet is emblematic of free information, free entertainment, and free services of all kinds. Its pre-Web history was defined by free sharing. While the "Information wants to be free" attitude was dimmed by the dot-com crash and the increasing no-bull commercialism of the Web, an undertone of entitlement persists online and is reinforced by a few prominent, articulate voices.

- **A song is not an album.** To the extent that average folks are aware of music as property, that awareness is pinned on the music CD as the essential product increment. When you buy music in a store, you usually buy an entire CD. Downloading music from free-sharing networks normally transpires on a song-by-song basis, with the "product" separated from its album companion songs and artwork. Copyright applies to songs as stringently as to albums, but the "feel factor" comes into play again here: downloading a song doesn't feel as lawless as taking a CD.
- **The extra effort seems like the purchase price.** Downloading songs through KaZaA and Gnutella programs isn't brain surgery, but it's not a nap on the couch, either. Rightly or wrongly, people have an instinctive sense that they earn downloaded music through the effort of searching for, sorting, and archiving songs—not to mention tolerating rampant pop-up ads, misnamed files, poor encoding quality, and all the other drawbacks of unauthorized sharing. Furthermore, they are paying for access to the Internet in the first place.
- **Resentment toward record labels.** Unauthorized downloading is partly driven by consumer revenge. No entertainment industry is as ill-respected as the music CD industry. File-sharing gives consumers a vote against stubborn retail prices, flimsy jewel cases, top-down marketing that provides few choices, and albums containing eleven undesired songs wrapped around a single hit.
- **Explicit desire for change.** A small portion of the free-downloading community has a high awareness of copyright issues and the consolidated corporate ownership of entertainment. These people are attempting to hasten a new world order by deliberately damaging the status quo. To that end, they boycott CDs from the major labels and gleefully download their content.
- **People buy CDs after downloading songs.** Don't laugh. The use of file-sharing as a means of auditioning new music is more common than you might think.

These points represent some—but by no means all—of the rationalizations, conscious and unconscious, that I know with certainty contribute to the startling wave of illegal behavior sweeping through the marketplace of music consumers. This book doesn't endorse any justification for infringing copyright. But taken as a group, these points do represent what industry observers like to call a new paradigm in action, in which technology has enabled millions of people to act out their dissatisfaction with the status quo, and in so doing establish certain requisites of the next-generation music marketplace.

Weren't We Taught That Sharing Is Good?

It's human nature to both hoard and share. Some people also create art that's worth hoarding and sharing. Copyright is the fence dividing the creators from the consumers. The height and durability of that fence have changed over years, decades, and centuries. It is a mistake to believe that current copyright law is somehow God-given, that it hasn't evolved through legislative battles from substantially different versions, or that it can't change in the future.

American copyright started as an attempt to balance the protection of both creators and society's desire to share. Early copyright law was based on the understanding that creators are motivated to create by financial gain, and therefore need a period of exclusive ownership to sell their work outright, publish it, syndicate it, and market it in any way of their choosing. During that exclusive period, a creator retained sole privilege to sell the work to a publisher, performer, or syndicator, as well as the sole right to copy it for any reason whatsoever. It still works this way, but the exclusive period is much longer than it used to be, tilting the balance of protection toward the creator.

The need for copyright has always been driven by technology, and in particular the technology of copying. The invention of printing brought the need for regulation to the forefront—before the printing press, books and other documents were painstakingly difficult to copy. (Even today, the book publishing industry is relatively untroubled by bootlegging, because copying a book is so hard.) As commercial printers slowly proliferated in England during the sixteenth and seventeenth centuries, the economic rights of authors were protected by royal decrees. The Licensing Act of 1692 was the first highly organized effort to track authors' works and regulate their use, by establishing a book registry. However, this law was tainted by the state's power to censor registered books it disapproved of, and it was repealed within two decades.

It was Britain's Statute of Anne, enacted in 1710, that established con-

Copyright outside the United States

The economic protection of artists and performers is a political issue handled by each nation independently. At the same time, some international guidelines exist that regulate how created work originating in one country must be treated by other countries.

The first across-the-pond copyright agreement involving the United States was a reciprocal arrangement between America and Britain launched in 1875, eventually resulting in the more formal International Copyright Act of 1886. Adjustments have been made in the meantime. Today, changes to international copyright are considered and addressed by the World Intellectual Property Organization (WIPO).

cepts of copyright that are still viable today, including the term (duration) of copyright and a public domain into which works pass when the copyright term expires. The Statute of Anne provided the basis of U.S. copyright as defined in the Constitution. In America, the Copyright Act of 1790 put the issue at the federal level by giving Congress the power to "promote the progress of science and useful arts . . . by securing for limited times to authors and inventors the exclusive rights to their respective writings and discoveries." In this sense, the term *author* includes songwriters and composers. In music, a separate copyright category identifies a specific performance of composed music, and it is both the authorship and performance copyrights that are infringed by online bootlegging.

Through a series of American copyright reforms, the copyright term (the period during which creators enjoy exclusive ownership) has been extended again and again. At this writing, the Supreme Court has announced its intention to rule on the constitutionality of the recent Sonny Bono Copyright Term Extension Act, which lengthened corporate copyright terms to ninety-five years, and personal copyright terms to the life of the author plus seventy years—an extension of twenty years from previous terms in both cases.

Legal and Illegal Copying

Though historically interesting, the length of copyright term doesn't bear much weight on music downloading controversies, because most recorded music is fairly new and easily falls within existing terms. Currently, you can share a music recording legally only in three circumstances:

The Right Length of Copyright Terms

How long should copyright last? The question touches on philosophy, sociology, history, and law, and generates fierce arguments that tend to pit media holding companies against consumers, and copyright fundamentalists against libertarians.

Some voices in this field recommend rolling back the length of copyright terms, and indeed the Supreme Court might do just that when it revisits the most recent twenty-year extension. Lawrence Lessig, a prominent advocate of copyright reform, proposes renewable five-year terms. Copyright owners turn a scornful eye toward attempts to shorten their ownerships, with many people and companies believing that intellectual property is no less substantial than physical property. In that view, copyrights should never expire, any more than your house or clothes should become public property after a certain period of ownership.

America's founders, their descendants, and the international community generally support the principle that a balance must be struck between protecting creators and enriching society with open access to culture. Expiring copyrights give everybody free access to centuries of classical music, new novels featuring vintage characters like Sherlock Holmes, and other benefits of public domain—all at the expense of the authors' estates. It's a tricky balance with no obvious solution.

- playing your only copy while others are present;
- giving away your only copy or buying a new copy as a gift; and
- waiting until the copyright expires and the work becomes public domain.

Because of this basic no-duplication directive of copyright law, it is fundamentally illegal to make and distribute copies of music, even informally and without any financial gain, even when the copies are analog (not digital), even when the songs are "oldies"—yet all these activities have been occurring for decades. The strictness of copyright law might come as a surprise to some people who have been sharing music, with no ill intentions, since they were teenagers. Although it might not seem intuitive, copyright law does indeed forbid taping a CD to give to a friend (or copying it to a blank CD)—and the fact that you're not selling the copy has nothing to do with it. In fact, the time-honored and labor-intensive practice of making a compilation tape of songs from several albums, and giving it away, infringes copyright and is illegal.

Taping CDs and compilations is perfectly legal when done strictly for personal use. In fact, that activity is called "personal use" copying, and is protected by U.S. copyright law. As soon as the tape becomes somebody else's possession it crosses over to the dark side of the law. Naturally, these copyright regulations apply to digital copies in exactly the same way. Hence the furor caused by Napster and online song-swapping.

So were our parents wrong? Is sharing bad, at least when it comes to music? This is a tricky and hotly debated question, one that asks us to consider the difference between harmless copying that is technically illegal and illegal copying that is also damaging to creators and copyright holders. Understanding who *might* get damaged by unauthorized song-sharing is the first step in taking a personal stand for or against it. The following section explores who really owns all this melodious intellectual property.

Artists, Labels, and the Musical Food Chain

It's natural to think that a musician owns his or her music. After all, the musician created it, and copyright is meant to protect creators. In fact, artists, songwriters, producers, publishers, and record labels are tangled in a knot of

Personal Use and Fair Use

Though U.S. copyright regulations are broad in principle and strict in application, two exceptions provide a limited right to copy music: personal use and fair use. The two are sometimes confused.

Personal-use copying has no length limit, but it does restrict what can be done with a copy. The owner of a song or album recording may copy the entire thing for the purposes of "space-shifting" and "time-shifting." Copying a CD for playback in the car is an example of space-shifting. Taping a radio program for later listening is an example of time-shifting. In all such cases the copy cannot be given away, sold, or republished.

Fair-use copying enforces length restrictions rather than usage restrictions. First developed in the nineteenth century, and written into U.S. copyright law in 1976, the concept of fair use is still somewhat slippery. When push comes to shove, fair-use legal defenses must concentrate on a variety of criteria, but in most instances it is the length of the copy that holds sway. In music, any copy of a recorded piece that remains under thirty seconds is generally considered fair use. Even so, distribution of short music clips usually proceeds with the permission of the copyright owner.

Uploading versus Downloading: A Fine but Important Distinction

Over the last few years, many newspaper articles and TV news features have focused on "illegal downloading" of music. The phrase embodies a glib inaccuracy, sometimes furthered by the recording industry. It might seem like a small detail, but it is the *creation and uploading* of song copies that infringes copyright, not downloading them. It is the double act of copying and distributing (even to one other person) a song that crosses the legal line. Taking an unauthorized song copy (either by downloading it or by accepting a tape) is not actionable behavior (that is to say, it's technically legal).

Don't get too excited. First of all, legal distinctions don't necessarily correspond to moral distinctions, and participating in one end of a copyright-infringing system supports the other end. Also, when it comes to file-swapping networks, the line between giving and receiving is blurred by the programs that link you into those systems. These programs usually set up a so-called shared folder (see chapter 5) to hold downloaded music, and the contents of that folder are automatically exposed to the system and made available to other users. It's always possible to change the default settings and isolate downloaded music, or, in some cases, to prohibit all uploads from occurring out of your computer. But the design of these systems, and the most common application of them, combines giving and receiving into an undistinguished loop of sharing, making it very easy to redistribute downloaded music without even knowing it.

contractual obligations so labyrinthine as to practically defy coherence.

To simplify the situation, it's safe to say that recorded music is mostly owned by record labels, with the artist owning a minority stake in every recorded product. This balance of ownership certainly applies to almost all mainstream music marketed by major labels. The label's role in producing the music we hear is basically threefold:

- to discover and sign musicians;
- to fund recording and CD manufacturing; and
- to promote the CD product by acquiring radio airplay, mounting performance tours, and otherwise advertising the artist.

In exchange for the cost of developing talent and creating a product, labels get most of the product revenue. The business model here is similar to that of other publishing fields: the artist gets an advance against future royalties. And, as in other publishing fields, most of the money, success, and power is concentrated at the very top of a pyramid, as labels attempt to maximize a few successes that ultimately pay for a great many failures.

Most musicians make sacrifices to participate in this business, most notably the copyright to their music, which is owned by the label. (Big, big stars like the Rolling Stones or Bruce Springsteen hold the copyright to their music and license their recordings to the labels, but this is hardly the norm.) Of course, they gain a lot too, most significantly the resources of a large corporation willing to create a good product and test it in the market-place. Even failures can be short-term success stories for the musicians who receive hefty advances for CDs that don't sell. At the same time, there exists raucous and intensifying discontent among recording artists, even among star musicians who have the most to gain from the success pyramid. The Recording Arts Coalition (RAC) exists to raise awareness for the founder-ing rights of musicians signed to major-label contracts.

Musicians are divided on the issue of online distribution. Several high-profile artists and bands publicly praised or expressed benign interest in Napster, including Courtney Love (a ragingly outspoken critic of record companies) and Limp Bizkit (which accepted Napster's sponsorship of its "Back to Basics" tour in 2000). Of course, outspoken musicians on the other side of the fence (Dr. Dre, Metallica) savaged Napster. Many musicians even withhold permission from their label to participate in authorized music subscription plans Pressplay and MusicNet, forcing those services to remove certain albums and tracks from the catalog and further slowing con-sumer acceptance of those subscriptions.

Consider, too, that every piece of recorded music represents both a com-poser and a performer. They might and might not be the same person or people. Different revenue-collection agencies track and distribute royalty payments to those two types of musician. While the sanity-defying tangle of artist and label payments has been worked out for CD sales, distributing individual songs online, unhooked from the CD, presents horrendous prob-lems in bookkeeping and paying.

The Gray Area of Recording Internet Radio

Recording media streamed into the home, for personal use, is perfectly legal in the United States under the Audio Home Recording Act of 1992. Thus protected, many people use VCRs and cassette recorders to time-shift TV and radio programs. When it comes to Internet streams, though, the legality of recording becomes problematic and is disputed on several fronts.

If computer recording were as linear as tape recording, perhaps there would be no controversy. But innovative software like Streamripper and Bitbop can go far beyond merely documenting a streamed program from start to finish. Roaming through the playlist databases at the source of streaming stations, searching for individual artists and songs, separating streamed songs into distinct files complete with accurate filenames, and other creative possibilities are a breeze for stream-recording software. Such programs deliver recorded music with a specificity and ease that rival file-sharing networks. While the process is quite different, the result is similar: local storage of unauthorized song copies.

Streamripper and Bitbop have both faced preliminary challenges to their operation, and have been partially disabled or sidelined at the time of this book's publication. Time will tell how this struggle develops. In the meantime, any listener can make a digital recording of an Internet stream using recording features found in Media Jukebox and Musicmatch, both described in chapter 9. Those programs enable the separation of songs into distinct files, but those files are not identified, named, or tagged with artist and track information. Beyond that pointer, I cannot be more explicit about this or any other gray-area use of software. Check with this book's Web site (www.digitalsongstream.com) for updates.

Are File-Sharing Networks Illegal?

As of this book's publication, no file-sharing technology, specific network, or company operating a network has received a definitive legal ruling that defines the legality of file-sharing tools. This might seem surprising considering that Napster, Madster, and KaZaA were driven out of business (and the first two driven out of operation) by litigation. But those three bankruptcies halted legal proceedings against the companies before a ruling could be handed down. Napster was forced to cease operations almost a year before its bankruptcy filing by court injunctions defining how it was required to operate, but its right to operate a file-sharing network within those requirements was not prohibited.

The Digital Millennium Copyright Act, enacted in 1998 to address certain issues of electronic distribution and virtual property, protects online services under a "safe harbor" section. Safe harbor removes initial liability from the service provider when its users break the law. In the case of file-sharing, the network is protected by safe harbor when its users make unauthorized uploads and downloads of copyrighted music. However, safe harbor has a limit, and the service's responsibility kicks in when a copyright holder complains of infringement. So, if a record label complains to the file-sharing network that copyrighted music is being transmitted without permission, the service must remove or disable access to the infringing music. This is pretty much how Napster's case proceeded, and it turned out that blocking content that existed concurrently on millions of individual hard drives was difficult to accomplish, and Napster was forced out of business.

If disabling the competition were that easy, the media companies would be less hysterical over file-sharing than they are. Napster was fairly easy to shut down because it was an American company with a somewhat centralized service. Its descendants are technologically more protected through a wily level of decentralization that can make a file-sharing network difficult to shut down even when ordered to. To make matters more pernicious, some companies running the new networks are incorporated in Europe and the Pacific islands, at a remove from U.S. copyright jurisdiction. The final straw is an open-source network like Gnutella or FreeNet, unowned by any entity that a plaintiff can get its hands on, thoroughly decentralized, and basically unstoppable whether technically legal or not.

While the networks operate in a legal gray area, individuals do not. This is the central, bracing upshot for online consumers. Like using a legally registered car to run a red light, unauthorized file-sharing uses legal Internet service providers to infringe copyright. In both cases, the individual is accountable. Granted, the record labels have not taken the step of suing an individual for sharing music online, although some of their advocates have urged them to do so. The day might come when we see an individual dragged into court by a multinational media conglomerate. But until then, each online music consumer must decide whether file-sharing is conscionable and damaging.

Consumer Sentiment

There is no question about it, average people harbor an unusual degree of ill will toward record companies. Part of the animosity derives from the unchanging price of CDs even as the cost of making them has reduced to pennies per unit. (Actually, CD prices have resisted inflation well, and discs that deliver years of pleasure are a bargain compared to more expensive and ephemeral entertainment products.) The massive consolidation of media holdings, resulting in top-down cultural choices such as boring radio and formulaic music production, likewise alienates customers from a business that has traditionally thrived on a personal relationship between artist and listener. Then there is the indefensible stubbornness with which media companies have refused to meet (or been unable to understand) consumer demand for new distribution channels that leverage mainstream Internet technology. As this book is published, the labels appear no closer to realistic efforts in that direction than they were five years before, when MP3 was unleashed as a consumer-friendly audio format.

This last point is particularly galling, and motivates rampant civil disobedience of copyright. Given a choice between political principle and technology, a free market will always choose the gadgets—especially when adopted technology delivers a greater supply of beloved culture. Speaking broadly, refusing to meet customer demand is a suicidal business practice, and it's no surprise that the record labels sometimes feel close to doom. At the same time, though, emerging studies reveal that the labels' strangled death rattle might be disingenuous, or at least glib. In mid-2002 an extensive study by Jupiter Media Metrix, a highly respected analysis company specializing in online behavior patterns, revealed that music file-sharing might actually *increase* the likelihood of CD purchasing. Many experienced observers of the digital distribution space found this result completely plausible, as P2P networks make superlative audition tools but poor mechanisms for delivering high-quality music files. Naturally, the Recording Industry Association of America (RIAA) disdained the study, but its own surveys often seem painfully undocumented compared to the scientific rigor that goes into a Jupiter Media Metrix investigation.

At any rate, the point is that the RIAA and its member labels suffer rock-bottom credibility with consumers in general, and particularly with online-savvy listeners. The more the labels scorn their customers as criminals, the more those customers continue to use underground technology while patiently explaining in survey after survey that they would gladly pay for authorized versions if they existed. And the more the labels float heinously inconvenient and ill-informed services like Pressplay and MusicNet (see chapter 4), or release copy-protected CDs that constrain personal-use rights, the more consumers tune out their entire anti-technology agenda.

12

The Future of Digital Music

Although the recording industry was born in the late nineteenth century, two major players dominated the two most common record formats: Edison, who released his recordings first on cylinders and then on vertical-cut discs, and Victor, who owned the rights to lateral cut discs, which by the 1910s had become the most popular format. Anyone who wanted to release records that would play on Victor's proprietary machines (known as Victrolas) had to pay the company a licensing fee. In 1919 the small independent label Gennett decided to challenge Victor's monopoly, and refused to pay the fee. In a foreshadowing of today's litigious climate, Gennet was sued by Victor. However, Gennett's lawyers discovered an earlier copyright that predated Victor's ownership claim, and won the lawsuit. From that point forward, the recording industry grew by leaps and bounds, unfettered by Victor's stranglehold on the technology.

A year later, David Sarnoff began pushing RCA into commercial radio broadcasting. Pittsburgh's KDKA received the first government-assigned call letters and launched the first on-air programming one hour a day. So, as the Roaring Twenties began, commercial records and radio arose at about the same time. To this day, over eighty years later, the push-pull of priced and free music, product-based and service-based business models, continues.

The Internet has proved an upsetting force, weakening the once supreme synergy of broadcast radio and per-unit sales of recorded music. The Net has driven a wedge between consumers and the music industry in two major ways:

- Webcasted music (Internet radio) gives listeners one-click access to thousands of alternative programmers around the world, rendering the geographic limitation of "terrestrial" broadcasting, and its corporate-controlled playlists, dated anachronisms.
- Effortless global distribution of recorded material at the grassroots level (file-sharing) peels the music from the disc and generally reduces the value of per-unit sales.

Apocalyptic thinkers believe that these forces represent a wrecking ball that has already crashed through the media world as we know it and destroyed any legitimate marketplace for commercial music. Captains of the media industries wish to save the day by rolling back the clock through litigation and government regulation, clamping down on technology and teaching those pesky music-loving consumers how to behave. Apologists believe that what is good for consumers is good for business in the long run, and hope for new revenue models that will capitalize on a high-volume, liquid world of instant digital media. What paths forward are emerging from the angry divides of the present? Which ones seem best lit by both history and a realistic assessment of the moment? How painful will this transition be for record labels, musicians, and consumers? What will life for everyone involved in music be like in two, five, and ten years?

Naturally, this chapter is the most speculative part of this book. It is informed by daily discussions among the most immersed professionals in the business: journalists, lawyers, CEOs of digital music companies, label executives, and the nuts-and-bolts geeks who rewire our lives. But the explicit conclusions and forecasts in this chapter, for better or worse, are mine.

The Triple Meaning of Free Music

Although many disagree, it is my view that digital music is not primarily about free music; it is about convenience and access.

However, there is no question that free music file-sharing publicized the MP3 format and pushed digital music from society's fringe toward the mainstream. Napster was the most vigorously adopted music technology in history, becoming more quickly popular than player pianos, sheet music, the phonograph, and the compact disc. As discussed in chapter 5, Napster's siren song played to a melody of availability and immediacy, in addition to the absence of price stickers. More than one study quantified that its users regarded unpriced music as a third priority, behind great selection and easy downloading access, and would have been willing to pay a monthly subscription price to use an authorized service built on the same foundation. In light of this consumer sentiment, the word *free* takes on an ironic triple meaning:

- liberated from the vaults of unavailable music;
- emancipated from the disc and CD player; and
- free of charge.

The first two meanings point to the future more assuredly than the third. The availability of rare music, and the untethering of all music from the disc, have to some extent already been accomplished, in both authorized and unauthorized music services. And while file-sharing has increased the scope of informal music bootlegging, price-free music is undesirable for everybody and untenable in the long run despite its giddy short-term attraction. Even without thinking too deeply about the business of music, it's obvious that a total lack of consumer dollars would drive out the best (or at least the most ambitious) creative talent, collapse all commercial distribution, and eliminate the considerable benefits of an orderly marketplace. There is little precedent for it. A strong tendency toward commercialization has sustained the many phases of the Western music industry for over four hundred years.

In all eras, there is a correspondence between the three aspects of music freedom: accessibility, flexibility, and inexpensiveness. When the release of music is tightly controlled and constrained in format (by decision or the natural limits of technology), it tends to be expensive. This formula is mere supply and demand. When the New York Philharmonic Orchestra plays a symphony in its concert hall, it is practicing the most tightly controlled and inflexibly formatted distribution of its music possible. Only a couple of thousand people will ever hear that performance, and they must physically get to Lincoln Center in Manhattan. Accordingly, the ticket prices are high—much higher than when buying a symphonic performance by the same musicians in wider distribution through more formats.

If the orchestra recorded that performance, it could be released in music stores around the world (greater access) on CDs and cassettes (more flexibility), and also sold to classical-radio syndicators (more access and extendibility). The resulting mix of prices would drive the average "ticket" cost of the performance sharply down, balanced by a much higher volume of sales and reliance on other revenue sources, such as advertising.

Now imagine that the doors of accessibility and flexibility are thrown wide open by new technology. (In fact, they have been.) That recorded performance can be perfectly copied by any moderately equipped computer user at home, and exposed to file-sharing networks where anyone searching for the New York Philharmonic, or the composer, or merely the word *symphony*, is likely to find the copy and possibly download it. With ultimate access and flexibility, the price is reduced ultimately as well—to zero.

The inverse formula of low access and low flexibility corresponding to high price is the basis of all music industry. (Indeed, it is a basis of all media industry and to some extent all industry, but let's not get too far afield.) Record labels exist partly to control the distribution and the formatting of music, thus keeping control of its price, and they have recently lost some of that control. Hence the uncertain call of the future, which, as always, seeks to accommodate both business needs and consumer demand for greater access and flexibility.

The Threat and the Threatened

Glib futurists can be heard saying that record companies are doomed, and that copyright is an obsolete cultural regulation. Both forecasts, while too simple, do contain cores of present-day reality.

Record labels are in the business of making copies—a rather mundane activity, when you think about it. Of course, copy-making isn't their only business. Labels also scout for talent, sign artists, invest in careers, fund and manufacture recordings, arrange distribution, fulfill orders, and publicize music. But the essential asset of the recording industry is copyright: the exclusive prerogative to make copies of a product. Record labels are incubators and warehousers of copyright, and they thrive when the occasional product creates so much demand that the label's copies rise in value. Accordingly, the label's ability to restrict supply is crucial.

Two disruptive inventions have drastically devalued the business of copying. Writeable CDs and CD-RW drives are one; they make possible the perfect replication of albums, without any generational loss. The other is file-sharing, which makes restriction of supply artificial and irrelevant. When the business of music copying is devalued, copyright itself is devalued, and that's exactly what industry and government are both facing.

Following this, it's easy to say that record labels are threatened to extinction. But a larger historical lesson is that ownership of musical property is always a viable basis of commerce. The question is not whether copyright should exist (it should) or whether music ownership can be commercial in the future (it always can be). The question is how to profitably distribute music assets through existing technology. That is always the question, whether the technology environment includes player pianos, sheet music, phonographs, broadcast radio, compact discs, or the Internet. The popular fixation on the Internet as uniquely threatening is merely the arrogance of the present moment, which always seems more consequential than the past.

To that end—capitalizing on modern technology—the record companies haven't even tried. If they were to die off tomorrow, one would have to attribute their extinction more to peevishness than technology. If the multinational corporations that own most recorded music could be granted a magic wish, it would probably be to turn back the clock and climb back into the womb of the 1980s and early 1990s. Virtually all major-label responses to digital music, from futile lawsuits to unrealistic subscription services, have represented an attempt to regain lost control of the supply of music.

Consumer adoption of technology is pushing media corporations in certain easily discernible directions, in both the short term and the long term. The initial panicky, reactive phase will continue for some period as everyone—labels, legislators, judges, musicians—comes to grips with new realities. The media companies have launched initiatives that will take some time to play out, in three main arenas:

- copy-protection;
- litigation; and
- lobbying for governmental regulation.

The following sections explore trends in these three areas.

The Future of Copy Protection

It is a natural reaction, when robbed, to install new locks. The record industry must be ruing the day it embraced the digital CD, with its unsecured music files that didn't seem to pose any threat at the time. Now that those files can easily be removed from the discs and shared rampantly online, the labels are trying to bolt them down with software locks. Copy-protected discs were first introduced in 2001 in limited releases, and as this book nears publication the trend is gaining industry support and momentum.

Two major issues arise with copy-protected CDs. The first is that they cannot truly be considered CDs, according to Royal Philips Electronics and Sony Electronics, which jointly control the CD technical specifications, trademark, and logo. Copy-protected CDs perform in such a defective manner—crashing some computers during normal playback, refusing to work at all in some CD players, and manifesting other bad behaviors—that the two companies disavowed any connection to them. The one unassailable benefit of commercial music CDs, namely the foolproof convenience of universal playback throughout the entire installed base of CD players, is disastrously abandoned with copy-protected discs.

Second, the security built into the first rounds of copy-protected discs removed their owners' lawful right to digital copying for personal use. That right is not mandated by copyright law, but it is preserved—which is to say that record labels are not *required* to provide unencumbered personal copying in all formats, but they are bound to infuriate a lot of people if they don't. To their credit, the media companies clearly label copy-protected discs as such, and prepare retail stores to accept higher numbers of returns.

A less quantifiable but no less realistic issue is that copy protection is utterly futile. Promoting these defective products betrays the labels' miscalculation of technology's reach, an underestimation of renegade ingenuity, and a misunderstanding of the viral nature of file-sharing. First of all, anything that can be played can be digitally copied. That central, irrefutable principle would be more productively accommodated than resisted. Second, it doesn't matter if 95 percent of unauthorized track duplication is eliminated, or even 99 percent. Content spreads online with ferocious speed and insatiable replicative zeal. Consider the Gnutella protocol (see chapter 5), which was posted by one person for a mere few hours before the door was slammed, yet nonetheless became an open-source movement of juggernaut proportions. One unauthorized song copy exposed to a file-sharing network (Gnutella, perhaps) can become ten, and a thousand, and potentially millions—within days.

Nevertheless, record labels will continue to tempt fate and taunt their customers with copy-protected discs (and online files as described in chapter 4's survey of music subscriptions) as a stubborn statement of principle. The latest word, as this book nears publication, is that research and development of copy-protected music CDs is continuing, and that a less troublesome version will eventually appear on the shelves.

The majors would be relieved to move the marketplace away from CDs entirely, and that's the thrust of new disc formats like DataPlay and Super

Audio Compact Disc (SACD). While each of these new formats conveys improvements in audio fidelity (SACD) or file storage (DataPlay), the real benefit for record labels is that they are copy protected. However, consumers might not be willing to adopt a new format and engage in the wholesale replacement of current music collections, as transpired in the migration from LP to CD.

The Future of Litigation

When Napster was sued by the big five record labels, and soon thereafter discontinued its service, most casual observers counted it a victory for the labels. Then, in 2002, KaZaA BV, the Dutch company that invented the popular KaZaA file-sharing network and was later sued by an alliance of movie studios and record companies, collapsed under the weight of the suit, going out of business—another apparent victory for the media ownership.

But two difficulties taint these victories. First, file-sharing technology cannot be litigated out of existence, even in the fondest daydreams of media lobbyists. Napster's demise merely spawned a new field of networks, cumulatively more trafficked than Napster ever was. And KaZaA's network had already been sold to another company (Sharman Networks), which reincorporated in a South Pacific island as protection from copyright regulations. The KaZaA network continued operating without so much as a blink.

A second problem with premature ends to these lawsuits involves the lack of established precedent. The labels are squashing companies, but they are not getting rulings. The Napster case was turning for the worse (at least from the labels' point of view) as its judge began investigating the labels' alleged antitrust behavior as vigorously as she was examining Napster's copyright compliance. Madster, another song-sharing service, was under the gun until it declared bankruptcy, bringing that suit to a skidding halt. Then KaZaA's corporate collapse left that case undecided in American courts, after a Dutch court actually ruled in favor of KaZaA's continued operation, pronouncing that while its users might be infringing copyright, the network itself was a neutral service provider. So, the only concrete adjudication to come from all this litigation that could be carried forward in court was a non-American ruling (and European copyright rules are generally stricter than those in America) that upheld one file-sharing network's right to continue operating.

Courtroom battles will continue, and so will unauthorized file-sharing networks. The only answer to reducing the popularity of such networks is to build more attractive alternatives. The renegade networks have a lot wrong with them in the usability department, so the labels have a window of opportunity. But if the labels don't start building into this globe-spanning technology, claiming leadership in doing it right, some new virtual technology company incorporated on an unreachable island will make the essential improvements first, illicitly and unstoppably. Then the game will really be lost.

The Future of Industry Lobbying

Increasingly, media companies are turning to the United States Congress for support in a battle that seems to pit copyright interests against technology interests. Traditionally, the government has been sympathetic to the lobbying agenda of copyright industries, most notably extending ownership durations far beyond the original mandate of copyright regulations.

In early 2001, Senator Fritz Hollings promoted a bill called the Security Systems Standards and Certification Act (SSSCA), the broad outline of which would mandate copy-protection systems built into every piece of hardware that could play any type of media: including computers, portable music players, Palm Pilots, and much more. The bill was launched in April of that year under a different name: the Consumer Broadband and Digital Television Promotion Act (CBDTPA). The Recording Industry Association of America, the Motion Picture Association of America, and individual media companies lauded the bill as forward-thinking and responsible lawmaking. The hardware and telecommunications industries savaged the proposed legislation.

Two main problems arise when considering government-mandated copy protection, and they are the same two problems that confound copy-protected CDs: copy protection constrains personal copyright, and it doesn't work anyway. It seems incredible that media owners haven't yet learned that copy protection of all types is routinely broken and tossed aside in short order. One mocking example of this truism was revealed in May 2002, when published reports revealed that Sony's expensive, high-tech copy protection used on certain music CDs could be disabled using nothing more sophisticated than a marking pen on certain portions of the disc.

Furthermore, the installed base of machines and devices that are unencumbered by copy protection is so enormous and pervasive that attempting to lighten its density by introducing new, unattractive consumer products is sheer folly. And that is exactly what the hardware and telecom companies fear: that consumers won't purchase hobbled machinery that misfires as badly as copy-protected CDs, thereby slowing the growth of technology sectors and the adoption of broadband connection services.

Intensive lobbying is a perennial characteristic of transition periods in which technology rocks the boat. The likely outcome of Congress's threatened involvement in setting technical standards is faster negotiation between conflicting industries, and off-the-books agreements that appease realistic needs of copyright owners while allowing technology to proceed.

Technology Takes the Lead

The most fervent technology advocates sometimes seem to rail against the status quo simply for the sake of a good rant. There is good reason to side with technology, though, when it seems that the status quo is taking up arms against it. For centuries, in many fields and certainly in the leisure industries, technology has held the power of initiative, driving consumer demand for new ways of purchasing entertainment. In free-market societies, consumer demand usually wins, and consumers generally want easier, more abundant, cheaper culture. In the long run, it so often turns out, a win for consumers turns into a win for everybody.

The baseball industry once faced a business crisis similar to that faced by record labels today. When television threatened to encroach on the game, carrying it directly (and free of charge) into the home, team owners screamed that their revenues—based on ticket sales—would collapse. Television seemed to threaten the owners' control of the game's access and format constraints (live attendance and radio listenership) and devalue the product. Very few visionaries, if any, foresaw a time when (as now) television licensing would provide a primary revenue source to baseball teams. The status quo was dedicated to making a bit of money from each consumer—baseball's version of CD sales. Unforeseeable as it might have been, baseball did shift from a local, low-traffic entertainment product to a global, high-traffic product of unimagined prosperity.

Closer to music, the movie industry was confounded by the appearance of VCRs in 1977, and as home taping grew popular the film business began worrying over the possible devaluation of its film properties. The situation differed from baseball's confrontation with TV, which transformed the game from an exhibition product to a hybrid live-broadcast product. In the case of movies, home recording threatened to devalue the aftermarket of an exhibition industry—namely, licensing of movies to television networks. If a family could tape one TV broadcast of a movie and archive it, future broadcasts (with their unskippable commercials) would suffer reduced market value.

Panic over new technology always obscures the lessons of history. Selected quotes from 1982 Congressional testimony of Jack Valenti, then and now the president of the Motion Picture Association of America (MPAA), recalls industry fear over new VCR technology:

> this property that we exhibit in theaters . . . is going to be so eroded in value by the use of these unlicensed machines, that the whole valuable asset is going to be blighted. In the opinion of many of the people in this room and outside of this room, blighted, beyond all recognition. . . .
>
> We are going to bleed and bleed and hemorrhage, unless this Congress at least protects one industry . . . whose total future depends on its protection from the savagery and the ravages of this machine. . . .
>
> I say to you that the VCR is to the American film producer and the American public as the Boston strangler is to the woman home alone.

In 2001, just over 1 billion prerecorded VHS and DVD products (movies plus music videos) were shipped into the marketplace. Jack Valenti's sky didn't fall after all; to the contrary, the secondary markets for movies have become so vibrant that many releases skip theatrical exhibition entirely and go straight to store shelves. As with baseball, the encroaching and evil Goliath turned into an unforeseeably beneficent Santa Claus.

In the suddenly challenged music business, what present-day rhetoric will seem as faulty in twenty years? What new market mechanics might develop to make current fears seem, in retrospect, like the mere petulance of an industry being forced to become more prosperous?

Toward an Unconstrained Future

The tectonic concussions that seem to be shaking the music industry are not illusory. The loss of control is real. Record labels can no longer restrict the accessibility and flexibility of music with any legitimacy. In attempting to do so, media companies are leaning on unenforceable copyright regulations. It is undeniably frightening for the labels to lose their grip on the business of making copies. The silver lining is that with a virtual, instantly transferable product comes an unlimited marketplace—one that is probably willing to pay for music that meets modern standards of accessibility and flexibility.

The essential characteristic of liberated media is liquidity. No longer needing to be packaged in earthbound, metallic containers, music as data resembles more a river than a stack of containers. Music labels are deeply involved in the supposition that an orderly marketplace cannot sell a liquid product. But nothing stops people from bottling water in all sorts of shapes, sizes, and marketing models. It's worth noting that multinational Coca-Cola, facing a decline of its core product, turned to new formulations that could diversify its previously single-tracked revenue stream. (Coke was *it*.) As fate would have it, bottled water (Dasani is Coca Cola's brand) turned out to generate higher profit margins than more complicated soda formulations.

Regarding music as a natural resource is absolutely abhorrent to media companies. But if they can eventually regard technology as a natural resource, the industry's developmental bog can be broken open. Technological tools to commercialize the digital songstream exist right now, and have for some time. If those tools, and the minds and companies that develop them, were liberated to the same extent as music has been, a bright future would emerge to the unfathomed benefit of consumers, musicians, and copyright owners. The following sections sketch the touchstones of that possible future.

Compulsory Music Licensing

It sounds dry, tedious, and irrelevant, but the lack of compulsory licensing has stopped legitimate digital music in its tracks. Compulsory licensing enables technological development by requiring content owners to negotiate in good faith with distribution channels that need attractive content. The exact parameters of "good faith" differ among industries; in some cases, licensing terms are set by law as Webcasting royalty rates were in mid-2002. (In those cases, the resulting, free-floating license is called a statutory license.) The cardinal point is that content copyright owners cannot hoard all the attractive content for themselves, which would constitute antitrust behavior. That's the hot water that was starting to create a steamy situation for the major labels in the Napster case, because Napster had gotten nowhere trying to license major-label songs for its service, while the big labels used their content to launch the competing services Pressplay and MusicNet.

Imagine if every brilliant tech startup, every good online service idea, were able to test the market with major-label music content, paid for under terms reached in a reasonable period that did not drain the company's resources in fruitless negotiations. Instead of a subscription environment in which each service is essentially identical to the others—all defective in the same general ways—there would be a constant stream of innovation similar to the development of the World Wide Web, in which information and certain services were liquified much as music has been.

Abundant Access to the Catalog of Recorded Music

While an amazing amount of new music is recorded and marketed each year, even more amazing is how much retired music is unavailable, or available in unsatisfactory packages. The difficulty in finding the beloved songs of youth, for example, drives the surprising adoption of file-sharing networks among the Boomer generation. Bundling a few songs into Time-Life CD compilations and their ilk is a painfully unsuitable marketing strategy in a digital age, and consumers know it. There is no reason for copyright owners to give away that music—and likewise no reason not to make money by creating channels of unprecedented access to individual songs.

The music catalog is about to undergo a redefinition. No longer does it imply a *current* catalog, as distinguished from a *past* catalog. All recorded music can be digitized and added to the stream. Only when it *is* added can it be packaged imaginatively, in formats and increments that people want to pay for.

The Reign of Single Songs

The music industry was built on singles, but marketed through more expensive albums. The album loses its coherence in the digital songstream, and this should be a cause for some celebration in all camps. All albums are compilations, and that's a useful but one-dimensional marketing format. Why shouldn't the miscellaneous single—perhaps a remarkable concert performance, or studio jam that didn't make the CD—be commercialized to an audience eager to get specialty products from a popular band? Even more to the point, why shouldn't a hit single be marketed by itself, without the encumbrance of an entire album that raises the retail price but slows sales?

If unauthorized file-sharing has taught the music industry a single lesson, it is that a mighty market exists for single songs. From Napster's first day to the present, file-sharing has been a lousy method of obtaining whole albums, and a superlative method of grabbing songs. The album might not be dead (yet), but a giant untapped marketplace stands ready to receive digitally marketed, online-distributed singles. As with any stream, the rushing river of digital media tends to break obstacles into smaller pieces, and that's what will happen to the large, ungainly song album.

Digitization of Ownership and Payment

Music is owned twice: primarily by the copyright owner, and just as substantially by the consumer who licenses a personal copyright with every purchase. An essential key to the digitally fluid future is universal, specific tracking of who owns what at both ends of that equation.

Recorded-music rights are complicated, involving composers, performers, producers, and manufacturers. It is this very complication that slows the development of digital music marketplaces, even among progressive and willing record labels. Building a universal database of all music rights pertaining to the entire recorded catalog is a tremendously daunting proposition. But the benefit would be so sensationally liberating, and so galvanizing of commercial potential, that the enterprise seems inevitable. Even now, song-identification systems are operating (as described in chapter 2), that instantly pinpoint a song or album when ripping a CD in any Internet-connected computer. Extrapolate a bit from that preexisting tracking system and imagine a next-generation file-sharing network that can identify every download and assign payment to the appropriate parties. No longer would unauthorized distribution be a problem, because *every* distribution could be tracked and accounted for. With the job of marketing and distributing music placed in the hands of those most suited to the job—music fans—viral marketing would lose its negative connotation and benefit all creators in a completely meritocratic system.

Corollaries to universal tracking are transparent payment systems (the best file-sharing services will always *feel* free, even if they are not in fact free), and a system of revenue distribution as accurate as the ownership database. Any such system would be a tremendous improvement over the artist agencies that currently approximate and distribute royalties. It is also essential to make the entire system easy to enter, so that independent musicians can participate in the songstream through an equal-opportunity registration system. Ideally, with all music registered, and with all consumers drinking from the same media stream (or many streams operating according to compatible standards), the current top-down enforcement of music culture would be wholly reversed. Hits and stars would be created as they should be, from the bottom up, reflecting the mandate of consumer preference, not the marketing boardroom.

Celestiality in Action

Rudimentary attempts to create this ideal musical universe have been thwarted by technical and legal obstacles, not least of which is a recording industry hoping to preserve the traditional system of enforced scarcity and attachment of music to physical discs. Progress toward the ideally transparent, universal system of legal music access must proceed along several lines at once: enormous databases of copyright data must be built, licensing standards must be agreed upon, and massive format conversions must be accomplished. Above all, an unprecedented level of cooperation among copyright holders must be forged, which might be the most unlikely exigency of all. The industry's alternative, though, is increasingly rampant use of unauthorized file-sharing networks, which provide a certain "celestial jukebox" experience that consumers have gotten used to.

Twenty years from now, the music industry will appear quite different, and will probably be more prosperous than ever—perhaps even facing its next technology shakeup. The only alternative to industry change is suffocating technology regulation. Such a development seems unlikely on the basis of historical precedent alone, and also because this particular technology—the global Internet—transcends the regulatory reach of any government.

The current transition is as painful as any other for an established industry forced to think in new ways. But, as the Borg say, resistance is futile. All the litigation, all the lobbying, all the attacks on personal-use copyright, all the wheedling and whining to the press, every agitated reinforcement of the status quo—this is not really a defense of copyright or legal principle. It is all meant to fortify a business model—nothing more. And while the CD-copying business is under assault, the larger business of copyright ownership has never appeared brighter. Demand for music is incredibly strong. The liquification of music's formats will, in the hindsight of ten or twenty years, seem like the best possible development in an industry ripe for change.

For music-lovers on the consuming end, the golden days begin right now, even with the frustrations of label-provided services. The selection has never been better, the field has never been more level, the products have never been more portable, the gratification has never been more instantaneous. New trends have been seeded in fertile soil, and the future is poised to bring a flowering of cultural access and empowerment.

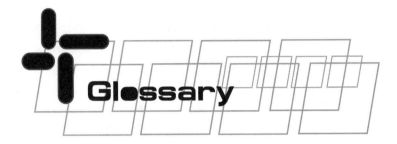

Glossary

Application: Any computer program that accomplishes a task. Applications can be desktop music players, CD labelers, file-sharing clients, the programs that access music subscriptions, and many other types. Music files such as MP3 songs are not applications.

Bandwidth: Capacity for transferring data from one computer to another. High-speed Internet connections provide more bandwidth than low-speed ones, allowing faster downloading of music files, and higher fidelity of Internet **streams**.

Beta: Preliminary, unofficial version of a program or service. Programs "in beta" are sometimes available to consumers on a preview, no-guarantee basis.

Bit rate: Number of data bits recorded, per second, in a digital audio recording. The higher the bit rate, the better (higher fidelity) the recording. Most MP3s are encoded at a bit rate of 128kbps (kilobits per second). MP3 encoders (rippers) let you set higher, lower, and **variable bit rates**.

Broadband: High-speed networking. Broadband Internet connections in the home are mostly cable modems and DSL lines. At the industrial level, broadband is usually implemented by T1 and T3 lines. As a general term, *broadband* refers to any networking connection that passes data substantially faster than telephone modems, and quickly enough to smoothly stream music and video.

Buffer: Type of data storage space. Internet music **streams** use a buffer to prevent interruption, just as CD players use a buffer to prevent skipping. After initiating a music stream, you can usually see the song or program "buffering" for a few seconds before playback starts.

Burn: To record data on a compact disc, by dragging files (as with a floppy disc) or using music software to create an audio CD. A burned CD may contain any type of computer file, but in the context of digital music a "burned CD" usually means either an audio CD or an MP3 CD.

Cable modem: High-speed modem connected to a household's cable-TV line, and to a computer. Cable modems provide download speed about ten times faster than the swiftest **dial-up** modems.

Cache: A portion of memory set aside for storing data used repeatedly. A cache may exist on a hard drive or in RAM memory. Web browsers deploy caches to store graphics and other elements of Web pages, in order to quicken loading during repeat visits. The Windows operating system establishes a hard drive cache as part of its normal operation, using it to store chunks of data that don't fit into RAM memory. Occasionally, an online music service creates a cache to store elements of the service.

CD burner: CD player that also can record music and other files on blank compact discs (**CD-R** and **CD-RW**). CD burners are typically built into modern computers, and are also available as stand-alone devices.

CD, audio and data: Audio CDs, such as those purchased in a music store, are playable in standard hi-fi CD players and computer CD players. Data CDs contain non-CDA files (the type of file on a standard audio CD). Data CDs can hold MP3 files, WMA files, or any other type of music or nonmusic computer file. Note that audio CDs are—technically speaking—data CDs as well, containing CDA files.

CDA file: Standard file type on audio CDs, playable in music CD players. Technically, the format is called CDDA, and renamed as CDA by the Windows operating system to make it recognizable by the computer.

CD-R: Recordable compact disc. Unlike the **CD-RW**, CD-Rs cannot be erased. Once burned, though, CD-Rs can be used in a wider range of devices than CD-RWs.

CD-RW: Rerecordable (rewriteable) compact disc. The files burned on CD-RWs can be erased, and the disc reused. However, some devices (including some music CD players) cannot read (or play) CD-RWs.

Celestial jukebox: Theoretical streaming music service providing access to a huge selection of recordings. Such services are usually envisioned as **music locker** systems or **on-demand, subscription** systems.

Client: Software program, running on a personal computer, that interacts with a **server**. Client-server programs lie at the heart of the online experience. Examples of clients include the AOL program, Web browsers, file-sharing programs like Morpheus, music streamers like RealOne, and **subscription** programs like Rhapsody.

Convergence: Combining features previously associated with different devices into a single device. Digital music represents a convergence of computer technology and music CDs. The convergent blending of technology has long been an ideal in the hi-tech industry.

Cookie: Small piece of software that, when placed on a user's hard drive, identifies that computer to an Internet server. Typically, cookies are used to automate sign-in at Web sites and online **subscription** services. Cookies are distrusted by some privacy advocates because of the potential for spying; cookies can be designed to gather information about a user's files and online activities.

Copy-protected CD: Audio disc whose tracks cannot be **ripped**. The first copy-protected CDs were introduced by Universal Music Group in late 2001, to great controversy within and without the record industry. Some copy-protected CDs do not play in all CD players.

Copy protection: Encoding of a digital music file to prevent copying by the end user. Copy-protected files cannot be **burned** onto a CD, nor can they be transferred to a portable player.

Copyright: Exclusive legal right to reproduce a creation. When applied to intellectual property such as music, especially when it comes to digital reproduction and online distribution, copyright is difficult to police and almost impossible to enforce. For this and other reasons, some copyright philosophers advocate rethinking U.S. copyright laws.

DAR: See **Digital audio receiver**.

Desktop player: Software program that opens and plays digital music files such as MP3, WMA, and Liquid Audio files. Popular desktop players include Winamp, RealOne, Windows Media Player, Media Jukebox, and Musicmatch. These and other such programs might include functions for **ripping** and **burning** CDs, and playing Internet music **streams**.

Dial-up: Internet connection by means of a telephone modem. Dial-up connections are low-**bandwidth**, slower than **cable modems** and DSL lines.

Digital audio receiver (DAR): Home networking device that transfers digital music files to and from the computer. Digital audio receivers enable MP3 and other music files to play through a shelftop stereo system.

Digital audio server: Stereo component offering dedicated ripping, burning, CD playback, and archiving of digital music files.

Digital Millennium Copyright Act: See **DMCA**.

DMCA (Digital Millennium Copyright Act): Enacted in 1998, the DMCA is a controversial addition to U.S. copyright law that introduces provisions covering digital distribution of intellectual property, including music.

Download: Transfer of a song (or any other computer file) from a **server** to a personal computer. Likewise, the transfer of a song from a personal computer to a portable device such as an MP3 player. **P2P** downloads proceed from one personal computer to another, without the file residing on a server.

DSL: Digital subscriber line. DSL refers generally to a group of related technologies (ADSL, HDSL, VDSL, and others), all of which deliver high-speed Internet connection through standard telephone wires. DSL provides download speed roughly equal to that of **cable modems**.

Encode: To convert one music file type into another. Most commonly, CD tracks are encoded as MP3 files.

EQ: Equalization. Like a sophisticated tone control, EQ allows the user to boost or lower different frequencies during music playback, giving the audio more treble, bass, or midrange. Many **desktop players** provide EQ controls.

Ethernet card: Specialized circuit board that connects a computer to high-speed data-transfer devices such as **cable modems**.

Fair use: Condition of U.S. **copyright** law that permits individuals to copy excerpts of intellectual properties and publish them for illustrative purpose. Although an allowable excerpt length is not specified by law, music samples under thirty seconds are generally considered fair use.

File type: Format in which a computer file is encoded. In digital music, the most common file type is MP3. File types are identified by their three-letter file extensions, such as *mp3* and *wma*. Not all playback programs and devices recognize all music file types.

File type assignment: Link between a music **file type** and the program assigned by the Windows operating system to play that file type. The assignment makes it easy to play a file simply by double-clicking it.

However, any desktop player can open any music file using the File menu, even if the file type isn't assigned to that program.

File-sharing: Uploading, downloading, and browsing files through a **P2P** network. File-sharing networks include **Napster, Morpheus, Gnutella,** Usenet newsgroups, IRC rooms, and others.

Firewall: A software barrier surrounding a network or online service. Firewalls attempt to protect extensive networks, company intranets, and single Web sites from outside intrusion. Typically, entrance through a firewall is accomplished by providing a correct username and password. Firewalls are relevant to downloading through file-sharing networks because files sometimes cannot be transferred through a firewall, such as attempting to download from a firewalled source (such as a corporate computer).

Firewire: A wireless standard for connecting hard drives and other peripherals to computers without cables.

Format: Music delivery platform. Digital music formats include file types such as **MP3** and **RealAudio,** as well as broad availability formats such as downloadable and streaming music.

Freeware: Downloadable software offered free of charge. In digital music, some **desktop players** are freeware, most notably **Winamp.**

Genre: Type of music. Popular genres include rock, jazz, hip-hop, folk, classical, and many others. Online music directories are often categorized by genre, and further divided into subgenres.

Gigabyte: Measure of file-storage capacity, 1,000 **megabytes.** A song in MP3 **format** typically uses about 1 megabyte per recorded minute, and 1 gigabyte would store about 250 four-minute songs.

Gnutella: A **P2P** file-sharing network, accessed by several **clients.** Gnutella is an **open-source** network that is not owned by a single entity, and operates in a decentralized fashion to connect users to each other's hard drives.

Hash: A sample of a media file used for identification. Hashes are typically very small, a second or less of the song or other content being sampled. Hashing is used by some file-sharing programs to identify identical files at multiple locations, for more efficient downloading.

Head: The CD player and/or radio tuner control section of a car stereo system.

Hi-fi and low-fi: High fidelity and low fidelity, referring both to the varying quality of music files and the connection speed used to **download**

or **stream** those files. Many Internet radio stations and on-demand streaming services allow the user to choose between hi-fi and low-fi options.

Hop: The physical distance traveled by transmitted data between two switching points. Hops are used to estimate the proximity of two personal computers connected to the same file-sharing network, and accordingly to estimate the reliability and speed of sending a file from one computer to the other.

ID3 tags: Song identifiers that allow **MP3** collectors to sort their music by artist, song title, album name, genre, or by one of several other categories.

Import: A databasing function used by desktop jukeboxes to store filenames and **ID3 tags** of **MP3** tracks in a personal collection. Tracks must be imported into the program in order to take advantage of sorting and playlisting features. Importing does not alter or move the files.

Indie: An abbreviation of *independent, indie* can refer to an artist, a record label, or a music genre. Indie artists are either unaffiliated with any label or signed to a label that in turn is independent of the major label conglomerates. The indie genre is associated with music produced free of corporate influence, focus testing, and targeted marketing.

Infringement: Violation of **copyright**. Copyright infringement occurs when a song is copied and distributed online, even without financial profit.

Internet radio: Any programmed music **stream**. Internet radio is not broadcast through the air as radio is; nonetheless, the term refers to both programming explicitly created for the Internet, and online streaming of **terrestrial stations**.

Kbps: Kilobits per second, a measurement of data transfer speed.

Kilobit: One thousand bits. A bit is the smallest increment of datum. One kilobit is a standard of measurement of data transfer, which defines the speed of an Internet connection.

Label: Record label. A company that produces music, owns its copyright, and distributes it. Most commercial music is recorded and owned by the five largest labels.

License: The purchased right to distribute copyrighted music. Music **subscription** companies license music catalogs, then make them available to subscribers in streaming or downloadable format.

Liquid Audio: Music file format and the company that developed and owns the format. Liquid Audio files are copy protected, and mostly unavailable on **file-sharing** networks.

Local files: Music files stored on an individual's personal computer.

Logged on and logged off: Connected to, and disconnected from, the Internet. Similarly, some music **subscription** services distinguish between being logged into the service and being logged out.

Majors: The five largest record **labels:** Warner Music, BMG, EMI, Sony Music Entertainment, and Universal Music Group. These five media companies (one of which is American) produce and own about 75 percent of all commercial music CDs.

Megabyte: Measure of file storage capacity. With typical encoding settings, a megabyte (meg, or MB) can hold about one minute of recorded music.

Morpheus: Popular **file-sharing** network. Morpheus filled a large part of the void left when the first version of Napster shut down.

MP3: Most popular file format for compressed digital music. The acronym stands for MPEG Audio Layer-3, and the format was based on the work of the Motion Picture Experts Group, later to be completed by the Fraunhofer Institut in Germany. MP3 files are about one-tenth the size of corresponding CD tracks, making them practical for sharing online. MP3 took off among consumers in 1998 when the **Winamp** player was developed and offered online as **freeware**.

MP3 jukebox: Program or device that plays large numbers of **MP3s**. Software jukeboxes are distinguished by their ability to organize large file collections. Portable hardware jukeboxes are distinguished from **MP3 players** by internal hard drives that store far more music than **RAM**-based portable players.

MP3 player: Portable music player with limited **RAM** memory that plays **MP3** files. Typically, these players can hold between thirty and sixty minutes of music.

MP3–CD player: Music CD player, usually portable, that recognizes MP3 files. These devices play both standard audio CDs, and data CDs burned with MP3 files, which can hold over 150 songs.

Music license: See **License**.

Music locker: Online storage space for music files. Music lockers enable verified CD owners to access their music from any Internet-connected computer.

Music subscription: See **Subscription**.

MusicNet: Record label alliance that **licenses** music catalogs to online distribution companies. Specifically, MusicNet provides the music content for **RealOne**, a **subscription** service. MusicNet was created by three of the five largest record labels: BMG, EMI, and Warner Music.

Napster: File-sharing program. Napster introduced **P2P** networking to millions of users, and made free, downloadable music both a reality and an expectation in mainstream consumerism. Napster was introduced in 1999, ceased operations two years later in the wake of litigation, and relaunched in early 2002 as a **subscription** service.

Netcast: See **Webcast**.

Network: Two or more computers connected to each other. The Internet is a network, and **P2P** systems such as **Napster** and **Morpheus** are networks that connect individual users to each other.

Ogg Vorbis: Digital music file format. An **open-source** alternative to **MP3**.

On-demand: Internet audio programming initiated by the individual user. On-demand song **streams** (such as in **RealOne, Pressplay,** and Rhapsody) allow users to demand individual songs; **Internet radio** streams allow users to demand individual stations. On-demand programming differs from broadcast programming in its freedom from any kind of schedule.

Open source: Software developed by a community that anybody can join. Nobody owns open-source products, and any developer can alter them or create a proprietary version.

Opt in and opt out: User's permission for contact; user's refusal of contact. Opt-in and opt-out choices are usually presented during the first sign-up or **subscription** to an online music service, and give (or deny) the service permission to send various newsletters and third-party promotions.

P2P: Peer-to-peer. **Networks** that connect individual users with each other, allowing them to share files. IRC rooms have allowed P2P **file-sharing** for many years, but it was **Napster** that made P2P networking rampantly popular.

Partition: A designated portion of a hard drive. Partitions are assigned drive letters as if they were separate physical drives, and are useful for separating music collections from other hard drive content.

Password: A unique identifier, usually used in combination with a **username**, that acts as a key in accessing online services. Passwords are always used in paid services such as online music **subscriptions**, and are sometimes used to access free services.

Peer-to-peer: See **P2P**.

Personal use: Condition of U.S. **copyright** law that permits individuals to copy purchased works for distribution among personally owned devices. For example, copying a music CD to a blank cassette for playing in one's own car stereo is allowable, but not if that cassette is given to another person.

Playlist: Order in which music files are played. Most **desktop players** allow the creation of playlists from a personal **MP3** collection.

Portable player: Hand-held music player that plays **MP3** files, and possibly other music file types. Typically, the RAM-based players hold between thirty and sixty minutes of music, and the disc-based players hold sixty to one hundred hours of music.

Pressplay: Record label alliance that **licenses** music catalogs to online distribution companies. Pressplay was created by two of the five largest record companies, Sony Music and Universal Music Group, and is distributed as a **subscription** service through Yahoo! Music, MP3.com, and other online destinations.

RAM: Random access memory. The type of memory used in computers to store programs and files currently in use. RAM memory is also used in portable **MP3 players**.

RealAudio: Digital audio format. RealAudio was the first **streaming** format, and remains one of the most popular among **Internet radio** programmers.

RealOne: Subscription service featuring the **MusicNet** catalog.

Redbook: The standard by which audio CDs are identified as universally playable in consumer CD players. The term is sometimes used when distinguishing burning an audio CD from burning a data CD.

Registration: Sign-in procedure by which a user claims a **username** and **password** for access to certain features of a site or service. Music **subscription** services all require registration, as do some free services.

RIAA: Recording Industry Association of America. Trade and lobbying group representing the five largest record **labels** plus many smaller ones. The RIAA is the most visible antagonist of, and legal combatant with, **file-sharing** networks and other services that facilitate music **copyright infringement**.

Rip: To encode a CD track in a compressed digital **format**, usually **MP3**. "Ripping" is not "ripping off," because copying CDs in other formats is allowed by **personal-use** aspects of U.S. **copyright** law.

Safe harbor: A condition of nonliability bestowed on online service providers in the Digital Millennium Copyright Act (DMCA). Safe harbor dictates that an online service is not immediately liable for illegal actions of its subscribers (such as infringing music copyright) if it wasn't aware of the actions.

SDMI: Secure Digital Music Initiative, a technology venture undertaken by an alliance of major record **labels** to create a **secure file** standard.

Hampered by technical and political troubles, SDMI has yet to reach completion.

Search engine: Automated keyword finder. General Web search engines scour Web pages for keyword matches. In music **subscription** services, localized search engines help members find music by artist, song title, and album title.

Secure Digital Music Initiative: See **SDMI**.

Secure file: Copy-protected music file. Secure files force the end user to comply with subscription or licensing terms. In some cases the **copy protection** prevents **burning** to CD, in other cases a limited number or type of burns is allowed.

Server: Hub computer that provides files to connected computers. Internet computers that house Web sites and music services are servers.

Set-top box: Specialized digital device residing atop a television set that provides interactive features or online services. ReplayTV, TiVo, and the Moxi Digital Media Center are examples of set-top boxes.

Shareware: Downloadable software offered for a trial period, beyond which the user must pay an ownership price to continue using the program. Some **desktop players** are provided in this manner, with the trial version missing some features that are activated after purchase.

Skin: Alternative window design. Skins became fashionable with **Winamp**, a **desktop player** that allows users to create colorful variations of the program's default windows. Many other music programs can be skinned, and skins are almost always freely downloadable.

Sound card: Circuit board inside a personal computer that provides audio to the speakers.

Space-shifting: Playing recorded media in a place removed from the recording source, such as playing a copied CD in the car.

Stations: In digital music, genre-specific audio **streams**. Not necessarily Internet simulcasts of broadcast radio stations, stations include a broad array of programming including home-built **MP3** streams and professional **subscription** streams.

Stream: Internet audio programming, often played **on demand**, usually not captured on the individual's hard drive. Streaming is one of two general formats of online music, the other being downloadable files.

Subgenre: See **Genre**.

Subscription: Payment for music delivered online. Subscription services allow members to download and/or **stream** tracks and entire CDs for a monthly fee. Terms of service—such as how many streams and downloads are included per month, and whether the downloaded files may be burned and transferred to portable players—vary among services.

Subwoofer: A compact speaker dedicated to reproducing low- and mid-frequency audio. Typically, subwoofers sit on the floor and are part of three-speaker integrated sets. The best of these amplified speaker sets make high-fidelity music reproduction from a computer possible and affordable.

Swarming: Downloading one file from multiple sources simultaneously. Swarming is a file-sharing technology used in the **Gnutella** and FastTrack networks, among others, to speed up the acquisition of files. Normally, the program downloads separate chunks of the file from different sources, then assembles the whole when all the chunks are completed.

T1: A high-speed network connection line capable of transferring data at about 1.5 megabits per second. Some cable-modem connection can approach this speed. T1 lines are typically used at the institutional level.

T3: An institution-grade, high-speed network connection line capable of transferring data at about 44 megabits per second.

Terrestrial stations: Broadcast radio stations, as distinct from **Internet radio**.

Time-shifting: Playing recorded media at a time removed from the original broadcast, such as playing a copied TV show the day after it aired.

Username: An on-screen identifier, usually consisting of a name or name-number combination, used to log into online services. Music subscriptions use the typical username-password combination, as do some file-sharing programs.

Variable bit rate: Encoding setting that increases the **bit rate** when necessary to preserve fidelity, and decreases it when possible to minimize the file size.

Virtual drive: A name for a hard drive **partition**.

Visualization: Abstract, moving designs played in accompaniment to music in some jukebox programs.

Watermark: Digital identifier applied to music files that either prevents copying or enables tracing copies back to the source.

WAV: Digital audio file format. WAV files are large—about ten times larger than corresponding **MP3** files.

Webcast: Internet audio and/or video **stream**, often of a live event, or an online simulcast of a broadcast signal. *Webcast* is something of a misnomer, as the streams do not rely on the underlying properties that define the World Wide Web. *Netcast* is a more accurate term, but a less popular one.

Winamp: Brand of **desktop player**. Winamp popularized the **MP3** format in 1998.

Windows Media: Digital audio file **format**, owned by Microsoft and built into the Windows operating system. Windows Media competes with **MP3, Liquid Audio,** and other formats.

WMA: File extension of the **Windows Media** audio format.

Zip: A file-compression system used mostly for application files downloaded from the Internet. Zip is rarely applied to MP3 files, which are already drastically compressed.

Index